CAREERS IN PSYCHOLOGY

Opportunities in a Changing World

THIRD EDITION

Tara L. Kuther
Western Connecticut State University

Robert D. Morgan
Texas Tech University

 **WADSWORTH**
CENGAGE Learning·

Australia • Brazil • Japan • Korea • Mexico • Singapore • Spain • United Kingdom • United States

WADSWORTH
CENGAGE Learning™

Careers in Psychology: Opportunities in a Changing World, Third Edition
Tara L. Kuther and Robert D. Morgan

Publisher/Executive Editor: to come

Editorial Assistant: Trina Tom

Executive Marketing Manager: Kim Russell

Marketing Coordinator: Molly Felz

Marketing Communications Manager: Talia Wise

Project Manager, Editorial Production: Jared Sterzer

Creative Director: Rob Hugel

Art Director: Vernon Boes

Print Buyer: Linda Hsu

Permissions Editor: Bob Kauser

Production Service: Pre-Press PMG

Copy Editor: Pre-Press PMG

Cover Designer: Andy Norris

Cover Image: © William Whitehurst/Corbis

Compositor: Pre-Press PMG

Library of Congress Control Number: 2008942956

ISBN-13: 978-0-495-60074-9

ISBN-10: 0-495-60074-1

Wadsworth
20 Channel Center Street
Boston, MA 02210
USA

Cengage Learning products are represented in Canada by Nelson Education, Ltd.

For your course and learning solutions, visit
academic.cengage.com

Purchase any of our products at your local college store or at our preferred online store **www.ichapters.com**

Printed in the United States of America
1 2 3 4 5 6 7 8 9 12 11 10

To JGM—TLK
To Stacy Morgan—RDM

BRIEF CONTENTS

CONTENTS

PREFACE

Are you wondering what to do with your psychology degree? Many students enter our offices asking the same question: "What can I do with a degree in psychology?" A baccalaureate in psychology is a highly flexible, marketable, and useful liberal arts degree. Psychology offers students insight into human behavior, which is useful to all careers and is perhaps why psychology is one of the most popular undergraduate majors, with over 88,000 baccalaureate degrees awarded annually. Graduate degrees in psychology offer additional career opportunities; approximately 19,000 masters and about 5,000 doctoral degrees are awarded in psychology each year (National Center for Educational Statistics, 2007).

Our goal in writing *Careers in Psychology: Opportunities in a Changing World* is to discuss the broad range of careers that psychology students might choose. Many students are unaware of the breadth of psychology and its many subdisciplines, and this book will introduce them to the wide range of possible undergraduate and graduate level careers in psychology. A guiding principle of *Careers in Psychology* is that education in psychology prepares students for careers in many fields; however, students have the onus of determining their career interests and tailoring their psychology degree with additional courses and experiences to round out their preparation and enhance their marketability for their chosen career. This principle holds true for undergraduate as well as graduate degree holders in psychology.

Careers in Psychology is appropriate for a range of students, including prospective and declared psychology majors. It complements a variety of psychology courses, including introductory psychology, careers in psychology, methodology courses, capstone courses, and seminars for psychology majors. We view this book as a resource for psychology students and their advisors, and we encourage students to discuss the career opportunities they find within these pages with their advisors and career counselors.

Careers in Psychology begins by discussing the nature of psychology and the diverse careers available to psychology graduates. In Chapter 1, students are guided through considerations in choosing a major and the benefits of majoring in psychology. Chapter 1 closes with a discussion of tips for succeeding as a psychology student. Chapter 2 discusses getting a job after graduation and includes advice on locating positions, writing a résumé and cover letter, and interviewing.

Each of Chapters 3 through 13 covers a psychology subdiscipline and presents related careers for baccalaureate and graduate degree holders. Chapters 3 and 4 explore the applied fields of clinical, counseling, and school psychology. In Chapters 5, 6, and 7 readers are introduced to baccalaureate- and graduate-level careers in three popular subspecialties: psychology and law, health psychology, andsport psychology. Chapter 8 covers careers related to biopsychology, cognitive neuroscience, and clinical neuropsychology. Chapter 9 discusses careers in industrial/organizationalpsychology and human factors, and Chapter 10 examines careers for students who are interested in experimental, cognitive, and quantitative psychology, and psychometrics. Chapters 11 and 12 present career options for students of social, consumer, and developmental psychology. Each discipline-specific chapter (Chapters 3 through 12) closes with a checklist to help readers evaluate their interest and aptitude for the field discussed within the chapter, as well as a list of courses and experiences that students interested in that particular area should obtain. Chapter 13 examines careers relevant to graduate degree holders in all areas of psychology in academic, research, and applied settings. Finally, Chapter 14 discusses how to apply to graduate school in psychology and provides an overview of the process, including the various graduate degrees that students may obtain, getting information about programs, the application, and interviewing.

The Third Edition of *Careers in Psychology* provides updated salary and career information for each subdiscipline of psychology as well as new undergraduate career paths. Sport psychology and health psychology are presented in two chapters rather than one as in prior editions. In addition, the book has been reorganized to emphasize the interests of undergraduate students of psychology. Specifically, several chapters have been rewritten with the questions and needs of undergraduates in mind. Information about job seeking is placed at the beginning of the book, in Chapter 2, so as to encourage students to consider the pragmatics of job seeking as they choose a career and plan a course of study. Each chapter closes with a table listing recommended courses, applied experiences, and research experiences for a given subfield of psychology.

It is our hope that *Careers in Psychology* will help prospective and current students develop and evaluate their interest in psychology, appreciate the myriad of career opportunities available with a degree in psychology, and take the steps needed to round out their education and experiences in order to obtain the careers they seek. We believe that psychology students are well-prepared for many careers. When students think outside of the box, seek out innovative opportunities, and acquire related skills they will be surprised at the opportunities that await them within our changing world.

ACKNOWLEDGEMENTS

We are most appreciative of the constructive comments and helpful suggestions that we received from reviewers: Mary Jo Carnot, Chadron State College; Keith Colman, California State University, Long Beach; Karen Jackson, Texas Lutheran University; Cheryl Lynch, University of Louisiana; Cynthia Magistro, Seton Hall University; Donna Stuber-McEwen, Friends University; Colleen Seifert, University of Michigan; Linda M. Subich, University of Akron; Frank Vattano, Colorado State University; Paula Waddill, Murray State University; Todd J. Walter, D'Youville College; and Valerie Whittlesey, Kennesaw State University.

In addition, we thank Vicki Knight, who first signed this project, and especially Trina Toni Tom, Senior Editorial Assistant at Wadsworth, for patiently and forcefully nudging us through the process. Thanks to Erin McDonald and Poonam Melwani for their assistance on prior editions of this book. We thank Catherine Serna for her work on this edition, especially her help with proofreading chapters and assembling the reference list.

Much of what appears in these pages is the result of conversations with students; I (Tara) thank them for asking the questions that prompted us to write this book. I thank my parents, Philip and Irene Kuther—especially my father, who was the first to ask me, "What can you do with a degree in psychology?" and trusted that I would discover the answer. Finally, I thank John Mongelluzzo for his support and companionship.

I (Robert) thank them (the students) for challenging me to explore the boundaries of psychology. I offer a special thanks to Robert Ax and Steven Mandracchia for teaching me to think outside of the box. Finally, I thank my family, Stacy, Taylor, Ryan, and Riley, for their unyielding support.

Choosing a Major and Career

CHAPTER GUIDE

Each semester that she teaches introductory psychology, one of the authors of this book begins the first class by asking three questions. First, "What is psychology?" Here are some typical student responses:

"Psychology is the study of the mind."
"Psychology helps people solve problems."
"Psychology looks at the things inside us that make us do what we do."

Then she asks: "What does someone trained in psychology do?"

"Studies the mind and thought processes of an individual to find the roots of a problem that cannot be explained by physiology."

"Works as a doctor who does not use medication or drugs to delve into issues that are causing a person to experience disharmony in life. That disharmony can range from difficulty in personal relations to sleep disruption to behavioral problems."

"Gets training in scientific and social analysis to help patients suffering from mental disorders and/or problems by listening."

Are these student responses accurate? Yes and no. Psychology is the study of mind and behavior and it permits us to help people who are experiencing problems; however, the discipline of psychology encompasses much more than therapy, as we will discuss in this chapter and throughout this book. Each of the roles described above are held by psychologists, professionals with doctoral training in psychology.

The final question she asks is: "What does someone with a bachelor's degree in psychology do?" This question is often met with silence. A student might cautiously respond, "Teach?" Another student might call out, "Get an MBA," or "Go to graduate school!" and the class usually laughs nervously. Sure, these are humorous responses, and are true in some cases, but are they accurate depictions of the average bachelor's degree recipient in psychology? No. Most students who major in psychology do *not* go on to graduate school. Yet students often are unaware of their career options. Nearly all psychology students are asked repeatedly, "What can you do with a psychology degree?" The authors of this book faced that very question a seemingly endless number of times. We found our answer to that question, and this book is intended to help you find yours. In this chapter we discuss the diverse field of psychology, how to figure out if psychology is the major for you, and how to succeed in your major and enhance your marketability for jobs after graduation.

WHAT IS PSYCHOLOGY?

Most of us first become acquainted with the field of psychology informally through our everyday experiences. Turn on the television to see a psychologist on *Oprah* explaining how parents can help their troubled teens. Change the channel and Frasier Crane, the lead character of the sitcom *Frasier*, is depicted as a psychiatrist dispensing advice on his radio show. Open a magazine and you may find an article written by a psychologist about how to love your body. Psychology has ingrained itself into American pop culture. But how much do you really know about psychology and the work of those trained in psychology? You may be surprised to learn that the field of psychology extends beyond therapy, self-help books, and parenting advice.

What is psychology, then? Psychology is the scientific study of behavior—anything an animal or a person does, feels, or thinks. Topics of psychological study include social relationships, the brain and the chemicals that influence it, vision, human development, the causes of normative and atypical behavior, and much more. Many students are surprised when they discover the broad range of activities that represent the field of psychology. Advanced training in psychology can lead to a research career studying animal behavior, the brain, personality, and more. At various levels of training, people with psychology degrees may work in business settings, developing training programs for employees, creating informational surveys, conducting interviews, and devising strategies to improve worker productivity. Psychologists, individuals with doctoral degrees in psychology, work as administrators, managing hospitals, mental health clinics, nonprofit organizations, government agencies, businesses, schools, and more. Some psychologists are employed as professors at universities, community colleges, and high schools. Others work as researchers in university, hospital, corporate, and government settings.

Of course, we can't forget the service-provider roles of psychologists. Psychologists work with people, providing intellectual and personality assessments, conducting therapy, and developing programs to prevent problems or to help people deal with and overcome problems. Although the average person is most familiar with this type of psychologist, the practicing clinical or counseling psychologist, only about one-half of psychologists work in these service provider roles (Wicherski & Kohout, 2007). Many different careers fall under the umbrella of psychology. Table 1.1 provides a list of all of the discipline subdivisions within the American Psychological Association, the most prominent professional organization for psychologists. As you examine the table, one thing becomes apparent: Psychology is diverse.

TABLE 1.1	DISCIPLINES WITHIN PSYCHOLOGY: AMERICAN PSYCHOLOGICAL ASSOCIATION DIVISIONS

Addictions

Adult Development and Aging

American Psychology-Law Society

Applied Experimental and Engineering Psychology

American Society for the Advancement of Pharmacotherapy

Behavior Analysis

Behavioral Neuroscience and Comparative Psychology

Child, Youth, and Family Services

Clinical Neuropsychology

Counseling Psychology

Developmental Psychology

Educational Psychology

continued

TABLE I.I | CONTINUED

Evaluation, Measurement, and Statistics

Experimental Psychology

Exercise and Sport Psychology

Family Psychology

Health Psychology

History of Psychology

Humanistic Psychology

International Psychology

Group Psychology and Group Psychotherapy

Media Psychology

Mental Retardation and Developmental Disabilities

Military Psychology

Psychologists in Public Service

Psychologists in Independent Practice

Psychology of Religion

Psychopharmacology and Substance Abuse

Psychotherapy

Population and Environmental Psychology

Psychoanalysis

Rehabilitation Psychology

School Psychology

Society for General Psychology

Society for Community Research and Action

Society for Consumer Psychology

Society for Industrial and Organizational Psychology

Society for Personality and Social Psychology

Society for the Psychological Study of Social Issues (SPSSI)

Society for the Psychological Study of Lesbian, Gay, and Bisexual Issues

Society for the Study of Peace, Conflict, and Violence

Society for the Psychological Study of Ethnic Minority Issues

Society for the Psychological Study of Men and Masculinity

Society for the Psychology of Aesthetics, Creativity, and the Arts

Society for the Psychology of Women

Society for the Teaching of Psychology

Society of Clinical Psychology

continued

TABLE 1.1	CONTINUED

Society of Consulting Psychology

Society of Clinical Child and Adolescent Psychology

Society of Pediatric Psychology

Society of Psychological Hypnosis

Theoretical and Philosophical Psychology

Trauma Psychology

Each chapter within this book examines one or more subdisciplines within psychology to provide a taste of the many fields in which people like you may find employment. Remember that most students who earn bachelor's degrees in psychology do not attend graduate school. Because of this, each chapter presents career options for students with bachelor's degrees as well as options for students with graduate degrees. Many of the career options that we will discuss reflect the content of two or more psychology subdisciplines; for example, a given job might be appropriate for students with interests in counseling psychology and developmental psychology. Whenever possible we will point out career options that overlap subdisciplines.

WHY MAJOR IN PSYCHOLOGY?

With over 88,000 baccalaureate degrees awarded each year (National Center for Education Statistics, 2008), psychology is consistently one of the most popular college majors. Why? The knowledge and skills that you'll develop as a psychology major apply to a variety of careers. The psychology major is a solid liberal arts degree, which means that it will teach you how to think and problem solve and will prepare you for lifelong learning (McGovern, Furumoto, Halpern, Kimble, & McKeachie, 1991). Psychology majors develop critical thinking and analytical skills, learn how to learn, and become independent thinkers. The skills and knowledge that you develop as a psychology major are generalizable outside the classroom and are desired by employers. Consider the range of skills and abilities that undergraduate programs in psychology seek to promote (American Psychological Association, 2002; Hayes, 1996; McGovern et al., 1991):

- **Knowledge of Psychology.** Students of psychology gain knowledge of psychological theories, facts, and modes of inquiry. Because psychology is a broad discipline encompassing biology, development, perception, thinking, emotion, and more, students of psychology develop a comprehensive understanding of the human condition that serves as a foundation for lifelong learning about human behavior. In other words, students learn about "how people work."
- **Critical Thinking and Analytical Skills.** Psychology students are exposed to multiple perspectives on behavior. They quickly learn that any phenomenon is addressed by many, often conflicting, theories. Psychology students learn to think flexibly and accept ambiguity. Often we don't know the "right" answer to questions about a given phenomenon but have research that supports several

theoretical perspectives or explanations. Exposure to diverse perspectives helps psychology students hone their critical thinking and analytical skills. Students learn how to weigh multiple points of view, compare and contrast evidence, and make reasoned decisions—valuable skills in today's complex world.

- **Communication and Presentation Skills.** Psychology students learn how to communicate: how to speak and how to write. Over the college years, psychology students write a great many papers and enroll in courses that require discussion and debate. They learn how to substantiate arguments with evidence and communicate arguments from a psychological standpoint. Certainly, other college majors require that students write papers and participate in class discussions, but the content of psychology papers often differs from that of other liberal arts disciplines because it draws not only from theory, but also empirical research. The ability to write about empirical research, whether from a journal article or from a study that the student has conducted, and to integrate theory and research, requires a different skill set than does the writing entailed in other liberal-arts majors.

- **Information Gathering, Evaluation, and Synthesis Skills.** Psychology students learn how to gather information through a variety of means, such as the library, computerized databases, the Internet, and data collection. More important, psychology students learn how to critically evaluate information to determine its credibility and relevance to the problem at hand. They learn how to extract information from multiple courses, summarize it, and synthesize it into a coherent and persuasive argument. Psychology students present the results of empirical research and analyses that integrate the findings of multiple research studies, which requires that they develop unique skills that set them apart from other liberal arts majors, as we will discuss. In this information age, the ability to selectively gather, sort, and manipulate information is valuable.

- **Research Methodology and Statistical Skills.** Psychology students learn how to pose questions and devise procedures to gather new information about human behavior. Undergraduate students in psychology gain a basic understanding of research methodology and statistics, and learn how to interpret data summaries. These skills in question asking and answering—problem solving— make psychology graduates unique among liberal arts graduates.

- **Computer Literacy.** Computers are an unavoidable part of daily life and, especially, work-life. College students learn a variety of computer skills, such as word processing, Internet browsing, and e-mail. Psychology students learn how to use statistical, spreadsheet, and presentation software. Moreover, psychology students know enough about thinking—their own thinking—to understand how to learn about new technology.

- **Interpersonal and Intrapersonal Skills.** Interpersonal skills—how to work with people—enable success in career and personal life. Psychology students develop skills to work with people and groups. They are aware of and sensitive to issues of culture, class, race, and ethnicity. Psychology students also develop intrapersonal awareness, or self-knowledge. They learn how to monitor and manage their emotions and behavior.

- **Adaptability.** Upon taking courses in research methodology, many students express dismay at all of the flaws they find in published research. Soon they learn that perfection in a research study is unattainable. Instead, researchers attempt to conduct the best research possible given limited resources. The ability to be flexible, adapting approaches and research techniques to fit current circumstances and opportunities, is valuable to the success of students in college and afterwards.

Undergraduate psychology programs emphasize all of these skills that will help you grow into a well-rounded and educated person who is marketable in a variety of fields. In that regard, psychology is a solid liberal-arts major that provides you with the thinking tools and skills to excel in life (Gehlhaus, 2007; Kierniesky, 1992). Other liberal-arts degrees, like those in English and history, also provide training in critical thinking and communication. However, psychology is unique among liberal-arts fields because it provides a blend of education in statistics, analytical skills, research, writing, and interpersonal skills. Knowledge of psychology—how people and groups function—as well as research methodology and statistics is a large part of what makes study in psychology different from that in other liberal-arts disciplines.

CHOOSING A MAJOR AND CAREER

Now that you've had a brief introduction to the broad field of psychology, let's talk about you. How do you decide what you want to do with your life? How do you determine your college major? How do you know if psychology is the right major for you? Lots of students find career planning stressful and confusing. Sometimes it seems like everyone else knows what they want to do with their lives—what about you? Finding the right major and determining your career goals doesn't require magic, innate abilities, or luck. What does it take? The willingness to do the hard work of looking deep within and disentangling what you think you should do, what others want you to do, what you truly want to do, and what you realistically have the ability to do.

THREE RULES FOR CHOOSING A MAJOR AND CAREER

Before we talk about how to select a major, understand that there are three general principles that should guide you through this process. The first guiding principle is to take an active role in choosing a major. "Of course I'm taking an active role. I've declared a major, haven't I?" Yes, declaring your major certainly is your decision, but taking an active role in choosing a major happens well before you formally declare your major and must extend well past. The process of considering and then narrowing down possible majors must be your own. You are the only one who will know what is right for you. Frequently students feel subtle pressure to select particular majors from family members or friends. Maybe your parent majored in finance and everyone's always told you that you're just like him or her. Or maybe several of your friends have decided to major in communications or theatre arts and share a number of courses in common. Expectations often are subtle. Regardless, the process of choosing and your choice of major are your own. No one cares as much about what major you choose as you do, because the only person truly affected by your choice is you.

Second, your college major does not determine your career. In that sense, your choice of major doesn't matter much. Liberal-arts majors provide solid foundations for all students. However, as we have discussed, a bachelor's degree in psychology provides students with specialized training that makes them stand out from other liberal-arts majors. That said, your college major is simply a starting point. It will not limit you to one career choice. Most people end up working in careers that are not closely tied to their majors; rather, they work in careers that are closely tied to their skills. Therefore, the current emphasis in career planning is skill-based: What skills do you have to entice an employer? Employers care about communication, computer, writing, speaking, and problem-solving skills. You have the opportunity to develop these skills in a variety of majors because these are general competencies that are encompassed within the goals of a college education. Don't worry that your choice of major will pigeonhole you or determine your lifelong career. It can, but it doesn't have to if you acquire a broad base of skills similar to those that you can obtain as a psychology major.

Finally, career planning is a process. It is not something that is done all at once and finished quickly, say in your first semester or first year in college. Instead, career planning is a lengthy process that may begin in college but persists through-out life. You likely will not decide what you want to do for the rest of your life suddenly and definitively—and your decision will likely change throughout your life. Most people have many careers over their lifetimes. To determine your life path, you must be willing to engage in the process and do the work of looking within and evaluating your aspirations, expectations, and opportunities.

One step in career planning is choosing a major; however, recall that your major will not dictate your career. The following sections of this chapter discuss the process of learning about yourself, determining your interests and abilities. Sometimes students engage in the career-planning process, choose a major, and later decide that the major is not right for them. If so, recognize that changing majors is common. If you choose a major that ultimately is not a good fit for you, it's perfectly acceptable to change your major to something that is more suitable. Recognize that a change of major will entail taking a new set of courses and occasionally may delay graduation. Speak with a faculty member or advisor in your new major to learn more and determine if it is right for you.

Your Interests, Skills, and Values

Your first step in developing career goals and choosing a major involves understanding yourself. What are your interests? What are you good at? Understand yourself and you'll be more likely to choose a major that fits you and makes it easier to succeed in your classes. Sometimes students choose a major without considering their interests. For example, they might choose a major because they think it looks good and is marketable, then take a few classes and realize that they are bored or that they simply don't like it. Don't complete this task backwards. Changing majors is common, but avoid it if possible. Consider your interests before you choose a major and you'll select one that fits you. It's easier to do well when you like what you're doing.

How do you determine your interests and skills? Try this exercise: Write about all of your accomplishments—any times you can think of when you encountered a problem and took action to solve it. Write freely, letting all of your achievements flow onto the page. The problems that you've solved don't have to be huge. Even learning to play a song on your guitar or managing your annoying roommate are accomplishments. In other words, the accomplishments that you list can be small, and they don't have to be acknowledged by anyone else. List as many as you can, and don't stop when it becomes challenging. Instead, probe further. When it becomes very difficult to add to your list, write whatever comes to mind, without censoring or editing. Even writing about the difficulty of thinking about additional accomplishments might jog your memory.

Once you have completed your list, take a close look at it and analyze it with regard to skills. What skills does each of your accomplishments entail? For example, sorting out problems with your roommate taps interpersonal skills. List your skills on a separate page. As you consider your accomplishments and their associated skills, your list will grow. After you have considered all of your accomplishments and noted the related skills and abilities, look at your list. Which skills do you prefer using? Which of these skills are most interesting to you? Which are you best at? Do any of your skills need more development? Are there any that you would like to develop further? Which are most important to you?

Now go back to your list of accomplishments. Which are most personally relevant to you? Why? Which have brought you the most satisfaction? Which do you value most highly and why? This exercise is important because by understanding which achievements you cherish you'll get a better idea about your interests and values, which is helpful in determining a major that will hold your interest. Understanding your skills, identifying strengths and areas in need of improvement, and identifying the skills you most enjoy using will also shed light onto possible careers.

Finally, as you evaluate potential careers, consider how they fit with your values—your principles regarding your life and experience. What do you believe is important in life? Consider your values regarding prestige, work hours, life-balance, job security, knowledge, autonomy, financial security, and more. This process of examining interest, abilities, and values is one that you should periodically revisit, because career planning and self-awareness are lifelong tasks.

YOUR PERSONALITY

Consider your own personality when choosing a major and career. One simple way to gain insight into your personality is to brainstorm traits that describe you. What are you like? Write down adjectives that describe at least part of you. List as many as you can think of without stopping to evaluate them. Once you've completed a long list and gathered all of the descriptors that you can, evaluate your list and choose the 10 traits that most accurately portray you. This list illustrates some of your personality traits.

Understanding your unique personality will help you to choose a major that's right for you. In one of the most widely used models of career development, Holland (1959) identifies six personality types and relates them to specific career choices. The six categories are presented in Table 1.2. Most people find that they are a combination of several personality types. How do you determine your type? Read the descriptions. Most people find that one or two descriptions seem to fit them well. Try Checklist 1.1 to help you determine which descriptors and personality style

TABLE 1.2	HOLLAND'S (1959) PERSONALITY TYPES
Realistic	Someone with a realistic personality type is athletically or mechanically inclined. He or she would probably prefer to work outdoors with tools, plants, or animals. Some of the traits that describe the realistic personality type include practical, candid, a nature lover, calm, reserved, restrained, independent, systematic, and persistent.
Investigative	The investigative type enjoys learning, observing, problem solving, and analyzing information. Traits that describe the investigative type include curious, logical, observant, precise, intellectual, cautious, introspective, reserved, unbiased, and independent.
Artistic	Imaginative and creative, the artistic personality type likes to work in unstructured situations that allow for creativity and innovation. Personality characteristics of the artistic type include intuitive, unconventional, moody, nonconforming, expressive, unique, pensive, spontaneous, compassionate, bold, direct, and idealistic.
Social	The social personality type enjoys helping and training others. Characteristics that describe the social type include friendly, cooperative, idealistic, perceptive, outgoing, understanding, supportive, generous, dependable, forgiving, patient, compassionate, and eloquent.
Enterprising	The enterprising personality type likes to work with people in persuasive, performance, or managerial situations to achieve goals that are organizational or economic in nature. Characteristics that describe the enterprising type include confident, assertive, determined, talkative, extroverted, energetic, animated, social, persuasive, fashionable, spontaneous, daring, accommodating, and optimistic.
Conventional	The conventional personality type is well-organized, has clerical or numerical ability, and likes to work with data and carry out tasks in detail. Characteristics that describe the conventional type include meticulous, numerically inclined, conscientious, precise, adept, conforming, orderly, practical, frugal, structured, courteous, acquiescent, and persistent.

Source: Kuther, 2006, pp. 20–21.

fit you. Another quiz based on the Holland personality types is available at Career Key (http://www.careerkey.org). Or consider taking the Self-Directed Search® (Holland, 1994), a formal assessment based on the categories listed in Table 1.2. The career development office at your university can provide you with more information about this tool, or consider taking the online version, which you can complete for a fee at http://www.self-directed-search.com.

Understanding your personality type can help you in choosing a major because some majors are better suited to particular personality types. Table 1.3 lists college majors organized by personality type. Note that not all possible majors are listed, and that the categories are flexible; some majors appear in more than one category because they reflect a variety of skills.

 WHICH HOLLAND PERSONALITY TYPE DO YOU MATCH?

Check off each trait that describes you

- ☐ 1. Assertive
- ☐ 2. Bold
- ☐ 3. Candid
- ☐ 4. Compassionate
- ☐ 5. Confident
- ☐ 6. Conscientious
- ☐ 7. Cooperative
- ☐ 8. Curious
- ☐ 9. Dependable
- ☐ 10. Determined
- ☐ 11. Energetic
- ☐ 12. Expressive
- ☐ 13. Friendly
- ☐ 14. Frugal
- ☐ 15. Idealistic
- ☐ 16. Independent
- ☐ 17. Introspective
- ☐ 18. Intuitive
- ☐ 19. Likes numbers
- ☐ 20. Logical

- ☐ 21. Meticulous
- ☐ 22. Nature lover
- ☐ 23. Observant
- ☐ 24. Optimistic
- ☐ 25. Orderly
- ☐ 26. Outdoorsy
- ☐ 27. Outgoing
- ☐ 28. Patient
- ☐ 29. Pensive
- ☐ 30. Perceptive
- ☐ 31. Persistent
- ☐ 32. Persuasive
- ☐ 33. Practical
- ☐ 34. Precise
- ☐ 35. Reserved
- ☐ 36. Spontaneous
- ☐ 37. Structured
- ☐ 38. Supportive
- ☐ 39. Talkative
- ☐ 40. Unconventional

Scoring: Add up your check marks for items measuring each personality type:

Realistic Personality Type: 3, 16, 22, 26, 31, 33, 35
Investigative Personality Type: 8, 16, 17, 20, 23, 34, 35
Artistic Personality Type: 2, 4, 12, 15, 17, 18, 29, 36, 40
Social Personality Type: 4, 7, 9, 12, 13, 15, 27, 28, 30, 36, 38
Enterprising Personality Type: 1, 2, 5, 10, 11, 13, 24, 27, 32, 36, 39
Conventional Personality Type: 6, 7, 9, 14, 19, 21, 25, 31, 34, 37

Did you score high in more than one personality type? That's common as many traits and qualities are useful in a broad range of careers.

EXPLORE OPTIONS

Self assessment is a process, so it may take time to understand yourself well enough to choose a major. What do you do in the meantime? Don't pressure yourself. Allow yourself opportunities to explore:

- Take a range of classes. You'll fulfill your college's general education requirements and learn about areas in which you might want to major. If you find a class interesting, take another in that discipline.
- Seek diverse research opportunities: If you are uncertain of your career track, don't get locked into one research lab. Research experiences afford you an opportunity to delve into a specific content area, but when exploring your options, it can be beneficial to learn about a variety of areas of study.

TABLE 1.3 | HOLLAND PERSONALITY TYPES AND COLLEGE MAJORS

Realistic	Investigative	Artistic	Social	Enterprising	Conventional
Agriculture/Forestry	Animal Science	Advertising	Audiology	Advertising	Accounting
Criminal Justice	Anthropology	Art History	Counseling	Agricultural Economics	Business
Engineering	Astronomy	Art Education	Criminal Justice	Broadcasting	Computer Science
Health and Physical Education	Biochemistry	Architecture	Elementary Education	Communications	Economics
Animal Science	Biological Sciences	Classics	History	Economics	Finance
Biosystems Engineering	Chemistry	Communications	Human Development	Finance	Mathematics
Plant and Soil Sciences	Computer Science	English	Human Services	Industrial Relations	Statistics
Architecture	Engineering	Foreign Language	Library Sciences	Insurance	
Recreation and Tourism Management	Forestry	Graphic Design	Occupational Therapy	Journalism	
Environmental Studies	Geography	History	Nursing	Law	
Geology	Geology	Interior Design	Nutrition	Management	
Medical Technology	Mathematics	Journalism	Philosophy	Marketing	

Exercise Science	Medical Technology	Music	Political Science	Political Science
Sport Management	Medicine	Music Education	Recreation and Physical Education	Public Administration
Aerospace Engineering	Nursing	Speech/Drama	Psychology	Speech
Civil Engineering	Nutrition		Religious Studies	
Electrical Engineering	Pharmacy		Sociology	
Industrial Engineering	Philosophy		Social Work	
Mechanical Engineering	Physical Therapy		Special Education	
Nuclear Engineering	Physics		Urban Planning	
Radiological Technology	Psychology			
	Sociology			
	Statistics			

Source: Kuther, 2006, pp. 21-22.

Furthermore, all researchers do not think alike, so you will also be exposed to some of the diverse methods with which to tackle a research question.

- Talk to others about potential majors and get feedback. Talk with students and ask why they chose their majors. Talk with graduates, parents, and professors to learn about how they chose their careers. Ask professors and advisors questions to learn what you can do with various majors, what each entails, and what skills you need to develop.
- Visit your college's career center to speak with a career counselor who can recommend assessment instruments to help you learn about careers that are suited to you as well as provide individualized attention and advice. The career development center may also offer alumni contacts who can tell you about their experiences and offer advice.

Remember that although you will seek input and advice from parents, friends, and professors, ultimately the decision of which major to select is your own. Choose a major that interests you, because passion will make difficult classes and endless term papers seem more manageable. Also, remember that you can change your major—it isn't set in stone.

TIPS FOR SUCCESS

We've seen that the psychology major offers students the opportunity to develop well-rounded skills. How do you take advantage of the opportunity? How do you ensure that you're prepared for your future after graduation, whether you will be entering the career world or graduate school? As we've seen, this is a difficult but essential task. Think about your career goals and where you would like to be in a few years. Then determine exactly what you need to do to get there. Throughout this book we discuss tips for students who are interested in careers related to specific areas of psychology and provide suggestions on helpful experiences to obtain for various jobs. Check out the chapters in this book that relate to your goals for more specific training advice and use this information as a guide, but also seek advice from faculty, advisors, and the career center to devise a strategy for getting the experiences that you need to be marketable for the jobs you desire. The following tips are intended to help students regardless of where their interests lay.

GET TO KNOW PROFESSORS

Most students see their professors only in the classroom. If this is true for you, then you're not taking advantage of your college's most valuable resource—the faculty. There's much more to learn from professors than content knowledge. Get to know your professors and you might get involved in their research, learn about professional development, learn about special opportunities like internships, and see what it's really like to work in the field. How do you get to know professors? Talk to them after class. Stop by during office hours. What do you talk about? Psychology. Ask questions about material—theories, research, cases—discussed in class. Ask about their experiences as students, how they decided to go to graduate school, what led them to their research interests. Share an interesting Web site on the brain, for example, or tell the professor about a relevant program that you viewed on the Discovery channel. The goal is to learn from these conversations and also to show your interest in their subject. Remember, professors are people too: smile and be friendly and you'll be surprised how easy it is to get to know faculty.

GET INVOLVED IN RESEARCH

Seek research experience by assisting professors with their research or by developing an independent research project. Research experience demonstrates your ability to work independently and sharpens your analytical and critical thinking skills. You will develop important skills, learn what it's like to generate new knowledge, and have an experience that looks great from the perspectives of employers and graduate school admissions committees. Research experience provides employers with evidence of your motivation, initiative, and willingness to go beyond basic requirements.

How do you seek research opportunities? Perform well in class and be motivated and visible in your department. Approach faculty during their office hours and ask who might be looking for research assistants. If you're interested in a particular faculty member's work, approach him or her and ask if you can help.

SEEK INTERNSHIPS AND PRACTICA

Secure an internship or practicum for hands-on experience. Internships provide wonderful opportunities to apply what you've learned in the classroom to the real world, have learning experiences that you'd never obtain in a classroom setting, and explore potential careers. Another advantage of an internship is that it lets you sample a potential career. Do you really want to work with people? Your internship experiences may surprise you. In addition, internships can provide contacts in the field, a possible offer for paid employment after graduation, and someone who can provide a reference or recommendation based on your ability to apply your knowledge of psychology in a real-world setting. Learn about internship opportunities by asking faculty in your department. Also visit the career development center at your college and you might learn about additional opportunities for hands-on experience.

TAKE ADDITIONAL CLASSES AND GET A MINOR

Regardless of your career plans, classes and experiences that enhance your communications skills (for example, courses in writing, speech, and communications; writing for the campus newspaper) are a good investment because employers view communication skills favorably (MSU Career Placement and Services, 2008; National Association of Colleges and Employers, 2008). After you have considered what types of careers interest you, take a few elective courses outside of psychology that are specific to your goals. For example, if you plan to enter the business world, a course in management or accounting would be useful. If you would like a job in human services, take courses in social work, communication, criminal justice, sociology, or anthropology. Throughout this book we will mention courses that students with particular interests may take to enhance their marketability. Many students find that declaring a minor permits them to obtain—and demonstrate—skills that can enhance the value of their bachelor's degree. For example, a psychology major with a minor in marketing or economics might be particularly attractive to employers in business settings. Once you know what you'd like to do, consider adding a minor to your curriculum to enhance your experience and skill set.

GET WORK EXPERIENCE

Work experience is invaluable because it helps you figure out what you're good at and what you like while gaining the experience that employers seek. There are plenty of part-time and summer jobs that allow you to hone your interpersonal skills and explore potential careers. Try a job as a camp counselor, residence-hall advisor, childcare worker, or human-services worker. According to the Collegiate Employment Research Institute, over four-fifths of employers rate career-related employment as extremely important for prospective hires (MSU Career Placement and Services, 2008), so your time will be well spent.

ENGAGE IN EXTRACURRICULAR ACTIVITIES

Extracurricular activities can help you develop useful skills and enhance your marketability. Like internships and work experience, extracurricular activities can provide you with opportunities to test career paths, develop contacts, and work on your communication skills. In addition, employers value volunteer work for campus and community organizations because it shows that you are a good citizen. Extracurricular participation provides employers with evidence about your leadership skills, ability to work effectively in a group, and your initiative and motivation.

As a final piece of advice, be open to new possibilities. Flexibility is an important life skill critical to coping and optimal development throughout adulthood. Employers rate adaptability as highly desired in new employees (National Association of Colleges and Employers, 2008). Adaptability and tolerance for ambiguity are important characteristics for graduate students because science, like life, isn't always clear-cut and obvious. As you read through the chapters in this book and explore various career opportunities, practice being open to new possibilities. Actively consider each subdiscipline and career opportunity to determine if it's a good fit for your interests and aspirations. Above all, keep an open mind and explore multiple possibilities. You will be more likely to find a job and career that you will love.

SUGGESTED READINGS

Halonen, J. S., & Davis, S. F. (Eds.). (2001). *The many faces of psychological research in the 21st century*. Retrieved July 1, 2008, from the Society for the Teaching of Psychology Web site: http://teachpsych.org/resources/e-books/faces/index_faces.php
Kuther, T. L. (2006). *The psychology major's handbook* (2nd ed.). Belmont: Wadsworth.

Landrum, R. E., & Davis, S. F. (2007). *The psychology major: Career options and strategies for success.* Upper Saddle River, NJ: Pearson Education.

Morgan, B. L., & Korschgen, A. J. (2009). *Majoring in psych? Career options for psychology undergraduates.* Boston, MA: Allyn and Bacon.

Sternberg, R. J. (2006). *Career paths in psychology: Where your degree can take you.* (2nd ed.). Washington, DC: American Psychological Association.

Zichy, S., & Bidou, A. (2007). *Career match: Connecting who you are with what you'll love to do.* Washington, DC: AMACOM.

WEB RESOURCES

Psychology: Scientific Problem Solvers—Careers for the 21st Century
http://www.apa.org/students/brochure/index.html

Eye on Psi Chi
http://www.psichi.org/pubs/search.asp

Careers in Psychology
http://www.psywww.com/careers/index.htm

Pursuing Psychology Career Page
http://www.uni.edu/walsh/linda1.html

Career Key
http://www.careerkey.org

American Psychological Association
http://www.apa.org

American Psychological Society
http://www.psychologicalscience.org

State Psychological Associations
http://www.apa.org/practice/refer.html

Psi Chi
http://www.psichi.org

Psi Beta
http://www.psibeta.org/

Eastern Psychological Association
http://www.easternpsychological.org/

Midwestern Psychological Association
http://www.midwesternpsych.org/

Rocky Mountain Psychological Association
http://www.rockymountainpsych.org/

Southeastern Psychological Association
http://www.sepaonline.com/

Southwestern Psychological Association
http://www.swpsych.org/

Western Psychological Association
http://www.westernpsych.org/

CHECKLIST: IS PSYCHOLOGY FOR YOU?

Do you:

- ☐ Have an interest in how the mind works?
- ☐ Want to learn how to think critically?
- ☐ Have an interest in research?
- ☐ Feel comfortable with computers?
- ☐ Want to learn how the brain works and its effect on behavior?
- ☐ Have an interest in mental illness?
- ☐ Like mathematics?
- ☐ Have an interest in how we grow and change over the lifespan?
- ☐ Have an interest in personality and what makes people unique?
- ☐ Wonder how we perceive stimuli in our environment?
- ☐ Have an interest in learning how research findings can be applied to solve real-world problems?
- ☐ Want to learn how to work well with others?
- ☐ Want a well-rounded education?
- ☐ Have an interest in biology and how physiology influences behavior?
- ☐ Have the ability to be flexible and deal with ambiguity?
- ☐ Want to help people?

Scoring: The more boxes you checked, the more likely it is that you're a good match for the psychology major.

Getting a Job After Graduation

Psychology is one of the most common bachelor's degrees awarded annually. Where do all of those graduates go? The majority do not go to graduate school. Instead, they enter the world of work and find jobs. In this chapter we discuss the job-search process, from locating positions to constructing résumés, preparing for interviews, and accepting a job offer.

19

WHAT DO EMPLOYERS SEEK?

What exactly do employers seek in new hires? Several research studies have examined this question (Appleby, 2000; Edwards & Smith, 1988; Grocer & Kohout, 1997; Lloyd & Kennedy, 1997; National Association of Colleges and Employers, 2000; Sheetz, 1995). Table 2.1 presents the results. In Chapter 1 we discussed the competencies that are typical of bachelor's degree holders in psychology. Do you notice any similarity between the skills employers seek and those that a major in psychology develops? You may be better prepared for the career world than you think; employers covet the skills that psychology majors develop. The interpersonal skills, research knowledge, and competence typical of psychology majors, honed through course work, practica, and extracurricular activities, provide an upper hand in the job market. Your major has helped you to develop a host of skills that employers want. To enhance your marketability and improve your employment options, review the tips for success discussed in Chapter 1.

TABLE 2.1 | SKILLS EMPLOYERS VALUE IN NEW HIRES

Reading and Writing Skills:

- The ability to extract important ideas through reading
- Writing skills to document ideas
- Ability to write reports, proposals, and summaries

Problem Solving Skills:

- Good judgment and decision-making skills
- The ability to apply information to solve problems and analyze problems on the basis of personal experience and psychological principles

Career-Related Work Experience:

- Hands-on practical experience through cooperative education, internships, practica, part-time jobs, or summer work experience
- A real-world work orientation and the ability to apply school-based knowledge in practical settings

Data Analysis Skills:

- Computational skills, the ability to reason numerically, and to identify problems in data
- The ability to collect, record, and report statistical information

Computer Skills:

- Knowledge of software applications including word-processing, spreadsheet, and database software
- Familiarity with the Internet and e-mail

Communication and Interpersonal Skills:

- Good listening skills
- The ability to communicate orally in a clear, concise, accurate, and logical fashion
- Sensitivity to social signals
- Group skills including discussion, team building, and conflict management
- Tolerance for, and an understanding of, individual differences

continued

TABLE 2.1 | CONTINUED

Psychological Knowledge:

- Specific psychological knowledge, such as how attitudes are formed and changed, or how people think, problem solve, and process information
- An understanding of group dynamics
- Knowledge about how people perceive and sense their environment

Self Management:

- Personal qualities and traits such as self-esteem, confidence, and social skills
- Tolerance for stress and ambiguity
- Ability to set and pursue goals, control one's emotions, and engage in appropriate behavior

Information Acquisition and Use:

- An understanding of how to absorb and retain information
- Understanding how to learn, where to find information, and how to evaluate and use it

Adaptability:

- The ability to be adaptable, be flexible, and handle multiple tasks
- A broad knowledge base outside of the field of psychology
- The ability to utilize resources in order to effectively complete tasks (e.g., creating a schedule, writing a budget, assigning space, and managing others)

Your skills are valued, but how do you find an employment setting in which to apply them? How do you get a job? In the following sections we provide an overview of the job-seeking process. Remember that this is simply an overview. There are many books and Internet sites devoted to job seeking, and we encourage you to explore the resources listed at the end of this chapter for additional, more detailed, job-seeking information.

LOCATE POSITIONS

Perhaps the most important thing to remember about looking for a job is that it is very unlikely that you will encounter a job ad seeking a psychology major. Generally speaking, most job ads do not mention specific majors. Although now and then an ad might list a preference for psychology majors, don't hold your breath waiting. Throughout the job-search process it is helpful to remember that most employers and the public at large have mistaken beliefs about psychology and psychology majors, such as those we discussed in Chapter 1 (psychology students become psychologists, psychology graduates do therapy, and so on). When looking for job openings, think in terms of skills rather than job titles. Job titles can be misleading—what skills are required? Your task throughout the job-search process is to educate potential employers by discussing the competencies that you have developed and how the psychology curriculum has improved your knowledge and skill base.

Your first stop in the job-hunting process should be the career services office at your college or university, where you'll find skilled professionals who can help you with all aspects of the job search, including locating positions. Employers often contact colleges seeking to hire new graduates. Read the job ads in your local newspaper; many newspapers maintain searchable online databases of job ads. Contact the human resources departments of major businesses, corporations, and agencies in your area to inquire about job openings. Note that many business and organizations advertise jobs on their Web pages, typically linked from the Human Resources Web page or on a page called "Employment Opportunities." The Internet has many sites devoted to job seekers. The internet resources at the end of this chapter offer a few examples of comprehensive job sites. Finally, remember that most jobs aren't advertised, so it's important that you use your personal networks to locate "hidden" positions. Through school, friends (and their parents), part-time jobs, and internships, you've already made many connections. Tap into these professional connections when scouting for positions and you may get leads on jobs that aren't advertised to the general public.

PREPARE A RÉSUMÉ

A well-written résumé is the ticket to getting an interview—and possibly a job offer. A résumé is a summary of your educational history, skills, and work experience. Employers always expect prospective employees to include résumés in their applications—even if they don't explicitly say so in their advertisement. Your résumé is your first, and sometimes only, contact with an employer. The sole purpose of a résumé is to convince an employer to interview you. It's a chance to present yourself: your strengths and unique fit to the position to which you're applying. Therefore, your task is to showcase your skills and competencies: What can you do for the employer and contribute to the organization?

As you prepare your résumé, carefully consider your experience and the corresponding skills. Employers study résumés with the awareness that prior behavior predicts future behavior. Think about your successful experiences and what characteristics and abilities influenced your success. What contributions have you made and what skills underlie those competencies? What transferrable skills (skills that are useful in many jobs) have you learned? The work that you describe need not be paid. Volunteer experiences that demonstrate your competencies are valuable. Employers care about whether you can do the job—it doesn't matter whether the evidence you give is from paid or unpaid experiences. There are many types of résumés, but chronological and functional résumés are the two most common.

CHRONOLOGICAL RÉSUMÉ

The chronological résumé presents your education and career in a chronological framework and is easy for employers to understand and read. A brief description of the content of each section of the chronological résumé follows; a sample chronological résumé appears in Table 2.2.

TABLE 2.2 | SAMPLE CHRONOLOGICAL RÉSUMÉ

CHRISTINE JONES

Student Dorms #321
Your University
Purchase, NY 11234
(914) 555-1414
Jones@yourstateu.edu

77 Pleasant Street
Pleasantville, NY 11245
(914) 555-6677
Fax (914) 555-9999

OBJECTIVE:	Entry-level position in human resources using interpersonal and organizational skills.
EDUCATION:	Your University, Purchase, NY Bachelor of Arts in Psychology, May 2001 Minor: Communications
EXPERIENCE:	Resident Assistant, Your University, Purchase, NY, May, 1999–present Assisted the director of a 360-resident living unit on campus. Assisted in creating and implementing policies and procedures for managing the residence. Developed and presented programs on a variety of subjects including alcohol awareness, career development, leadership, and safety. Intern, *Purchase Daily News*, Purchase, NY August, 1998–May, 1999 Researched and wrote weekly articles on breaking news. Interviewed and researched local residents for weekly "Local Profile" articles. Cashier, Purchase Delicatessen, Purchase, NY June, 1997–August, 1999 Assisted customers in locating products, operated computerized cash register, handled large sums of cash, stocked shelves, and monitored store inventory.
ACTIVITIES:	Theater Society, active member, two years, chorus member in three plays Psychology Club, active member, three years, organized fund-raisers, participated in tutoring groups, and invited local speakers to club meetings.
REFERENCES:	Available upon request.

Source: From Kuther, 2006.

- **Contact information.** Include your name, permanent address, phone number, fax number, and e-mail. Be sure to use a professional e-mail address, not a nickname. An e-mail address such as "HotTamale101" will be perceived poorly. Also, if you use a free e-mail account (for example, Hotmail, Yahoo), you should know that some employers' mail services may mark mail from free e-mail services as spam. Only include your Web site if it looks professional and is relevant to your career goals. Generally, it's a good idea not to list your MySpace or Facebook accounts.

- **Education.** Include the name of the degree you will receive, institution, and date, major and GPA (only if it's higher than 3.0). Also include any academic honors that you've received.
- **Experience.** Present all relevant employment experiences: part-time and full-time, internships, cooperative education, self-employment, or volunteer, listing your most recent position first and working backwards. Include the title, company, address, and dates of employment. Briefly describe your duties and responsibilities as they relate to the position you are seeking, and emphasize specific skills and achievements. Use active words to describe your duties and the results that you produced.
- **Activities and affiliations.** List professional affiliations and activities that illustrate your skills. List leadership activities and extracurricular activities on campus if they demonstrate useful competencies (for example, team work, leadership, problem solving). Only include those things to which you can draw a connection with your employment goals.

The main disadvantage of a chronological résumé is that applicants who are just starting out usually do not have many professional experiences to list, resulting in a résumé that may appear skimpy. Employers may not easily recognize your skills when you have limited work-related experiences. In these cases, a functional résumé is often recommended.

FUNCTIONAL RÉSUMÉ

The functional résumé organizes your experiences and work history by highlighting skills and accomplishments that might not be obvious in a chronological résumé. Table 2.3 illustrates the functional résumé.

The functional résumé begins with a listing of contact information, similar to the chronological résumé. The next section, *Specific Accomplishments*, is what makes a functional résumé radically different from a chronological résumé. Rearrange your employment, volunteer, and internship experiences into subsections that highlight areas of skills and accomplishments. Each skill or accomplishment subsection must contain statements supporting your experience in that category. You might list bullet points noting specific experiences that illustrate the skill (for example, worked as a team with four colleagues to prepare a presentation of the weanis; sold 600 widgets in two days), and then list employers and work dates towards the end of the résumé along with education. Or you might list the employer and work dates under each skill section, as is shown in Table 2.3. The drawback to this is that each employer may be associated with only one skill. Organize accomplishments in their order of importance with regard to the position that you seek. The *Experience* and *Education* sections follow and are identical to those in the chronological résumé. The caveat of the functional résumé is that employers tend to be less familiar with them. Some employers dislike functional résumés because they prefer to see a direct link between employment position and specific skills and duties.

Take great care in crafting your résumé; most employers glance at a résumé for 20 to 30 seconds (Krannich, 2002). If the first few lines of your résumé don't catch the employer's attention, your opportunity is lost. Make it past the 20-second test

TABLE 2.3	SAMPLE FUNCTIONAL RÉSUMÉ

CHRISTINE JONES

Student Dorms #321	77 Pleasant Street
Your University	Pleasantville, NY 11245
Purchase, NY 11234	(914) 555 -6677
(914) 555-1414; Jones@yourstateu.edu	Fax (914) 555-9999

Interpersonal Experience
Resident Assistant, Your University, Purchase, NY, May, 1999—Present

Assisted the director of a 360-resident living unit on campus. Assisted in creating and implementing policies and procedures for managing the residence. Developed and presented programs on a variety of subjects including alcohol awareness, career development, leadership, and safety.

Cashier, Purchase Delicatessen, Purchase, NY June, 1997—August, 1999
Assisted customers in locating products, operated computerized cash register, handled large sums of cash, stocked shelves, and monitored store inventory.

Leadership and Organizational Experience
Psychology Club, active member, three years, organized-fund raisers, participated in tutoring groups, and invited local speakers to club meetings.

Writing Experience
Intern, *Purchase Daily News*, Purchase, NY August, 1998—May, 1999

Researched and wrote weekly articles on breaking news. Interviewed and researched local residents for weekly "Local Profile" articles.

Public Speaking
Theater Society, active member, two years, chorus member in three plays

Education
Your University, Purchase, NY
Bachelor of Arts in Psychology, Minor: Communications, May 2001

Source: Adapted from Kuther, 2006.

by considering the main question that employers ask themselves as they read résumés: Why should I read this or contact this person for an interview? Keep this in mind as you prepare your résumé; make sure that you answer it, and you'll have a unique résumé. Employers look for applicants who stand out and often simply skim résumés looking for something of interest. If you have special experience or skills, list them towards the top of your résumé—put them up front to increase visibility. All of this hard work is essential; a good résumé gets you to the next stage, whereas a poor résumé stops you from going anywhere.

Professionalism, or rather a lack of it, is one thing that can stop you from getting an interview, regardless of your experience. Make your résumé look professional by using a laser printer and remembering that errors are the kiss of death for your application. Because employers are often inundated with résumés, they look for reasons to remove a résumé from the pile. Typos will get you the boot. See Table 2.4 for more résumé tips. Also, there are many books and Internet resources that provide advice for writing résumés. See the recommended readings and Web sites at the end of this chapter for more information.

TABLE 2.4	RÉSUMÉ CHECKLIST

- Clearly communicate your purpose and value.
- Communicate your strongest points first.
- Don't make statements that you can't document.
- Be direct, succinct, and expressive with language.
- Don't use lengthy sentences and descriptions; this is the only time that sentence fragments are acceptable, but use them judiciously.
- Don't use the passive voice.
- Don't change the tense of verbs throughout the résumé.
- Confine your information to one page.
- Use space to organize your résumé; it should not appear cramped.
- Aim for overall visual balance on the page.
- Use a font size of 10 to 14 points.
- Choose a simple typeface and stick to it (don't change fonts).
- Use ample spacing and bold for emphasis (but don't overdo it).
- Don't fold or staple your résumé.
- Check spelling, grammar, and punctuation.
- Proofread.
- Ask someone else to proofread.
- Get outside help. Get feedback from two or three people, including someone who regularly evaluates résumés and hires employees.
- Do not include your reference information on your résumé (see sample).
- Before giving their names to a potential employer, ask your references if they are willing to serve as references.

Source: From Kuther, 2006.

SOLICIT REFERENCES

Nearly all positions to which you apply will require you to provide several references—people who can verify your qualifications and abilities. Who should you use as a reference? Employers are interested in your potential as an employee, so your references should be able to comment on your professional abilities and personal characteristics that directly relate to job performance, like dependability, resourcefulness, and attitude. Professors, supervisors for your practica or other applied experiences, and former employers are good choices for references. As you choose your references, remember that you must ask before listing them on your résumé or application. Specifically, ask if they are able to give you a good recommendation (you don't want just any recommendation). Provide them with a copy of your résumé and ask them what other materials they may need. Whenever you go on the job market (especially after graduation), contact your references to fill them in on your experiences as well as to request their assistance and simply remind them of who you are. When a prospective employer contacts one of your references, you don't want that person to ask, "Who?" Don't surprise your references; ask their permission first so that you make a good impression and ensure that they feel comfortable recommending you for a job.

TABLE 2.5	COVER LETTER CHECKLIST

- Address the letter to an individual, using the person's name and title. If answering a blind newspaper advertisement, use the following address: "To Whom It May Concern."
- Indicate the position for which you are applying and explain why you are qualified to fill it.
- Include a phone number where you can be reached.
- Ask someone to proofread your letter for spelling, grammar, and punctuation errors.
- Indicate how your education and work skills are transferable and relevant to the position for which you are applying.
- Keep a copy of each cover letter for your records; write notes from any phone conversations that might occur on your copy of the cover letter.
- Make a connection to the company through a person you know, some information you've researched, or a specific interest.

Source: From Kuther, 2006.

WRITE A COVER LETTER

Your résumé highlights your skills, but you must also explain why you are well-suited to a particular job. The cover letter is an introduction to your résumé that enables you to tailor your application to the prospective employer. Your cover letter must be concise, and explain who you are and what you can offer an employer and organization. Usually three paragraphs will suffice. First, explain your reason for writing (for example, "to apply to the research assistant position advertised in the *Daily News*"). Demonstrate interest in the employer and position—why do you want to work there? Then, discuss what you can offer an employer. Highlight the most important aspects of your background that are relevant to the position and/or organization. Show that you have done some homework and learned about the employer. Finally, summarize your main points, provide contact information, thank the reader, and reiterate your interest in the position.

Your cover letter should motivate the reader to examine your résumé. Keep your audience in mind and address their needs. Continually ask yourself, "What is the purpose of this letter? What are the needs of the reader? What benefits will an employer gain from me? How can I maintain the reader's interest? How can I end the letter persuasively, so that the reader will want to examine my résumé and contact me?" Communicate what you can do for the employer, not what the job will do for you. Table 2.5 presents a cover letter checklist.

ACE THE INTERVIEW

If your résumé shows a good fit to the position, you may be invited for an interview. The interview is the most important criterion for hiring; it beats out grades, related work experience, and recommendations (Krannich, 2002). The interview helps companies to identify which applicants they'd like to take a closer look at. Often second, and sometimes even third, interviews occur. This is your chance to impress the prospective employer. How do you do it? Present a professional image, good communication skills, clearly defined professional goals, honesty, and cheerfulness. Be sure to prepare beforehand because your interviewer is interested in understanding why you want to work for them, what you're suited for, and your qualifications. Interviews are stressful, but you can increase your confidence by being thoroughly prepared.

PREPARATION

Keep the purpose of the interview and the interviewer's objectives in mind. From your perspective, the purpose of the job interview is to get a second interview or job offer; for employers, the purpose is to whittle down the list of applicants to one or two finalists. The interviewer seeks to learn the following:

- Why does this person want to work for us?
- What position is this person suited for?
- What are his or her qualifications?
- Why should I hire him or her?
- Does this person meet my employment needs?
- Is he or her trustworthy?

He or she looks for reasons why you should not be hired. Interviewers are interested in identifying your weaknesses. Your job is to communicate your strengths. To do so, you need to understand yourself and the company or organization to which you are applying.

Conduct research in order to understand the needs of the organization and to demonstrate that you are interested and knowledgeable. What is the relative size and growth of the industry? What product lines or services are offered? Where is the headquarters? Identify the competition. Be familiar with any recent items in the news. Try to predict what will be asked during the interview, and prepare answers. Table 2.6 presents common questions asked during interviews. Essentially, employers want to know if you are able to do the work, want to do the work, and are able to work with others. Be prepared to talk about your experiences, interests, and fit to the position and organization. You also will be judged on the questions that you ask. Naïve applicants underestimate the significance of asking good questions—you should ask thoughtful and intelligent questions about the company and position. Table 2.7 provides sample questions that an applicant might ask on an interview.

DRESS APPROPRIATELY

Dress appropriately for your interview; your appearance communicates messages about your level of seriousness and professionalism. During the first five minutes of an interview, interviewers make initial judgments or create expectations about your professionalism and "fit" for a position based on your appearance and demeanor. Do you look like you belong here? Use this to your advantage by dressing appropriately. Even if you are applying to a company with a casual dress code, dress up a bit for the interview to communicate your enthusiasm for the position. One rule of thumb is to dress one step above the expected dress code. If, for example, the setting is business casual (slacks, shirts, no ties), you might wear dark slacks and a tie.

TABLE 2.6 | COMMON INTERVIEW QUESTIONS

- What do you hope to be doing five or ten years from now?
- Why did you apply for this job?
- Tell me about yourself.
- What are your strengths and weaknesses?
- What can you offer to us and what can we offer to you?
- What are the two or three accomplishments in your life that have given you the greatest satisfaction?
- Do you work well under pressure?
- Have you ever held any supervisory or leadership roles?
- What do you like to do in your spare time?
- What other jobs are you applying for?
- Is there anything else we should know about you?
- Why do you feel that you will be successful in this position?
- What courses did you like best? Least? Why?
- What did you learn or gain from your part-time and summer job experience?
- What are your plans for graduate study?
- Why did you choose your major?
- What can a psychology major do for this organization?
- How did you finance your education?
- If you could do it all again, what would you change about your education?
- Did you do the best you could in school? Why or why not?
- Why did you leave your last employer?
- What job did you like the most? The least? Why?
- Have you ever been fired?
- Why do you want to join our organization?
- Why should we hire you?
- When will you be ready to work?
- What do you want to do with your life?
- Do you have any actual work experience?
- How would you describe your ideal job?
- Are you a team player? Explain.
- What motivates you?
- Tell me about some of your recent goals and what you did to achieve them.
- Have you ever had a conflict with a boss or professor? How did you resolve it?
- Tell me about a problem you faced and how you solved it.
- If I were to ask one of your professors to describe you, what would he or she say?
- Why did you choose to attend your college?
- What qualities do you feel a successful manager should have?
- What do you know about our company?
- What kind of salary are you looking for?

Source: Adapted from Kuther, 2006.

Whether you're a man or a woman, you can't go wrong with an understated classic navy or gray suit. Men should wear a white or blue oxford shirt with an understated tie. Women should wear a modest blouse, with understated hair

TABLE 2.7 | QUESTIONS TO ASK DURING AN INTERVIEW

Tell me about the duties and responsibilities of this job.

How long has this position been in the company?

What would be the ideal type of person for this position?

What kinds of skills or personality characteristics are ideal for this position?

With whom would I be working?

What am I expected to accomplish during the first year?

How will I be evaluated?

Are promotions and raises tied to performance criteria?

What is unique about working for this company?

What does the future look like for this company?

Source: From Kuther, 2006.

and makeup. Keep jewelry to a minimum: a watch, simple earrings (for women only), and a ring. Remember that these are merely general rules. Look to how others in your field dress for cues about appropriate attire. Dress codes vary by employment setting and employer; some settings permit more creativity and self-expression. However, during an interview it is best to err on the side of conservatism.

DURING THE INTERVIEW

Greet the interviewer with a firm handshake and say their name after they introduce themselves (for example, "Pleased to meet you, Sally."). Be enthusiastic. Remember that your interviewer is committed to his or her position and the company, and wants to hire someone who is similarly committed. Discuss what you've learned from your research and preparation. Ask questions to fill in any gaps in your understanding. Convey a sense of long-term interest by asking about opportunities for further professional education and advancement, but make it clear that you are interested in the job in question, likely an entry-level position.

Throughout the interview, be aware of your body language and keep fidgeting to a minimum. Lean very slightly toward the interviewer to communicate your interest in what he or she is saying (Krannich, 2002). Maintain eye contact to convey interest and trustworthiness. Smile to convey your positive attitude. Don't forget that your tone of voice can indicate how interested you are in the interview and the organization. Here are some other helpful tips for acing interviews:

- Bring a copy of your résumé. It comes in handy if you have to fill in applications and provides initial information for your interviewer.
- Allow the interviewer to direct the conversation.

- Answer questions in a clear and positive manner.
- Never speak negatively about former employers or colleagues, no matter what.
- Let the interviewer lead the conversation toward salary and benefits. Try not to focus your interest on these issues (at least not during the initial interview).
- When discussing salary, be flexible.
- If the employer doesn't say when you'll hear about their decision, ask about when you can call to follow up.
- Thank the employer for the interview and follow up with a thank-you letter.

THE JOB OFFER

Usually job offers are made over the phone or in person (for example, toward the end of an interview). No matter how the offer is delivered, you're likely to be surprised. The most appropriate response to an offer in person or by phone is to ask any questions that come to mind, and then request time (a day or two) to think about the offer.

Before accepting an offer, be sure that you understand the conditions and elements of the job. In many cases, salaries for entry-level positions leave little room for negotiation. Take your lead from the employer as to whether the salary is negotiable. If it isn't, you must decide whether you're still willing to accept the position, and what, if anything, would make it more attractive. As you think about whether to accept the job offer, consider the scope of the position, how it fits your career goals, opportunities for professional growth, and pragmatics (geographic location, benefits, salary, work hours, and so on).

If you decide to accept the offer, be sure to inform any employers still actively considering you. Do not continue to interview and apply for other jobs. It is dishonest and unethical to continue a job search once you have committed to an employer. Contact your references to inform them of your new job as well as to thank them for their assistance.

If you decide not to accept the job, notify the employer as soon as possible, by telephone. Timeliness is important because other applicants also are waiting for a response. Be polite, thank the employer for the offer, and wish him or her success. Remember that the career world is often quite small. Someday you again may find yourself in contact with someone who has interviewed you. Don't burn bridges. The contact you make now may influence your career later. Reject job offers with gratitude and grace.

SUGGESTED READINGS

Bolles, R. N. (2007). *What color is your parachute? A practical manual for job-hunters and career-changers*. Berkeley, CA: Ten Speed Press.

DeGalan, J., & Lambert, S. (2006). *Great jobs for psychology majors*. Chicago, IL: VGM Career Horizons.

Fry, R. (2001). *Your first résumé: For students and anyone preparing to enter today's tough job market*. Thomson.

Greene, B. (2008). *Get the interview every time: Fortune 500 hiring professionals' tips for writing winning resumes and cover letters*. Kaplan.

Kuther, T. L. (2006). *The psychology major's handbook* (2nd ed.). Wadsworth.

Morgan, B. L., & Korschgen, A. J. (2009). *Majoring in psych? Career options for psychology undergraduates*. Boston, MA: Allyn and Bacon.

Sher, B. (1995). *I could do anything if only I knew what it was: How to discover what you really want and how to get it*. Dell.

WEB RESOURCES

Quintessential Careers
http://www.quintcareers.com

College Grad Job Hunter
http://www.collegegrad.com/

JobWeb
http://www.jobweb.com

MonsterTrak.com
http://monstertrak.com/

Headhunter/Job Seeker
http://www.headhunter.net

JobTrak
http://www.jobtrak.com

CareerBuilder
http://www.careerbuilder.com

Psi Chi: Eye on Psi Chi
http://www.psichi.org/pubs/eye/home.asp

CLINICAL AND COUNSELING PSYCHOLOGY

CHAPTER 3

CHAPTER GUIDE

Clinical Psychology

Counseling Psychology

Other Mental Health Professions

Opportunities with a Bachelor's Degree

Human Services Worker

Social Worker

Substance Abuse Counselor

Opportunities with a Graduate Degree

Graduate Education and Training Considerations

Practice

Program Development and Evaluation

Administration

Suggested Readings

Web Resources

Checklist: Is Clinical or Counseling Psychology for You?

Did you know that about 61 percent of psychology doctoral graduates are from the subfields of clinical, counseling, or school psychology (American Psychological Association Center for Workforce Studies, 2008)? Clearly, mental health service providers comprise the largest subfields in psychology. Why are these subfields so popular? Many students explain their career choices by stating simply,

"I want to help people." The mental health service provider subfields afford students opportunities to gain specialized skills and knowledge that can assist people suffering from mental illness, emotional or behavioral problems, or other psychological distress. Because the mental health service field is so large, we'll discuss it within the next two chapters; in this chapter we examine clinical and counseling psychology, and in Chapter 4 we'll explore the subfield of school psychology. Do clinical and counseling psychologists do the same thing? Do they have the same jobs? If not, how are they different? These are important questions for students at the baccalaureate, masters, and doctoral levels considering careers as mental health service providers.

Before reviewing the two subdisciplines of clinical and counseling psychology, it is worth exploring the question of how are they different. Results of empirical research suggested that there are few quantitative differences between clinical psychology Ph.D., Psy.D., and counseling psychology Ph.D. programs (Morgan & Cohen, in press). In fact, there appear to be greater discrepancies within each specialty than between the two specialties of clinical and counseling psychology (Cobb et al., 2004; Morgan & Cohen, in press). Nevertheless, subtle differences exist in training requirements (see Morgan & Cohen, in press, for a detailed description of these differences) as well as historical and philosophical differences (see Roger & Stone, n.d.).

CLINICAL PSYCHOLOGY

Clinical psychology is the integration of science, theory, and practice to explain and understand, predict, and alleviate psychological problems and distress, as well as promote healthy human development (American Psychological Association Society of Clinical Psychology, n.d.). Assessment and diagnosis, intervention or treatment, consultation, research, and application of ethical and professional principles are the necessary skills developed by training in clinical psychology (Resnick, 1991). In other words, clinical psychologists work to help people alleviate distress or to improve their functioning via (1) psychological practice, or the provision of services such as assessment, diagnosis, and treatment (for example, psychotherapy); (2) consultation; or (3) by conducting research aimed at understanding human phenomena with the goal of helping people. But where are clinical psychologists found and how do they spend their time?

Primary employment settings of clinical psychologists include: private practice (40%), university settings (19%), hospital settings (9%), outpatient clinics and community mental health centers (8%), medical schools (9%), Veteran's Administrative (VA) Medical Centers (3%), and "other" settings such as correctional facilities, child and family services, rehabilitation centers, and so on (11%) (Norcross, Karg, & Prochaska; 1997). Clinical psychologists spend approximately 37% of their time involved in direct client intervention (for example, psychotherapy) and approximately 15% of their time in assessment- and diagnostic-related activities (Norcross et al., 1997). Somewhat less frequent activities of clinical psychologists include administrative responsibilities (11%), research/writing activities (10%), teaching (9%), supervision of other mental health service providers (7%), and professional consultation (7%) (Norcross et al., 1997).

COUNSELING PSYCHOLOGY

Counseling psychologists, like their clinical psychology colleagues, work to alleviate distress and emotional or behavioral difficulties associated with psychological problems; however, counseling psychology maintains an equal focus on helping people improve their well-being across the lifespan, including emotional, social, vocational, health-related, developmental, and organizational concerns (Society of Counseling Psychology, Division 17: American Psychological Association, n.d.). Additionally, counseling psychologists have been instrumental in sensitizing psychologists to an understanding and appreciation of human diversity, particularly as multicultural issues relate to human functioning. Defined more simply, counseling psychology is a field of study that works to improve human functioning, either by enhancing current functioning or by alleviating distress.

The roots of counseling psychology can be found in five unifying themes: (1) focus on intact or normative functioning rather than profoundly disturbed functioning; (2) focus on client's assets and strengths, and positive mental health; (3) emphasis on brief interventions (for example, counseling sessions of fewer than 15 sessions); (4) emphasis on person-environment interactions, rather than focus on person or environment as separate entities; and (5) emphasis on educational and career development and vocational environments (Gelso & Fretz, 2001). It is not surprising then, that based on these unifying themes, counseling psychologists are more likely to identify themselves primarily as clinical practitioners (48%) than other professional roles such as academicians (28%), administrators (11%), consultants (6%), and researchers (3%) (Watkins, Lopez, Campbell, & Himmel, 1986); however, like their clinical psychology colleagues, counseling psychologists are employed in a variety of settings: colleges and universities, including university counseling centers; private practice; community mental health centers; psychiatric hospitals; medical facilities; correctional facilities; VA medical centers; health maintenance organizations; family services; business and consulting firms; and rehabilitation agencies.

OTHER MENTAL HEALTH PROFESSIONS

It is also worth noting that there are mental health professions that are not based in the discipline of psychology. That is, some mental health training does not have psychology as the disciplinary root. Many students may find marriage and family therapy (MFT) programs, rehabilitation or rehabilitation counseling programs, social work programs, or addictions counseling programs a better fit for their career interests (for more information see: American Association of Marriage and Family Therapy, 2002; American Counseling Association, 2008; National Association of Social Workers, 2008; and National Rehabilitation Counseling Association, n.d.). A student in one of these programs may earn a doctoral-level degree (for example, Ph.D., Ed.D.), but a terminal masters degree (M.S. or M.A.) is more common. Licensure as a mental health professional (for example, Licensed Professional Counselor, LPC; Licensed Master Social Worker, LMSW) is then typically required to provide counseling or related clinical services.

Overlap exists between marriage and family therapy, rehabilitation counseling, social work, and clinical and counseling psychology, in the form of professional services provided and employment settings. The primary distinction with regard to clinical services is that psychologists are trained to administer and interpret psychological tests. Additionally, psychology-based programs at the masters and doctoral levels typically place greater emphasis on conducting research. This is not to say that students in other mental health programs are not trained in research—they are, particularly at the doctoral level; however, research appears to be more heavily emphasized in clinical and counseling psychology training programs than in social work programs. Regarding employment settings, these mental health professionals overlap with clinical and counseling psychologists and will be found in: community mental health centers, psychiatric hospitals, private practice, medical facilities, correctional facilities, family services, and rehabilitation agencies.

OPPORTUNITIES WITH A BACHELOR'S DEGREE

Although a graduate degree is the entry-level degree to practice professional psychology, several opportunities to help people exist for undergraduate psychology majors who choose not to pursue graduate education. Let's take a look at service opportunities for bachelor's degree holders in psychology.

HUMAN SERVICES WORKER

Human services workers occupy a range of positions, including social service worker, case management aide, social work assistant, community support worker, mental health aide, community outreach worker, life skills counselor, and gerontology aide (Bureau of Labor Statistics, 2008). These positions are paraprofessional positions with "a support role that overlaps with job duties and responsibilities of a psychologist; however, the paraprofessional does not have the education, responsibility, nor salary of the psychologist" (Landrum, Davis, & Landrum, 2000, p. 17). Human services workers provide services, both direct and indirect, to clients that typically include: assessing clients' needs and eligibility for services, helping clients obtain services (for example, food stamps, Medicaid, transportation, and other human services programs), and providing emotional support (Bureau of Labor Statistics, 2008). In community settings (such as group homes or government-supported housing programs), human services workers assist clients in need of counseling, assist with daily living skills, and organize group activities. In clinical settings (for example, psychiatric hospitals, outpatient clinics), human services workers support clients participation in treatment plans, assist with daily living skills, help clients communicate more effectively, and promote social functioning (Bureau of Labor Statistics, 2008).

Advantages to a position in human services are the opportunity to help others in need, as well as a steady job market. In fact, human services positions are expected to increase much faster than the average for all occupations through 2016, with an expected growth rate of 36 percent (Bureau of Labor Statistics, 2008). Unfortunately, long hours, difficult cases, and low income often lead to burnout. In 2006, the median salary of human services workers was $25,580, with a range of $20,350 to $32,440 for the middle 50 percent, and a peak salary of approximately $40,780 for human services workers (Bureau of Labor Statistics, 2008).

Notably, positions with local and state governments tend to offer better salaries than individual or family service agencies, vocational rehabilitation agencies, or residential mental health, substance abuse and mental retardation facilities (Bureau of Labor Statistics, 2008).

SOCIAL WORKER

Although a degree in social work is sometimes a prerequisite, entry-level social worker positions often can be obtained with a bachelor's degree in psychology. Social workers aim to help people improve their lives through counseling and identifying needed resources (such as housing or food stamps). Frequent duties include individual and group counseling sessions, identifying federal and state program assistance as needed (for example, housing assistance, disability benefits, food stamps, and so on) (Bureau of Labor Statistics, 2008). Social workers are employed in a variety of settings: hospitals, schools, community mental health centers, social service agencies, and courts and correctional institutions; thus, social workers can seek settings that best suit their needs and abilities.

Salaries for social workers tend to be moderate, with a median yearly salary in the mid-thirties (approximately $35,000); however, salaries are quite variable depending on education, location and agency with a median salary range of $32,490 to $48,420 (note that higher salaries are likely for positions at the masters degree level; Bureau of Labor Statistics, 2008). Other benefits of this career choice include an increasing job market (expected to increase by 22 percent by 2016; Bureau of Labor Statistics, 2008) and the satisfaction of helping people at the grass-roots level. A primary limitation of this career is the stress or feelings of helplessness resulting from difficulty identifying or securing appropriate resources for clients.

Although it is possible to obtain many social work positions with a bachelor's degree, continuing education in the form of a part-time masters program will increase your job security, opportunities for advancement, and ability to start a private practice. Salary will also increase with increased education. All states have licensing or certification requirements for private practice and the use of the title "social worker." Standards for licensing vary by state, so it's a good idea to check with your school's career development office and the Association of Social Work Boards (http://www.aswb.org/), to ensure that you are not disappointed.

SUBSTANCE ABUSE COUNSELOR

Although most counseling professions require graduate degrees (at least a masters degree) for employment, substance abuse counselors are a common exception. Substance abuse counselors provide counseling or rehabilitation services in residential treatment programs or as part of comprehensive outpatient substance abuse programs. The substance abuse counselor often is the primary therapist working with clients on their alcohol or drug dependence or abuse. Substance abuse counselors may spend their days facilitating therapy groups (particularly focused on educating clients about addiction and its related problems), as well as meeting individually with clients. Individual sessions allow therapists one-on-one time to focus on a client's specific problems.

The demand for drug and alcohol abuse counselors is strong, with an expected growth of 34 percent by 2016 (Bureau of Labor Statistics, 2008). Salaries for substance abuse counselors are consistent with other undergraduate positions listed in this chapter, with a median 2006 income of $34,040 per year, with the middle 50 percent earning between $27,330 and $42,650 (Bureau of Labor Statistics, 2008). It should be noted, however, that similar to social worker positions, higher salaries for substance abuse counselors are likely for positions that require a masters degree. Job availability and salary varies across the country, so examine the range of opportunities in your desired location as you plan for a career as a substance abuse counselor.

As with other mental health positions, one of the primary benefits of this career lies in the opportunity to help disturbed people who are in desperate need of help. In addition, the opportunity to enter the helping field at the baccalaureate level is attractive for students who want to enter the mental health profession but don't want to go to graduate school. Limitations of this career choice include the

TABLE 3.1	PREPARATION FOR B.A.–LEVEL CAREERS RELATED TO CLINICAL AND COUNSELING PSYCHOLOGY

Coursework
  Abnormal Psychology or Psychopathology
  Communications
  Community Mental Health
  Developmental Psychology
  Family Systems
  Interviewing, Counseling, or Helping Skills
  Professional Issues
  Psychological Assessment
  Psychopharmacology
  Social Work
  Substance Abuse
  Writing

Applied Experiences: Volunteer, intern/practica, or paid part-time positions in any of the following settings
  Any Mental Health Setting
  Big Brother/Big Sister Programs
  Boys and Girls Club
  Inpatient Psychiatric Unit
  Mental Retardation Facility
  Residential Treatment Facilities
  Substance Abuse Center

Research Experiences: Experiences studying and participating in research in any of the following areas*
  Abnormal Behavior
  Psychopathology
  Substance Abuse
  Specific Disorders (for example, Schizophrenia, Bipolar Disorder, Depression, Anxiety)
  Any treatment-, assessment-, or diagnostic-oriented research

*Note that the content area of the research is less important than the experience itself, which enhances reasoning, quantitative, writing, and organizational skills.

difficulty of professional advancement at the bachelor's degree level and the challenges of working with substance abusers, who often are resistant clients and can be difficult to work with.

Substance abuse counselors often are employed at the associate or bachelor's level, with certification. The requirements for certification as a drug and alcohol abuse counselor vary by state. Most states require the completion of four courses in drug and alcohol abuse counseling and 300 to 600 hours of supervised training. For more information about certification as a drug and alcohol abuse counselor, contact the National Association of Alcoholism and Drug Abuse Counselors (NAADAC) at http://www.naadac.org.

Although applied career opportunities exist for students who earn a bachelor's degree in psychology, many more opportunities exist for those earning a graduate degree. For example, students completing their masters (MA, MS), Ph.D., or Psy.D. may pursue applied careers as practitioners, program developers or evaluators, or consultants.

OPPORTUNITIES WITH A GRADUATE DEGREE

Your career options and financial prospects in clinical- and counseling-related careers expand dramatically with a graduate degree in psychology. Before we discuss graduate-level careers for students with interests in clinical and counseling psychology, let's take a look at graduate training and related issues. Students interested in these fields have several choices with regard to training. Following our discussion of graduate education in clinical and counseling psychology, we discuss three career trajectories for applied psychologists: practice, program development and evaluation, and administration.

Graduate Education and Training Considerations

Do your homework before entering graduate programs in counseling or clinical psychology. The most successful students are those who enter programs that are right for them (meaning, there is a good fit between the type of graduate program and their professional interests). As you read this book, you will realize there are many different types of programs available to you—clinical and counseling, but also non-service fields such as experimental or cognitive psychology. In this chapter, we examine the issue of choosing a graduate program in clinical and counseling psychology, but recognize that the decision-making process is similar in other fields (see Chapter 14 for more about applying to graduate school). Critically evaluate programs in light of your interests and career goals. Ask yourself:

- Do I understand the differences between the various programs? (How are clinical and counseling psychology different? What is a combined program?)
- What type of degree program is right for me (for example, Ph.D. or Psy.D.)?
- How do I get licensed after graduation?
- Are there other practice-related issues of which I should be aware?

DIFFERENTIATING CLINICAL AND COUNSELING PSYCHOLOGY.   Although the fields of counseling and clinical psychology overlap significantly (Cobb et al., 2004), subtle differences may be gleaned from the definitions provided earlier in this chapter.

It has commonly been suggested that one difference between the two disciplines is that clinical psychology is based on the medical model (meaning, assess, diagnose, and treat an ailment) whereas counseling psychology is less pathology-focused, favoring a holistic perspective emphasizing all aspects of a client's life. Not surprisingly, counseling psychologists, compared to their clinical psychology counterparts, tend to work with healthier individuals who are experiencing less psychopathology or distress (Norcross, Sayette, Mayne, Karg, & Turkson, 1998).

Consistent with a holistic perspective across the lifespan, counseling psychologists are more likely to conduct career and vocational assessments, whereas clinical psychologists, who focus on assessment and diagnosing pathology for treatment purposes (meaning, the medical model), are more likely to receive training in projective personality assessment (for example, the Rorschach or Thematic Apperception Test [TAT]) (Norcross, et al., 1998). Counseling psychologists tend to be employed in university counseling centers more often than clinical psychologists, whereas clinical psychologists are more likely to be employed in hospital settings (Gaddy, Charlot-Swilley, Nelson, & Reich, 1995; Watkins, et al., 1986). Another difference between the disciplines of clinical and counseling psychology is found in therapists' theoretical orientations. Clinical psychologists are more likely to endorse a behavioral or psychodynamic theoretical orientation, whereas their counseling psychology colleagues are more likely to endorse a person-centered (or Rogerian) theoretical orientation (Norcross, Prochaska, & Gallagher, 1989a; 1989b; Watkins et al., 1986).

With regard to training, results of empirical research suggest that there are few differences in clinical psychology Ph.D., Psy.D., and counseling psychology Ph.D. programs (Morgan & Cohen, in press). Two important differences are, first, that counseling psychologists are more likely to receive training in group psychotherapy than are clinical psychologists (Weinstein & Rossini, 1999) and, second, that counseling psychology programs tend to rely on external practicum sites for their graduate students, whereas clinical psychology programs are more likely to have in-house training clinics (meaning, psychology clinics operated by the department, which offers graduate student therapists opportunities to provide psychological services under close supervision of the faculty) (Morgan & Cohen, in press; Romans, Boswell, Carlozzi, & Ferguson, 1995). Given the few differences between training in clinical and counseling psychology, there appears to be more variation within each specialty than between the two specialties (Cobb et al., 2004; Morgan & Cohen, in press). Despite this, there are subtle differences in training requirements (see Morgan & Cohen, in press, for a detailed description of these differences) as well as historical and philosophical differences (see Roger & Stone, n.d.). Carefully evaluate each subdiscipline and each program to determine how each fit your interests and needs.

OPPORTUNITIES FOR GRADUATE EDUCATION.   If you're planning to seek graduate training in clinical or counseling psychology, understand that there is a large discrepancy in the number of graduate programs for each discipline. There are 232 American Psychological Association (APA)–accredited doctoral programs in clinical psychology compared to 72 APA–accredited doctoral programs in counseling psychology (American Psychological Association, 2007). It is not surprising that clinical psychology students accounted for 47 percent of all psychology doctorate degrees granted in 2003 (Center for Psychology Workforce Analysis and Research, 2008).

Both clinical and counseling psychology programs remain very competitive for admission, with an average admission rate of 6 percent for clinical psychology programs and 8 percent for counseling psychology programs (Norcross et al., 1998).

Admission criteria for clinical and counseling psychology programs are very similar, with some differences. Clinical psychology programs tend to require slightly higher verbal and quantitative Graduate Record Examination (GRE) scores than do counseling programs (Norcross et al., 1998). Another significant difference is in the percentage of students admitted with a masters degree versus a bachelor's degree. Counseling psychology programs are much more likely to admit a student who has already obtained a masters degree than are clinical psychology Ph.D. programs, which tend to admit students who have a bachelor's degree (Norcross et al., 1998). Counseling psychology programs also appear to be more ethnically diverse than their clinical counterparts (Morgan & Cohen, in press).

Somewhat less common than clinical and counseling programs are combined programs that integrate training from two or three of the subfields (counseling, school, and clinical psychology programs) without distinguishing among the disciplines. In other words, students in combined programs are trained in the principles of each of the specified subfields (for example, both clinical and school subfields). It should be noted that all combined programs are not alike; some integrate all three of the applied psychology disciplines (clinical, school, and counseling), whereas other programs incorporate either clinical or counseling psychology with school psychology. Although fewer combined programs (N = 11; American Psychological Association, 2007) exist compared to traditional counseling and clinical psychology programs, combined programs may offer increased diversity and a broader-based training experience for students; however, this has not been empirically examined.

PH.D. VERSUS PSY.D. DEGREES.   There are two types of doctoral degrees that a student interested in clinical psychology may obtain: the Ph.D. and Psy.D. How can we distinguish between these degrees? The first level of distinction can be found in their history. Generally speaking, the history of the Psy.D. is in training practitioners; thus, graduate training focuses more heavily on service provision than research. The history of the Ph.D., on the other hand, is based equally on science and practice (that is, the Boulder model), and so Ph.D. programs provide a greater focus on research skills than do Psy.D. programs. Students earning a Ph.D. complete a doctoral dissertation based in empirical research, whereas only a written project is often sufficient to complete requirements for the Psy.D. Alternatively, students in Psy.D. programs often accrue many more hours of clinical experience than do students in Ph.D. programs. So how do you know which degree is for you?

Consider two key issues. First, what do you hope to be doing in ten years? Although programs offering both the Ph.D. and Psy.D. train students to be clinicians, Ph.D. programs are more likely to train students to be scientists. If you're interested in becoming a practitioner and seek a program that emphasizes practice, the Psy.D. may fit your needs. However, if you're interested in developing your skills as a scientific researcher as well as your clinical skills, then the Ph.D. is in order. Which degree you choose is your decision, but recognize that there are very few noticeable differences in applicant quality between students in Psy.D. versus Ph.D. programs (Norcross et al., 1998). In other words, both options are highly competitive.

The second issue to consider is whether you prefer to attend a professional school or a more traditional university. The majority, albeit not all, of Psy.D. programs are housed in professional schools, whereas programs offering the Ph.D. are primarily housed in major state or private universities. What's the difference? We've already discussed the educational differences between the Ph.D. and Psy.D., but there's one more difference to consider: finances. Universities and private school based Ph.D. programs generally are less expensive and offer more funding to students (Norcross, Castle, Sayette, & Mayne, 2004). Professional schools, on the other hand, are not only more expensive but also tend to offer less financial assistance in the form of research and teaching assistantships (Norcross et al., 1998; 2004). While you should not base your decision solely on finances, it's important that you understand the economic realities of graduate education. For more information about graduate education, see Chapter 14.

LICENSURE.   The title of "psychologist" is protected; in order to provide psychological services (meaning, therapy, assessment, consultation) as a psychologist, you must be licensed in the state in which you wish to practice. Each state has a slightly different path to licensure; however, the basic process is roughly equivalent for all states.

First, a potential licensee must complete a doctoral program in clinical or counseling psychology (in a small minority of states, masters-level psychologists can seek licensure). Most states require that the doctoral degree is obtained in a program accredited by the APA, thereby certifying its rigor and training emphases, but it is possible in some states to seek licensure with a degree from a program that is not APA-accredited.

In addition to a doctoral degree, at least two years of supervised practice are required. Most students complete the first year as part of their degree requirements, the one-year full-time internship (or a two-year part-time internship) in which they receive supervision for providing psychological services (for example, therapy, assessment, crisis intervention). After completion of the doctoral degree (including completion of the internship), the licensee must acquire an additional year of supervised experience. This experience can be in the form of a formal postdoctoral program, but it can also be less structured (for example, in a private practice setting) as long as it includes providing psychological services under the supervision of a doctoral-level licensed psychologist.

After all degree and supervision requirements are met, the next step is to apply for licensure, which entails a national written examination and a jurisprudence examination. The national examination is multiple-choice, covering a broad range of issues and topics relevant to the practice of psychology. Because this is a national examination, the test is written for licensure applicants in all states and is thus of a generalist nature. A 70 percent accuracy rate is necessary to pass in most states, although states vary slightly in score requirements. The jurisprudence examination is also a written test; however, it is specific to the ethical code and licensure laws of each state. Thus, if you're applying for licensure in California, you will be asked questions regarding California law and its ethical code, but if you're applying for licensure in New York, you'll answer questions about New York statutes and ethics code.

After completion of the written examinations, many states require an additional oral examination in which licensees are presented with a case vignette and asked questions regarding diagnosis, treatment planning, and ethical concerns, as well as what multicultural issues might impact the case. As you can see, the process of obtaining licensure is time-consuming; it's also costly. For example, for one of the authors, the expense of pursuing licensure from start to finish cost approximately $1,300 (in 2000; adjusted for inflation, about $1,600 in 2007) after the examination and application fees. Furthermore, the expense and time commitment increases if a licensee doesn't pass a particular examination and therefore must repeat it (people fail the exams for various reasons). Despite the challenge of seeking licensure, it enables you to earn your stripes, so to speak. With licensure you are eligible to practice psychology without supervision.

INNOVATIVE TRAINING OPPORTUNITIES. Technological advances (for example, telemedicine), marketplace demands (such as managed care or prescription privileges for psychologists), and informational gains (for example, empirically-supported practice, formerly referred to as empirically based practice) continue to alter the face of psychology with the potential to profoundly impact the future of psychological practice. Two current issues that are gaining increased attention in psychology are prescription privileges and telemedicine or telehealth.

Prescriptive authority for mental health professionals has historically been limited to physicians and psychiatric nurses; however, psychologists in the United States military and several states recently gained prescription privileges, the ability to prescribe psychotropic medications to clients independent of psychiatrists or physicians. This opportunity not only meets a mental health service need in these agencies, states, or territories (for example, legislation was initiated in New Mexico because of a drought of psychiatrists in rural areas), but also creates many new practice and research opportunities for psychologists.

Similarly, the delivery of psychological services via computer networks is referred to as *behavioral medicine*, *telehealth*, or *telemental health* and is significantly expanding professional practice opportunities. In telehealth, a psychologist remains in one location and provides a psychological service (for example, therapy) to a client in a hospital, prison, or community agency in another location. This practice significantly alters the service delivery area of psychologists and may afford clients care from a specialist whom they would otherwise be unable to visit.

As relatively new and innovative practice strategies, many issues (including ethical and legal issues) must be navigated regarding training and competency in prescription authority as well as telehealth; however, for the innovative student the doors are wide open. If you have interests in these or other innovative opportunities, seek specialized experiences during graduate school that will best facilitate your future opportunities. For example, you may elect to complete coursework in psychopharmacology and seek practicum placements that require collaboration with psychiatrists. You might seek practicum opportunities in hospitals that rely on telehealth, or complete elective coursework in computer science to become as familiar as possible with computer technology. These are just a couple of examples of the myriad professional opportunities currently evolving in psychology, and students planning on pursuing a graduate degree in psychology are strongly encouraged to maintain an open mind and to seek innovative opportunities that may enhance future career possibilities.

PRACTICE

Undoubtedly, the greatest number of applied psychologists use their knowledge and skills as practitioners. Practitioners work in a variety of settings including private practices, hospitals, community mental health centers, schools, university or college counseling centers, criminal justice settings, and specialty clinics, to name just a few examples. In addition to selecting the setting where they will practice, psychologists also have an opportunity to decide if they want to specialize in a particular kind of client or problem. For example, some practitioners prefer to specialize in forensic or sports psychology practices, whereas other psychologists prefer to specialize in a particular type of presenting problem (for example, depression, anxiety, relationships).

One of the primary benefits of a graduate degree in clinical or counseling psychology is the flexibility to pursue career opportunities that match one's own interests and skills or abilities. Advanced degrees also afford practitioners salaries that are competitive with other psychology-related positions. In 2003, the median salary of all clinical psychologists (regardless of experience) was $75,000, and counseling psychologists earned a median salary of $65,000 (Pate, Frincke, & Kohout, 2005), varying by geographic location, setting, and clientele.

Another benefit for those interested in the practice of psychology is the expansion of the field. Psychology continues to break new ground and recent advances include delivering mental health services via telehealth and legislated prescription privileges. Although the days of seeing individual clients in one's private office are not extinct, neither is this type of service delivery necessarily the all-encompassing method of mental health services in the future. This is exciting for current students; innovative opportunities abound for those of you with imagination and foresight.

PROGRAM DEVELOPMENT AND EVALUATION

In addition to direct service delivery, clinical and counseling psychologists often pursue career opportunities in program development and evaluation. Psychologists may choose to develop the programs that schools or community placements offer, for example, rather than being the practitioner who provides the service.

Careers in program development and evaluation offer several benefits that practitioners don't always have. First is the opportunity to identify and develop the types of programs that are warranted for a particular agency or type of client. Working at the grassroots level such as this can be extremely rewarding, especially when a program is successful in helping the intended audience. Second, program developers avoid the stress of daily service provision to clients. On the other hand, psychologists involved in program development may miss the intimate contact and satisfaction from client progress that practitioners experience regularly. Typically, psychologists who take positions in program evaluation work as research associates at nonprofit organizations or as consultants. In 2007, research associates and consultants in private companies and government earned $85,000 and $77,000, respectively, with 2 to 4 years of experience. Those in nonprofit organizations, with 5 to 9 years of experience, earned $76,000 (American Psychological Association 2008).

ADMINISTRATION

ADMINISTRATIVE CAREERS.   In addition to careers in practice or as researchers, many clinical and counseling psychologists choose careers in administration. Administrators may be specialists who manage clinical services, or generalists who manage an entire agency or organization (Bureau of Labor Statistics, 2008). Administrators are responsible for overseeing the operation of an agency, including staffing and budget issues, healthcare delivery systems and technological advances, as well as daily operations (for example, mental health service delivery). If you're interested in a career in administration, take additional coursework in business administration, finance, and management.

Psychologists work in administrative roles within hospitals and clinics, community mental health centers and community organizations, correctional and rehabilitation centers, and nursing homes, to name just a few examples. Administrative positions in medical and mental health settings offer an attractive salary, with a median salary of $73,340 in 2006 with a slightly higher salary for those in general medical settings, and slightly less for those in outpatient service centers (Bureau of Labor Statistics, 2008). Another benefit of an administrative career is the direct influence administrators have on the services an organization delivers and the care clients or patients receive. On the other hand, administrative work typically requires long hours and job-related stress, particularly when dealing with personnel and budgetary issues (Bureau of Labor Statistics, 2008).

In this chapter we've covered just a few of the myriad possibilities available with a graduate degree in clinical or counseling psychology. Opportunities also exist for careers in writing and publishing (Chapter 13), research and academia (Chapter 13), corrections (Chapter 5), public health (Chapter 6), consulting (Chapter 9), marketing (Chapter 11), and social policy (Chapter 12), to name just a few.

SUGGESTED READINGS

Brown, S. D. & Lent, R. W. (Eds.). (2008). *Handbook of counseling psychology* (4th ed.) New York: Wiley.

Collison, B. B., & Garfield, N. J. (1996). *Careers in counseling and human services*. New York: Taylor & Francis.

Gelso, C., & Fretz, B. (2001). *Counseling psychology* (2nd ed.). Orlando: Harcourt.

Ginsberg, L. H. (2000). *Careers in social work*. Boston: Allyn & Bacon.

Kuther, T. L., Habben, C. J. & Morgan, R. D. (2005). "Today's new psychologist: Traditional and emerging career paths". In R. D. Morgan, T. L. Kuther & C. Habben (Eds.), *Life after graduate school in psychology: Insider's advice from new psychologists* (pp. 1–11). New York: Psychology Press.

Landrum, R. E. (2001). *I'm getting my bachelor's degree in psychology—what can I do with it? Eye on Psi Chi*, 6, 22–24.

Morgan, B. L. & Korschgen, A. (2001). *Majoring in psych? Career options for psychology undergraduates* (2nd ed.). Boston: Allyn & Bacon.

Srebalus, D. J. & Brown, D. (2000). *Guide to the helping professions*. Boston: Allyn & Bacon.

Woody, R. H. & Robertson, M. H. (1997). *A Career in clinical psychology: From training to employment*. Madison, CT: International Universities Press.

WEB RESOURCES

Division 12 of the American Psychological Association (Society of Clinical Psychology)
http://www.apa.org/divisions/div12/homepage.html

Society of Counseling Psychology (Division 17) of the American Psychological Association
http://www.div17.org/

So You're Considering Graduate Study in Clinical Psychology
http://www.wcas.northwestern.edu/psych/undergraduate/clinical.html

Marky Lloyd's Careers in Psychology Page
http://www.psywww.com/careers/

Choices: Careers in Social Work
http://www.naswdc.org/pubs/choices/choices.htm

Appreciating the PsyD: The Facts
http://www.psichi.org/pubs/articles/article_171.asp

Clinical versus Counseling Psychology: What's the Diff?
http://www.psichi.org/pubs/articles/article_73.asp

Counseling Psychology: Making Lives Better
http://www.psichi.org/pubs/articles/article_97.asp

CHECKLIST: IS CLINICAL OR COUNSELING PSYCHOLOGY FOR YOU?

Do you:

- ☐ Like working with people?
- ☐ Have an interest in helping people with problems?
- ☐ Want to work with healthy people to improve their current functioning?
- ☐ Have an interest in why people do the things they do?
- ☐ Have an interest in identifying people's abilities or personality functioning?
- ☐ Think you would enjoy working in a hospital, clinic, university counseling center, or other health care setting?
- ☐ Find that you are a person others feel comfortable talking to about their problems?
- ☐ Find yourself interested in other people's problems?
- ☐ Have good listening skills and avoid tuning out when people talk about their lives?
- ☐ Have an interest in mental illness?
- ☐ Enjoy reading about abnormal psychology?
- ☐ Enjoy reading research about mental illness?
- ☐ Think you would enjoy a career providing psychotherapy and assessment?
- ☐ Have an interest in applied research that can be used to better people's lives?
- ☐ Keep secrets and protect information that others feel is personal?
- ☐ Find that people consider you trustworthy?
- ☐ Have compassion and feel for other people when they are suffering?

Scoring: The more boxes you checked, the more likely it is that you're a good match for clinical or counseling psychology.

SCHOOL PSYCHOLOGY

CHAPTER 4

CHAPTER GUIDE

Opportunities with a Bachelor's Degree

    Teacher

    Childcare Worker

    Teacher Assistant

    Early Childhood Behavioral Specialist

Opportunities with a Graduate Degree

    School Psychologist

    School Counselor

Suggested Readings

Web Resources

Checklist: Is School Psychology for You?

As we have discussed, the majority of psychology graduate students specialize in the mental health service provider subfields (American Psychological Association Research Office, 2003). We have discussed the fields of clinical and counseling psychology; school psychology is a third mental health service provider subfield of psychology. School psychology offers unique training and professional opportunities that diverge from those of counseling and clinical psychology.

    School psychology overlaps with clinical and counseling psychology with regard to job activities, but school psychologists work with a more specific population. Trained in both psychology and education (Silva, 2003), school psychologists work with children, families, and school systems (American Psychological Association Division 16, 2005). Consistent with the title "school psychologist," the majority of school psychologists are found in school districts or school systems. School psychologists are also employed in clinics (such as community mental health centers), medical centers, correctional facilities, colleges and universities, and private practices.

School psychologists provide assessment and treatment services for children and families, consult with teachers and school officials, develop and evaluate programs, conduct research, and promote health in children and adolescents (American Psychological Association Division 16, 2005; Trull, 2004). School psychologists work with children and adolescents who present a broad array of psychological needs that are of a developmental or school-related nature. Approximately one in five children and adolescents experience significant mental health problems during their school years (Costello et al., 1996), and typical presenting problems school psychologists work with include: fears about starting school, time management and study skills deficits, family and relationship problems, psychopathology (such as depression or anxiety), drug and alcohol problems, developmental and life stage problems (for example, sexuality, college, and work issues), and concerns regarding academic aptitude and intellectual abilities (Silva, 2003). The school psychologist's task is to help families, teachers, and the educational system understand and resolve these problems while promoting the child's overall health and development.

OPPORTUNITIES WITH A BACHELOR'S DEGREE

Many psychology students are interested in working with and helping children and adolescents. If these are your interests, consider a career in teaching, school counseling, or childcare.

TEACHER

Few career paths enable you to have as much day-to-day contact with children as teaching. Teachers clearly need an understanding of behavior, learning, and development. If you're interested in a position where you can make a difference in the lives of others, consider teaching.

Given your school experiences, you're probably aware of the teaching duties required of teachers, but there are many other duties and obligations that occupy a teacher's day. Teachers are responsible for supervising study halls, homerooms, and extracurricular activities, all of which provide extended contact with students and therefore afford teachers the opportunity to identify physical or mental health problems and refer the child for the appropriate services. Thus, a background in psychology may assist teachers, not only in their work in the classroom but also in identifying and helping students who are experiencing problems.

Salaries for public educators are respectable, with an average income between $43,580 and $48,690 (Bureau of Labor Statistics, 2008), which is based on a nine-month salary ($58,106 to $64,920 extrapolated to 12 months). Note that salaries vary with geographical location and school system, but a career as a teacher can afford financial stability. In addition to a comfortable salary, an important benefit of a teaching career is parallel to that of the college professor: time off.

Schools routinely allow for traditional holidays (such as Thanksgiving), with extended holiday leave around Christmas (approximately two weeks) as well as spring and (of increasing frequency) fall breaks. So, during the nine-month academic year, it is reasonable that an educator may expect to receive anywhere from two to four weeks of time off. In addition, as the educator is tied to a nine-month salary, summers are unaccounted for. This allows for extra vacation time, pursuit of additional occupational interests, family time, or any other number of ways in which you wish to spend time.

As we've indicated, the primary benefit of a career as a schoolteacher may be the opportunity to be involved in and influence the lives of the children or adolescents who will lead our country into the future. As a schoolteacher, you'll have the opportunity to make a difference in a young person's life. The primary drawback to a career as a schoolteacher is the limited availability for professional advancement. Although some opportunities exist for advancement (for example, administration, teaching mentor), these positions are less common than teaching positions and require additional education. Thus, most schoolteachers remain in the classroom for the majority of their careers, which may lead to burnout for some.

If you're considering a career as a schoolteacher, understand that all teaching positions require the completion of a bachelor's degree and an approved teacher education program, plus certification, which is obtained after completing a specified number of courses in education and passing a standardized exam. An education major usually is not required as long as the required classes and experiences are obtained. Many universities offer a one-year program for bachelor's degree holders who wish to re-specialize and become teachers. The exact requirements for becoming a teacher vary by state, so consult your advisor and the Education Department at your college or university.

Childcare Worker

Students who are interested in school psychology often seek positions as childcare workers in childcare centers, nursery schools, preschools, public schools, private homes, and after-school programs. Childcare workers care for children and engage them in activities that promote their development while their parents are at work. They teach children and stimulate physical, emotional, intellectual, and social development (Bureau of Labor Statistics, 2008). They keep records on children's progress and maintain contact with parents to discuss children's needs and progress. In other words, childcare workers provide children with care and opportunities to learn through play and more formal activities. As a childcare worker, you'll prepare day-to-day and long-term schedules of activities that include quiet and active time, and individual and group play.

Childcare is strenuous work that can be physically and emotionally taxing (Bureau of Labor Statistics, 2008). Although childcare workers interact with parents or guardians, the majority of the work is with children. Thus, the work requires high energy with frequent bending and stooping as well as lifting of children in times of need (for example, the child who is sad when his parent drops him off). The work may become routine and hours may be long because childcare centers are open year-round and typically have extended hours to allow time for child drop-off and pickup that is flexible for parents' schedules (Bureau of Labor Statistics, 2008).

An important disadvantage to a career in childcare is that there is a high degree of burnout and employee turnover. In a large childcare center or preschool, you might advance to a supervisory or administrative position; however, other opportunities for advancement are limited. Other disadvantages of a career in childcare are dealing with children who have behavioral problems and working with difficult parents (unless difficult family situations and childhood behavioral problems are a specialty or interest of yours).

Nevertheless, few careers are as intrinsically rewarding as that of a childcare worker. Few careers allow for greater influence in the learning, growth, and development of children. The working conditions will vary by agency or employment setting (for example, one's own home versus an agency), and turnover in childcare work is high. High turnover, however, creates excellent job opportunities for those recently graduating from college and may provide a professional stepping-stone to other opportunities or career paths (Bureau of Labor Statistics, 2008).

Unfortunately, childcare workers often earn income that is low relative to their education (Whitebrook & Phillips, 1999). The median salary for a child worker in 2006 was $17,630; however, salary is contingent upon education and experience such that employees with more education typically receive higher salaries (Bureau of Labor Statistics, 2008). Salaries also vary by setting (for example, public or private childcare, home-based or center-based) and geographic location. In 2008, a typical daycare teacher earned a median salary of $27,294 (Salary.com, 2008). Unfortunately, benefits are also relatively poor (Bureau of Labor Statistics, 2008). For many, however, the disadvantages of a career in childcare are outweighed by the joy they experience in helping young children grow and flourish.

If childcare interests you, take additional courses in child development and early childhood education. It's essential that you develop an understanding of normative childhood development because childcare providers often help to identify children with disabilities or special needs. A career in childcare can be demanding because you must be enthusiastic, alert, and have lots of physical energy and endurance (for lifting, holding, carrying, and playing with all those kids!). Good communication skills with children and parents are important, and childcare workers must be able to anticipate problems and act to promote children's welfare.

TEACHER ASSISTANT

Teacher assistants typically perform a combination of instructional and clerical duties (for example, monitoring students in non-academic activities such as recess and eating) to allow teachers more time for lesson planning and teaching (Bureau of Labor Statistics, 2008). Assistant teaching is a rewarding career with opportunities to significantly impact the learning and well-being of children without the daily responsibilities of developing lesson plans and serving as the principal monitor and communicator of student progress to administrators and parents.

Teaching assistant positions offer a stable employment opportunity with solid growth, as teaching assistant positions are expected to grow by 10 percent by 2016 (Bureau of Labor Statistics, 2008). Although salaries for teaching assistants tend to be low with a median 2006 income of $20,740 (Bureau of Labor Statistics, 2008), increased salaries are available with increased education and experience. Furthermore, upper levels of teaching assistant salaries are not substantially below those of first-year teachers, who have a mean salary of $31,753 (American Federation of Teachers, 2007).

EARLY CHILDHOOD BEHAVIORAL SPECIALIST

Early childhood behavioral specialists develop behavioral interventions for children, generally from infancy to seven years-of-age, experiencing a variety of behavioral difficulties. Behavioral interventions are developed in consultation with parents, daycare providers, and early childhood teachers, and include observations of the child in his or her natural environments, including home and childcare or educational settings. Children served may suffer from serious mental disorders (for example, autism, Asperger's syndrome, or attention deficit/hyperactivity disorder), or evidence severe acting-out behavior (such as aggression or self-injurious behavior). Early childhood behavioral specialists will work with parents, other family members, and the identified child to implement planned interventions.

Although many early childhood behavioral specialist positions require a masters degree, many positions are available for graduates with a bachelor's degree. Early childhood behavioral specialists understand theories of childhood development, including social, emotional, cognitive, and other verbal and non-verbal domains, and are grounded in theories of early childhood interventions.

TABLE 4.1	PREPARATION FOR B.A.–LEVEL CAREERS RELATED TO SCHOOL PSYCHOLOGY

Coursework

- Abnormal Psychology/Child Psychopathology
- Child Psychology
- Communications
- Developmental Psychology
- Early Interventions
- Education courses focusing on assessment and intervention
- Family Systems
- Human Development/Child Development in non-psychology departments
- Math
- Other courses related to practical application of psychology for children
- Professional Issues
- Special education courses
- Writing

Applied Experiences: Volunteer, intern, or paid part-time positions in any of the following settings

- Any Child/Adolescent Mental Health Setting
- Big Brother/Big Sister Programs
- Child/Adolescent Psychiatric Unit

continued

TABLE 4.1	CONTINUED

Day Care and Preschool Settings
Head Start
Mental Retardation Facility for Children
Boys and Girls Club
Residential Treatment Facilities for Children with Behavioral Disorders
Teaching Assistant (Particularly in Special education)

Research Experiences: Experiences studying and participating in research in any of the following areas*

Child Psychology or Child Psychopathology
Early Intervention
Childhood Behavioral Problems
Education

*Note that the content area of the research is less important than the experience itself, which enhances reasoning, quantitative, writing, and organizational skills.

Advantages of this career choice include a strong employment outlook, as "Early childhood mental health specialists are desperately needed" (Bryans, 1999). Furthermore, salaries are very competitive in this field, as graduates with a bachelor's degree in psychology can expect to earn approximately $38,995 (PayScale, 2008). Disadvantages of this job are the emotionally taxing client load which often includes abused and neglected children; however, opportunities for significant progress are available that can be extremely professionally and personally rewarding.

OPPORTUNITIES WITH A GRADUATE DEGREE

If you're interested in school psychology and desire a wide range of professional opportunities, consider earning a graduate degree in school psychology or school counseling (often available through departments of education). Training in school psychology emphasizes mental health services (such as assessment and counseling), child development, school organization, and learning/behavior and motivation theory (Silva, 2003). Like their counseling and clinical psychology counterparts, many school psychologists earn doctoral degrees; however, a school psychologist may practice with a masters degree and/or receive national certification (from the National Association of School Psychologists) as a school psychologist, which requires a more advanced degree called a specialist's degree. A specialist's degree falls between the masters and doctoral degrees and typically adds from an extra semester to an extra year of study beyond the masters degree. Because a specialist's degree is required for certification, if you're interested in school psychology at the masters degree level, plan on taking the time to earn the specialist's degree. Now let's take a look at graduate-level careers in school psychology.

SCHOOL PSYCHOLOGIST

Although school psychologists are known for their work in schools, they are found in a variety of settings and in private practice.

SCHOOL SETTINGS. The primary responsibilities of the school psychologist in a public or private school setting are to provide consultation, assessment, intervention and prevention, educational or training services, and research and program development (Silva, 2003).

Consultation and educational services are primary tasks of the school psychologist in a school setting (Bardon, 1989). School psychologists consult with administrators, teachers, and parents to help them better understand how child development affects learning and behavior (Silva, 2003). For example, a school psychologist in a school setting may facilitate coordination between parents and the school system to ensure that all parties are promoting the best interest of the child. Similarly, educational services are offered to administrators, teachers, and parents to facilitate effective learning environments and address problem behaviors. Educational services may take the form of classroom management techniques, teaching educators new learning strategies or ways to identify at-risk children.

Assessment is also an emphasis of the school psychologist in school settings (Bardon, 1989). School psychologists use a myriad of instruments and techniques to evaluate the nature of a student's problem and identify the most appropriate intervention. School psychologists may be asked to evaluate students' academic skills and learning aptitudes, personality and emotional development, social skills, learning environment and school climate, eligibility for special education, and effectiveness of intervention strategies (Silva, 2003). In other words, although school psychologists provide direct services (such as counseling), they more typically assess a problem and then teach other people (for example, parents, teachers) more directly involved with the student how to be helpful to the child.

School psychologists also provide direct services via preventive and intervention strategies. Prevention strategies are designed to identify at-risk children and provide services to prevent the onset of learning or behavioral problems. Prevention services that school psychologists may provide include: program development and teacher education for identifying children at risk for learning disorders or mental health problems, skills training for parents and teachers to cope with disruptive behavior, developing school initiatives to facilitate school safety (for example, preventing bullying and aggression), and facilitating tolerance of individual differences and diversity (Silva, 2003). Intervention services, on the other hand, are designed to help children who already have learning or behavioral problems. Examples of intervention services a school psychologist may provide include: individual or group counseling, skills training (for example, social skills, time management, study skills, problem-solving skills, coping strategies), crisis management, grief counseling, family therapy, and substance abuse counseling.

Finally, school psychologists may be involved in research and program development within school settings. School psychologists evaluate the effectiveness of their services, academic programs, and behavior management systems, as well as develop new programs (for example, best practices) to facilitate student learning and development or for educational reform or restructuring (Silva, 2003).

Salaries for school psychologists in elementary and secondary school settings are comparable to counseling and clinical psychologists, with school psychologists earning a 2006 median salary of approximately $61,290 annually (Bureau of Labor Statistics, 2008; see Chapter 3 for more information on salaries in the applied areas of psychology, including clinical and counseling psychology). A primary benefit for the psychologist in a school setting is flexibility. Because school psychologists engage in a range of activities, they have diverse daily schedules and routines. An additional advantage is that psychologists in school settings adhere to the academic schedule, which affords extended leaves for winter holidays, fall and spring breaks, and summer breaks. Some school districts may employ their psychologists throughout the summer, although this usually includes increased pay.

A disadvantage for psychologists working in the school system is lack of access to colleagues. Most school districts employ one school psychologist (although this is tied to the size of the school district, with larger districts employing more school psychologists), so a sense of professional isolation may occur. One school psychologist may be responsible for all students in the district and across all grade levels, which can easily amount to overseeing the needs of hundreds and perhaps greater than a thousand students spread across several schools, requiring frequent travel between settings. Traveling among schools can leave some school psychologists feeling that they lack a "home base;" however, this diversity and travel between schools may be refreshing for some, preventing feelings of boredom or staleness.

PRIVATE PRACTICE. School psychologists in private practice engage in similar activities to those in school settings. Although some psychologists debate the appropriateness of school psychologists in private practice, a child's behaviors at school are not always directly related to the school or educational system. Thus, private practitioners are equally capable of providing consultation, assessment, and prevention and intervention services for learning and behavioral problems as are psychologists employed in school settings. Therefore, school psychologists in both private practice and school settings provide similar services and perform similar tasks.

Alternatively, school psychologists in private practice have unique advantages over their counterparts in the schools. First, school psychologists in private practice have greater flexibility in the scheduling of their appointments, with the exception that many students will not be seen until after 4:00 P.M., which often requires evening work. Nevertheless, this schedule may prove desirable for individuals who aren't "morning people." Second, school psychologists in private practice spend less time traveling from school to school and are more likely to see clients in their office. Thus, they have a central office from which to work and are less distracted by shuffling about. Finally, school psychologists in private practice are not limited in their clientele by an agency. Therefore, they have opportunities to branch out and provide other services (for example, relationship counseling, individual counseling to non-students) if they receive the appropriate training and supervision. Salary for school psychologists in private offices may also be slightly higher than for those working in elementary and secondary school settings.

A limitation for the private practitioner is the lack of availability and access to a child's learning environment. Whereas a school psychologist employed in a school setting has immediate access to a child and the classroom, the private practitioner must seek permission and approval from the school to observe a classroom and must wait for the student to be transported to his or her office. An additional disadvantage for the private practitioner is the overhead cost of maintaining a private practice (for example, office space, clerical assistance, and so on). Psychologists in school settings have little to no overhead costs, because the school district provides office space, computer access or computing services for report writing, and testing materials. The private practitioner must cover these expenses as business costs.

OTHER SETTINGS.   In addition to school settings and private practice, school psychologists are found in many other settings, including clinics and hospitals, criminal justice settings, universities and medical schools, businesses, and residential settings (see D'Amato and Dean, 1989, for a review of school psychologists in these settings). Similar to graduate degrees in counseling and clinical psychology, a graduate degree in school psychology affords great flexibility with regard to professional settings and responsibilities. Regardless of where a school psychologist works, however, he or she focuses on providing services that help students (children, adolescents, or adults) succeed academically, emotionally, and socially (Silva, 2003) by engaging in consulting and educational services, providing assessments, developing prevention and intervention programs, and conducting research.

SCHOOL COUNSELOR

Remember the school counselor in your high school—a trusted professional who would help you or your friends when you needed information about colleges and college admissions, or who offered assistance in times of need, or who simply offered a friendly smile and a comfortable place to talk about "stuff" that was occurring in your life? This, in essence, is the career of the school counselor.

As described in the Occupational Outlook Handbook (Bureau of Labor Statistics, 2008), school counselors help students understand and cope with social, behavioral, and personal problems. School counselors use counseling skills to emphasize prevention of problems before they arise, as well as skill development to enhance personal, social, and academic growth. School counselors may provide special services such as substance abuse prevention programs, conflict management, and parenting education training, as well as supervising peer counseling programs.

School counselors may work with individuals, small groups, or entire classes. Although this job description may appear to overlap with the school psychologist's, the school counselor is vastly different. Whereas school psychologists work with children with special needs, school counselors are available for all children and maintain regular school hours to help students as they navigate the educational process. Furthermore, unlike school psychologists, school counselors typically have less formal training in psychopathology, assessment, and counseling skills. When students are encountering severe problems or distress (academic, personal, behavior, social) the student is referred to the school psychologist, who has specialized training to deal with such issues.

Career opportunities for the school counselor are very good. The job outlook for school counselors is expected to remain steady through 2016 (Bureau of Labor Statistics, 2008). Other advantages of a career as a school counselor include the salary and work schedule. School counselors earn salaries with a 2006 median income of $53,750 (Bureau of Labor Statistics, 2008); however, it should be noted that this annual salary is typically based only on a nine- or ten-month contract. An additional benefit is the work schedule. School counselors, like teachers, have two or three months off every year to pursue other interests or other employment. In addition, they receive generous vacation packages that include major holidays, as well as spring and fall breaks, and an extended Christmas break.

A few states allow bachelor's degree holders to work as school counselors; however, all states require school counselors to hold state school counseling certification (Bureau of Labor Statistics, 2008), which usually requires additional training and credentialing beyond the bachelor's degree. The amount of education varies and some can be completed as part of the bachelor's degree. Some states require public school counselors to have both counseling and teaching certificates (Bureau of Labor Statistics, 2008). The opportunities available to you will vary by geographic location, as there are substantial differences in requirements across the nation. A growing number of states require school counselors to hold masters degrees in school counseling (usually available within departments of education). If you're considering a career as a school counselor, look into the education and certification requirements in your state (the American School Counselor Association is a great place to start your research: http://www.schoolcounselor.org/).

SUGGESTED READINGS

Burden, K. (2000). Psychology in education and instruction. In K. Pawlik & M. R. Rosenzweig, (Eds.), *International handbook of psychology* (pp. 466–78). Thousand Oaks, CA: Sage.

Esquivel, G. B., Lopez, E. C., & Nahari, S. G. (2007) *Handbook of multicultural school psychology: An interdisciplinary perspective*. Mahwah, NJ: Erlbaum.

Fagan, T. K., & Warden, P. G. (Ed.). (1996). *Historical encyclopedia of school psychology*. Westport, CT: Greenwood Publishing Group.

Gilman, R., & Teague, T. L. (2005). School psychologists in nontraditional settings: Alternative roles and functions in psychological service delivery. In R. D. Morgan, T. L. Kuther, & C. Habben (Eds.), *Life after graduate school in psychology: Insider's advice from new psychologists* (pp. 167–180). New York: Psychology Press.

Jimerson, S. R., Oakland, T., & Farrell, P. T. (2006). *The handbook of international school psychology*. Thousand Oaks: Sage.

Moffatt, C. V., & Moffatt, T. L. (1999). *How to get a teaching job*. Boston: Allyn & Bacon.

Renolds, C. B., Gutkin, T. B. (1999). *The handbook of school psychology* (3rd ed.). New York: Wiley.

Saklofske D. H., & Janzen, H. L. (1993). Contemporary issues in school psychology. In K. S. Dobson & D. J. C. Dobson (Ed.), *Professional psychology in Canada* (pp. 313–50). Seattle: Hogrefe & Huber.

Talley, R. C., Kubiszyn, T., Brassard, M., & Short, R. J. (Eds.). (1996). *Making psychologists in schools indispensable: Critical questions & emerging perspectives*. Washington, DC: American Psychological Association.

WEB RESOURCES

American Academy of Child & Adolescent Psychiatry (AACAP)
http://www.aacap.org/

Canadian Association of School Psychologists (CASP)
http://www.stemnet.nf.ca/casp/

Division 16 of the American Psychological Association (School Psychology)
http://www.indiana.edu/~div16/index.html

Division of Educational and Child Psychology of the British Psychological Society
http://www.bps.org.uk/decp/decp_home.cfm

European Agency for Development in Special Needs Education
http://www.european-agency.org/

International School Psychology Association (ISPA)
http://www.ispaweb.org

National Association of School Psychologists (NASP)
http://www.nasponline.org/

American School Counselor Association
http://www.schoolcounselor.org/

Selections from: A Complete Guide to the Advanced Study in and the Profession of School Psychology
http://www-gse.berkeley.edu/program/sp/html/spguide.html

Becoming a School Psychologist
http://www.nasponline.org/certification/becoming.aspx

CHECKLIST: IS SCHOOL PSYCHOLOGY FOR YOU?

Do you:

- ☐ Want to work with healthy people to improve their current functioning?
- ☐ Find that you are a person others feel comfortable talking to about their problems?
- ☐ Have good listening skills and avoid tuning out when people talk about their lives?
- ☐ Think you would enjoy a career providing assessment?
- ☐ Have an interest in applied research that can be used to better people's lives?
- ☐ Keep secrets and protect information that others feel is personal?
- ☐ Find that people consider you trustworthy?
- ☐ Have compassion and feel for other people when they are suffering?
- ☐ Have a preference for working with children, rather than adults?
- ☐ Have an interest in working in a school system?
- ☐ Prefer identifying the source of peoples' problems rather than working with them directly to resolve their problems?
- ☐ Enjoy working with children?
- ☐ Have the courage to report people who abuse children?
- ☐ Like to see children succeed?
- ☐ Enjoy developmental psychology?
- ☐ Enjoy watching children play?
- ☐ Consider children and their problems to be as important as adult problems?

Scoring: The more boxes you checked, the more likely it is that you're a good match for a school psychology career.

CHAPTER GUIDE

Arriving at a crime scene with badge in hand, analyzing the scene, exploring the intimacies of the alleged offender's life, and ultimately assisting in the offender's apprehension—certainly this must be the interface of psychology and the law, right?

It is not surprising that when we think about careers in psychology and law, forensic psychology, especially criminal profiling, comes to mind. Based on our experiences, an increasing number of psychology majors express the desire to become forensic psychologists, consequently more courses are being offered in psychology and law (Bartol & Bartol, 2004; Liss, 1992). But what exactly is a forensic psychologist? Popular films like *Silence of the Lambs* and television shows like *Profiler* depict forensic psychology as an action-packed career of apprehending dangerous criminals. Understandably, these exciting dramas pique the interest of many psychology students. Although the media portrays forensic psychology and careers in psychology and law as action-packed, this is rarely the case. So, then, what is the field of psychology and law? This chapter explores career opportunities for students at all educational levels who are interested in psychology and law.

PSYCHOLOGY AND LAW: WHAT IS IT?

Psychologists study human behavior, whereas judges and attorneys study the legal system. Clearly, each discipline is its own distinct field. Yet both disciplines aim at improving the quality of human life. Psychology, for example, studies human behavior to assist people in understanding their own behavior and to maximize human functioning. The law provides a recognized set of rules to ensure that we may all coexist equally. *Psychology and law*, then, is the interface or merging of these two disciplines.

Before we discuss career options in psychology and law, let's consider a further distinction in the field: *forensic psychology*. Forensic psychology is a narrow application of psychology to the legal system. Though many undergraduate students express interest in becoming forensic psychologists with the explicit intent to engage in criminal profiling, understand that criminal profiling is a rare professional activity and very few forensic psychologists do it. Forensic psychology is a mental health discipline, whereas profiling is a criminal investigative technique (American Psychology-Law Society, 2004). Students specifically interested in the opportunity (albeit rare) to be involved in profiling are encouraged to pursue a career in law enforcement.

Although forensic psychology does not typically include profiling activities, it remains a dynamic and challenging field. A forensic psychologist is any psychologist (although usually trained in clinical or counseling psychology) who works within the legal system (Brigham, 1999) including the following settings: secure forensic units, jails, prisons, court-related services and/or community mental health centers, other specialized agencies, and private practice (providing forensic assessment and treatment services). Forensic psychologists are probably best known as practitioners; however, researchers (for example, attorney consultation, jury selection) and educators (for example, in colleges, medical schools, law enforcement agencies) can also be engaged in forensic psychology–related activities. Forensic psychology refers to any application of psychology (by a doctoral-level psychologist) to the legal system, whereas psychology and law also includes broader applications such as social/public policy, trial consultation, and law enforcement, to name just a few.

OPPORTUNITIES WITH A BACHELOR'S DEGREE

A doctorate in psychology is not required to be involved in the legal or the criminal justice system. Bachelor's-level positions that incorporate aspects of psychology and law include law enforcement positions such as police or correctional officers, probation and parole officers, and juvenile detention workers, to name a few. Few professions are as noble or vital to societal functioning as law enforcement and support. Police and correctional officers work within the legal system to enforce the law, and psychology is an important component of their job. This is particularly true today because the mentally ill are increasingly present within the criminal justice system (Condelli, Bradigan, & Holanchock, 1997; Ditton, 1999; Hodgins, 1995; Steadman, Morris, & Dennis, 1995; Torrey, 1995). Police, correctional, probation, and parole officers, and juvenile detention workers are responsible for controlling human behavior and frequently must de-escalate volatile situations. Psychology, with its understanding of human behavior, is clearly essential to their success and safety.

POLICE OFFICER

Policing is one of the most demanding and taxing of all service positions, because officers hold the ultimate responsibility of protecting our lives and property. Depending on seniority and promotional opportunities, typical activities of police officers include: maintaining regular patrols, responding to calls for service, directing traffic as needed (for example, at the scene of a fire), investigating a crime scene, or providing first aid to an accident victim (Bureau of Labor Statistics, 2008). As an officer matures through the police ranks, other opportunities develop. For example, a police officer may be promoted to detective with a primary responsibility of investigating crime scenes. Also, with experience, administrative positions (Sergeant, Captain, Chief of Police) may be available in which an officer can more directly influence or administer policing within a given community. In large police departments, officers usually are assigned to a specific type of duty. Many urban police agencies are becoming more involved in community policing, a practice in which an officer builds relationships with the citizens of local neighborhoods and mobilizes the public to help fight crime. Given the diversity of activities and the direct nature of public service, an understanding of the principles that govern human behavior (psychology) is beneficial to the law enforcement officer.

Unfortunately, salaries in law enforcement aren't commensurate with the level of professional responsibility or job-related stress; however, law enforcement officers earn respectable salaries. For example, the median salary for police officers in 2006 was $47,460 (Bureau of Labor Statistics, 2008). If you are interested in criminal profiling, remember that, with advancement, a police officer may become a detective, and detectives occasionally use profiling as an investigative technique. In addition to increased professional opportunities, promotions carry financial incentives. The median income of police and detective supervisors in 2002 was $69,310 (Bureau of Labor Statistics, 2008). As you might imagine, the primary disadvantage to policing is job-related stress (Anson & Bloom, 1988; Birmingham & Morgan, August, 2001). Other disadvantages include security and safety concerns, as well as the public's occasional negative stereotypes about police officers. Perhaps the primary advantage of law enforcement is that few professions offer such a direct opportunity for public service; rarely does anyone have as great an opportunity to influence others as does the police officer.

CORRECTIONAL OFFICER

Correctional officers are similar to police officers in that they protect public safety as well as being responsible for the safety and well-being of others; in this case, "others" refers to offenders. Once arrested, offenders are housed in jail and prison facilities, and these facilities are stressful (and dangerous) for other inmates as well as staff (Morgan, Van Haveren, & Pearson, 2002). Correctional officers maintain peace in a violent world by monitoring the activities and work assignments of inmates, searching inmates and their living quarters for contraband (such as drugs or weapons), enforcing discipline, settling disputes between conflicting inmates, and maintaining security by routinely inspecting locks, window bars, doors, and gates for malfunction or signs of tampering (Bureau of Labor Statistics, 2008).

Because correctional officers work in the offenders' living environment, it's easy to see why an understanding and healthy appreciation of psychology is beneficial. In a typical day, for example, a correctional officer might resolve a dispute between inmates, console an inmate who has lost a family member and is unable to attend the funeral, and work with inmates on correcting their behavior to increase the likelihood that they will be successful upon release. Correctional officers rely on interpersonal skills and knowledge of human functioning to navigate these difficult situations.

An advantage of this career is the opportunity to serve those typically forgotten by the rest of society as well as protect society from those too dangerous to live in our world. Another advantage is relative job security, given the increasing prison population. However, few occupational environments present as many challenges as a penitentiary. Correctional officers work in a potentially volatile environment, and although this may add a level of excitement and novelty to one's job, stress and burnout are occupational hazards (Anson & Bloom, 1988; Cheek & Miller, 1983; Harris, 1983; Lindquist & Whitehead, 1986; Morgan et al., 2002). Salaries for correctional officers are slightly less than those of police officers with a median salary of $35,760 in 2006 (range, $23,600 to $58,580); however, the job market is strong with expected growth of 16 percent by 2016 (Bureau of Labor Statistics, 2008).

PROBATION AND PAROLE OFFICER

Probation and parole officers also work with offenders within the criminal justice system, but they don't work within correctional settings, nor do they enforce the law like police officers. Rather, probation and parole officers supervise offenders while they are in the community, to ensure that they are in compliance with the stipulations of their parole or probation.

At times, probation and parole officers must enforce the law (for example, when offenders fail to comply with the conditions of their parole or probation and must be returned to prison or the court), but they also aim to assist offenders in getting the help or treatment needed to remain in the free world. These job activities necessitate an understanding of human behavior, and an appreciation of the mental health and psychological needs of offenders. The primary advantage of this career is that, while it is a law enforcement position, it typically affords greater safety than does policing; however, like all law enforcement positions, it is a stressful occupation. Probation and parole officers earn salaries comparable to other law enforcement

TABLE 5.1	PREPARATION FOR B.A.–LEVEL CAREERS RELATED TO PSYCHOLOGY OF LAW AND FORENSIC PSYCHOLOGY

Coursework

    Abnormal Psychology or Psychopathology

    Communications

    Community Mental Health

    Criminal Justice or Criminology

    Interviewing, Counseling or Helping Skills

    Juvenile Delinquency

    Law

    Professional Issues

    Psychological Assessment

    Psychopharmacology

    Social Work

    Substance Abuse

    Writing

Applied Experiences: Volunteer, intern, or paid part-time positions in any of the following settings

    Any mental health or criminal justice setting

    Big Brother/Big Sister Programs

    Boys and Girls Club

    Inpatient Psychiatric Unit

    Juvenile Treatment Facilities

    Residential Treatment Facilities

    Substance Abuse Center

Research Experiences: Experiences studying and participating in research in any of the following areas*

    Antisocial Personality Disorder

    Correctional Psychology

    Forensic Psychology

    Juvenile Delinquency

    Study of Abnormal Behavior

    Study of Aggressive Behavior

    Substance Abuse

*Note that the content area of the research is less important than the experience itself, which enhances reasoning, quantitative, writing, and organizational skills.

officers, with a median salary of $42,500 in 2006 (range, $28,000 to $71,160; Bureau of Labor Statistics, 2006).

JUVENILE DETENTION WORKER

Like correctional officers, juvenile detention workers work within a setting of confinement, but they focus on juveniles (meaning, offenders typically younger than 18 years of age) rather than adults. Juvenile detention workers have many of the same responsibilities as correctional officers and probation or parole officers, but they may have a more desirable work setting because many hold the hope that juveniles can change. It is commonly believed in the adult criminal justice system that "nothing works," and that offenders don't change—that prisons are merely warehouses (Martinson, 1974). This belief isn't accurate because rehabilitation programs do increase the post-release functioning of inmates (Andrews et al., 1990; Andrews & Bonta, 1994; Garrett, 1985; Gendreau & Andrews, 1990; Gendreau & Ross, 1979, 1981; Lipsey, 1992), yet working with juvenile offenders who are stereotypically seen as less hardened offers the perceived potential for effective change. A primary disadvantage of juvenile detention work is coping with juvenile attitudes and impulsivity, which often results in frustration and feelings of futility. Salaries and benefits for the juvenile detention workers are generally consistent with those of correctional officers.

If you're interested in any of these careers in law enforcement, a psychology major will suit you well. Seek additional coursework in criminal justice and political science. Sociology classes in criminology, deviance, the criminal justice system, policing, and corrections can provide background knowledge that will be useful in deciding whether law enforcement is for you. Political science classes on the legal and criminal justice system will provide you with a broader understanding of how the legal and criminal justice systems operate. Also, seek practicum experiences (field experiences taken for course credit) with local police or sheriff's departments, or in the local jail to get some experience and determine whether this really is the career for you.

FORENSIC SCIENCE TECHNICIAN

Forensic science technicians work for or in conjunction with law enforcement agencies to investigate crime scenes and analyze physical evidence to solve crimes (Bureau of Labor Statistics, 2008). Forensic sciences offers an exciting career with opportunities to specialize in specific crime type evidence (for example, DNA analysis, firearm examination) with opportunities to solve crimes and testify in court as an expert witness (Bureau of Labor Statistics, 2008). Although popular media (such as CSI) have glamorized forensic sciences, this career choice affords law enforcement agencies a critical criminal investigation technique.

In addition to exciting professional challenges and the opportunity to work high-profile criminal cases, a career in forensic sciences affords a respectable salary with a median 2006 income of $45,323 (Bureau of Labor Statistics, 2008). Also, forensic sciences is a growing profession with employment opportunities predicted to grow much faster than average through 2016 (Bureau of Labor Statistics, 2008). Disadvantages of this career include job stress resulting from law enforcement work (law enforcement is consistently rated as one of the most stressful occupations), testifying as an expert witness, high case loads, and exposure to emotionally disturbing evidence (for example, decomposed or severely traumatized bodies).

OPPORTUNITIES WITH A GRADUATE DEGREE

At the graduate level, there are a variety of career opportunities in psychology and law. Practitioners may conduct forensic assessments, provide treatment services for offenders, or assist law enforcement officers. Research psychologists may seek opportunities to be directly involved in the legal system through trial consultation, or may conduct research that impacts the legal system (for example, research about children's developmental level and their ability to participate in court proceedings). Psychologists of any discipline (such as counseling/clinical, developmental, social, or cognitive) may pursue political careers. Psychologists have been elected to both federal and state legislative bodies (Sullivan, 2001), and opportunities for psychologists to be active in public policy have never been greater. The doctoral degree provides even greater flexibility for those seeking careers in psychology and the law. More specifically, the Ph.D. in psychology (typically in counseling or clinical psychology) affords much greater flexibility in forensic psychology than does the masters degree.

CORRECTIONAL PSYCHOLOGY

As the prison population continues to rise (Boothby & Clements, 2001; Irwin, 1996), correctional psychology is becoming an increasingly frequent career option for many psychologists with forensic interests. In fact, psychologists have been encouraged to seek employment in correctional facilities (Hawk, 1997) and prison and jail settings may become leading employers of psychologists, especially if the current incarceration rate continues to climb. Correctional psychologists report enjoying their jobs (Boothby & Clements, 2001; Ferrell, Morgan, & Winterowd, 2000); however, working in correctional environments is stressful for both inmates (Hassine, 1996; Toch, 1992) and staff (see Morgan et al., 2002), including health professionals (Brodsky, 1982; Inwald, 1982). Nevertheless, correctional mental health can be an enjoyable and rewarding career choice through its opportunity to make a difference with an underrepresented population.

OPTIONS FOR MASTERS DEGREE HOLDERS.   Although the doctorate in psychology is the entry-level degree for many psychology and law-related activities, several options exist for graduates with masters degrees, particularly in forensic psychology. Masters degree holders in clinical and counseling psychology frequently work as treatment providers for offenders in institutional or correctional settings, such as prisons (for example, Boothby & Clements, 2000; Morgan, Winterowd, & Ferrell, 1999). Such correctional settings provide basic mental health services to all inmates and include both assessment and treatment services that focus on symptom reduction and coping within the correctional environment (Morgan, 2002). The hiring of masters-level clinicians is debated (for example, Morgan et al., 1999), but it remains a common practice, particularly for state correctional systems, and affords mental health professionals with job security.

An important benefit of correctional mental health is that the salaries are slightly higher than similar entry-level positions in non-correctional settings. While the median salary for a masters-level clinician in 2002 was approximately $32,618 annually (Singleton, Tate, & Kohout, 2003), in corrections, this salary jumps to an average of approximately $40,000 and over (Boothby & Clements, 2000). No specific training beyond psychotherapy and assessment skills is generally required to secure employment in a correctional facility; however, any practicum experience working with offenders or other difficult clients (for example, clients mandated to attend treatment, psychiatric inpatients) is beneficial, even recommended.

OPTIONS FOR DOCTORAL DEGREE HOLDERS. Similar to masters-level clinicians, doctoral-level psychologists in correctional facilities typically are involved in direct service (Boothby & Clements, 2000), but doctoral-level providers have more opportunities to become involved in rehabilitative efforts through program development (Morgan et al., 1999). In other words, masters-level correctional mental health professionals frequently engage in service delivery, while doctoral-level providers may become more involved in developing specialized programs for offenders and evaluating the effectiveness of these programs. Doctoral-level psychologists in correctional settings generally are compensated well for their time, with a substantial benefits package and a 40-hour work week. Job security is an advantage as the U.S. prison population continues to increase with no slow-down in site. The primary disadvantages of correctional mental health are job-related stress and a potential feeling of dissociation from correctional administrators who have a goal of incarceration (by necessity) as opposed to the rehabilitative preference of most mental health professionals (Morgan et al., 1999).

A scan of classified ads (for example, *The Monitor on Psychology*) indicates that correctional psychology positions are readily available and have been for several years. Whereas masters-level clinicians earn on average $40,000 in correctional settings, their doctoral-level counterparts earn significantly more. In the Federal Bureau of Prisons, for which the doctoral degree is the entry-level degree, the starting salary is approximately $42,000, with an average salary of $61,800 (Boothby & Clements, 2000). Employment in state correctional facilities appears to provide a slightly lower average income for doctoral-level providers ($53,400); however, it was recently noted that California was offering a salary nearing six figures for entry-level psychology positions. No specialized experience beyond doctoral training is required for employment as a correctional psychologist. Nevertheless, field experience is always a plus. If you're interested in this career, consider pursuing internship or postdoctoral experiences in correctional settings (for example, the Federal Bureau of Prisons currently have nine accredited doctoral-level internship sites) or secure forensic institutions.

FORENSIC EXAMINER

Many forensic psychologists seek employment opportunities conducting forensic examinations. In fact, many doctoral-level interns apply to forensic sites to conduct criminal evaluations such as sanity evaluations (Ax & Morgan, 2002). Masters- and doctoral-level psychologists also conduct examinations for other types of court cases, including divorce and child custody, family and children's courts, civil commitment, personal injury cases, and anti-discrimination and entitlement laws (Ackerman, 1999; Melton, Petrila, Poythress, Slobogin, & Lyons, 2007).

Because of such high-profile cases as John Hinckley or the Unabomber, most students are familiar with psychologists' involvement in criminal cases. In criminal cases, psychologists may be asked to assess a defendant's competency to stand trial or mental state at the time of the alleged offense (evaluating the insanity plea); however, other issues may be raised regarding a defendant's competency during the criminal justice process. For example, a defendant's competency to consent to search or seizure, to confess, to plead guilty, to waive the right to counsel, to refuse an insanity defense, to testify, and to be sentenced and executed may also be questioned. (Several sources provide much greater detail on the nature and purpose of these evaluations, including Huss, 2001; Melton et al., 2007.)

Forensic psychologists are also heavily involved in noncriminal cases. Child custody evaluations and personal injury assessments are common forms of noncriminal forensic work. These cases differ from criminal cases in that a person's liberty is not in jeopardy; instead, a plaintiff seeks to obtain something that is in dispute (for example, custody of children, financial compensation for damages in personal injury suits). Child custody evaluations are often requested in divorce proceedings. When this occurs, a psychologist is often asked to assist the court by conducting a child custody evaluation. Such evaluations are requested in approximately 10 percent of custody hearings with the aim of assisting the court by investigating the facts that would be relevant to a judge or jury making a custody decision (Melton et al., 2007).

Psychologists are becoming increasingly involved in personal injury litigation cases (Butcher & Miller, 1999). Personal injury cases include any situation where a person is injured either physically or psychologically, and compensation for damages are sought (Ackerman, 1999). Worker's compensation cases, medical malpractice suits, and sexual harassment cases are just a few of the examples of personal injury cases where a psychological evaluation may be requested as part of the legal process. The role of the psychologist in personal injury cases, in general, is to assist the court in determining if a mental injury occurred as a result of some specific incident. This evaluation is similar to the insanity evaluation, because the examiner conducts a retrospective study (Melton et al., 2007); that is, the examiner determines the plaintiff's mental functioning before and after said incident.

In what setting do forensic examiners work? Many are in private practice, and some criminal forensic psychologists work in state institutions such as secure units, community mental health centers, and hospitals. Entry-level psychologists providing forensic services in hospitals and community settings may begin at approximately $40,000 annually, but salaries tend to vary by state and jurisdiction (American Psychology-Law Society, 2004). Forensic psychologists in private practice typically bill between $100 and $300 per hour (American Psychology-Law Society, 2004), but are without the benefit of a steady income. The primary advantages of forensic evaluation are the job satisfaction that most evaluators experience and the potential to earn a relatively lucrative income. One disadvantage of this career path is the necessity for advanced training beyond academic coursework, such as internship and/or postdoctoral training that specializes in forensic assessments. Another disadvantage is the potential for lawsuits and ethics complaints (for example, Kirkland & Kirkland, 2001) filed against forensic examiners. Even frivolous lawsuits or ethics complaints can be costly in terms of finances, time, stress, and professional image.

In order to conduct forensic evaluations, you must receive training in psychological assessment (for example, personality assessment, intellectual assessment, or mental status examinations), as well as specialized training in forensic issues. Most forensic psychologists receive their training during the predoctoral internship (a field experience obtained while pursuing the doctoral degree) or in specialized postdoctoral training programs where the focus is specific to forensic psychology. There are very few training programs that provide specialized training in forensic psychology practice, so field experience in the form of predoctoral and postdoctoral internships is essential. Some masters-level practitioners receive training in assessment on the job; however, without a doctoral degree and license, independent practice is not possible in most states.

POLICE PSYCHOLOGY

Police psychology has become increasingly necessary in law enforcement (Birmingham & Morgan, 2001) despite law enforcement officers' sometimes negative perceptions towards such services (Max, 2000). Police psychologists provide a variety of services, including: management consultation (consulting on administrative decision making that has agency-wide implications); pre-employment psychological assessments and fitness-for-duty evaluations (evaluations to help determine if a person is suitable for law enforcement work or fit for continued duty); special unit evaluations (assessments to assist with promotional decisions for specialized police assignments such as Special Weapons and Tactics [SWAT], Tactical Response Teams [TRT], and Hostage Negotiation Teams [HNT]); hostage negotiation team consultations (consulting and assisting with hostage negotiations); deadly force incident investigations (assisting with investigations regarding the appropriateness of an officer's use of deadly force); field consultation such as assisting an officer in the apprehension or security of a mentally ill person (Super, 1999); and, less frequently, investigative activities (Bartol, 1996), although investigative activities, such as criminal profiling, appear to be increasing (Bartol & Bartol, 2004).

Stress is a prevalent problem in law enforcement (Anson & Bloom, 1988; Birmingham & Morgan, 2001) and police psychologists provide counseling services to help officers cope with their stress. The most common activity of police psychologists is to provide pre-employment evaluations (Super, 1999). Pre-employment evaluations are requested to determine if would-be officers have the disposition and personality style to cope with stress and serve in the capacity of law enforcer. Typically, police psychologists hold doctoral degrees and may be consultants to law enforcement agencies or may be employed (often actually sworn in as law enforcement officers) by an agency (Bartol, 1996). Entry-level salaries appear commensurate with other entry-level doctoral psychology positions. As with other forensic psychology positions, if you're interested in police psychology, seek specialized training through predoctoral internships or postdoctoral training, because there are few formal opportunities for training in police psychology during graduate school.

Trial Consultant

Yet another potential occupational opportunity exists in trial consultation, and is of equal interest for psychological practitioners and other psychologists. In fact, social and cognitive psychologists have particular skills and expertise that translate well to courtroom consultations (American Psychology-Law Society, 2005). *Trial consultation* refers to any service provided to assist in the process of a trial (for example, focus group research; exploratory focus groups; experimental, quasi-experimental, and comparative studies; mock trials; or pretrial case analysis) (Andrews, 2005). Trial consultations usually include case analysis, review of reports and forensic evidence, identification of expert witnesses, development of examination (direct and cross) strategies, and preparation of expert and lay witnesses for testifying (Drogin & Barrett, 2007) with a primary goal of developing a better understanding how the judge or jury will understand and process information (Andrews, 2005).

A trial consultant may conduct research that influences trial process, such as that regarding decision making by the trier-of-fact (meaning, judge or jury), the impact of evidentiary psycholegal research, and eyewitness identification and recall (American Psychology-Law Society, 2004; Andrews, 2005; Huss, 2001). In addition to research, psychologists may advise attorneys regarding jury selection and the effects of courtroom trial procedures on jury decision making (Andrews, 2005; Huss, 2001). For example, trial consultants often use jury simulations or mock jurors (Andrews, 2005; Huss, 2001) to assist attorneys in developing strategies for jury selection, as well as trial strategy itself. Trial consultation occurs in both criminal and civil trials, and although high-profile cases such as the tobacco settlement bring notoriety to this profession, it appears to remain a relatively infrequent occupational consideration for psychologists in training.

The largest advantage of a career as a trial consultant is the potential income; however, it may be difficult initially to establish yourself in the private industry, limiting income in the early years of a career as a trial consultant. Nevertheless, psychologists with appropriate experience and legal connections who are fortunate enough to be hired for high-profile cases have been known to earn incomes in excess of $1,000,000 annually. Remember that this is the high end of the salary spectrum; entry-level positions appear comparable to other entry-level psychological positions. As in most careers, doctoral degrees afford additional opportunities and autonomy over masters degrees.

Politics

A bachelor's degree in psychology may enable you to become involved in the political process in a limited fashion. Masters degrees provide similar opportunities; and the Ph.D. provides many more. Psychologists are increasingly politically aware and active. In fact, by 2004, 17 psychologists were serving as United States legislators, 12 in state legislatures, and 5 in Congress (Sullivan, 2005). Although this represents a significant improvement over psychologists' political contributions of the past, much work is yet to be done—or, stated more provocatively, *must* be done. Considering the social and public-policy implications of our work, it is not simply an opportunity; rather, it is our duty, and psychologists should seek to apply the techniques of their trade to meet the larger public needs (DeLeon, 1988). Just as professional (clinical, counseling, or school) psychologists seek to achieve the betterment of the client, so can the political psychologist use psychological principals to the betterment of the public.

What do psychologists do in politics? They may assist in developing briefs, conduct psycholegal research, or become involved in planning strategies and drafting laws. To prepare psychologists for politics, the American Psychological Association developed a congressional fellowship program in 1974. The purpose of this fellowship program is to provide "psychologists with an invaluable public policy learning experience, to contribute to the more effective use of psychological knowledge in government, and to broaden awareness about the value of psychology-government interaction among psychologists and within the federal government" (American Psychology-Law Society, 2005). Psychologists who enroll in this training program spend one year assigned to a member of Congress or a congressional commit-tee and have the opportunity to perform such tasks as assisting in congressional hearings and debates or preparing briefs (American Psychology Association, 2005). Initially, this program was geared exclusively to entry-level psychologists; however, it now targets advanced (senior-level) psychologists as well (Fowler, 1996).

Salaries of psychologists holding political positions are governed by the United States or the state they represent, and vary accordingly. On the high end, a United States senator earns $154,700 (Bureau of Labor Statistics, 2004). Salaries of political employees vary according to level of government and jurisdiction. Entry-level psy-chologist fellows in the American Psychological Association fellowship program earn approximately $60,000, with the range increasing to $75,000 depending on level of experience (American Psychological Association, 2008). In addition, fel-lows receive the cost of relocation and/or travel expenses during the fellowship year. Although any United States citizen has the opportunity for political involvement, spe-cialized training such as that provided by the American Psychological Association fellowship program affords psychologists specialized knowledge and experience that is directly applicable to their political interests.

Throughout this chapter we've examined many opportunities for those who are interested in the interface of psychology and law at both the baccalaureate-degree or graduate-degree levels. Crime and social problems remain. Psychologists' specialized training as scientists, and in many cases practitioners, offers opportunities for com-bating these problems. In many cases, no additional training beyond the tradition-ally academic is necessary. Furthermore, many of the career options described here offer job security and salaries competitive with comparable positions. While psy-chology and law rarely includes activities such as analyzing a crime scene or con-ducting profile analyses, it does afford exciting and rewarding career options.

SUGGESTED READINGS

American Psychology-Law Society. (2005). *Careers in psychology and law: Subspecialties in psychology and law: A closer look*. Retrieved July 28, 2008 at http://www.unl.edu/ap-ls/student/careers_closerlook.html.

American Psychology-Law Society. (2004). *Careers in psychology and law: A guide for pro-spective students*. Retrieved July 28, 2008 at http://www.ap-ls.org/students/careers%20in%20psychology.pdf.

Andrews, C. K. (2005). Trial consulting: Moving psychology into the courtroom. In R. D. Morgan, T. L. Kuther, & C. J. Habben (Eds.), *Life after graduate school in psychology: Insider's advice from new psychologists*. New York: Psychology Press.

Fagan, T., & Ax, R. K. (2003). *Correctional mental health handbook*. Thousand Oaks: Sage.

Huss, M. T. (2001). Psychology and law, now and in the next century: The promise of an emerging area of psychology. In J. S. Halonen & S. F. Davis (Eds.), *The many faces of psychological research in the 21st century*. Society for the Teaching of Psychology: retrieved from http://teachpsych.org/resources/e-books/faces/script/Ch11.htm.

Kuther, T. L. (2004). *Your career in psychology: Psychology and the law*. Belmont, CA: Wadsworth.

Melton, G. B., Petrila, J., Poythress, N. G., & Slobogin, C., Lyons, P. M. (2007). *Psychological evaluations for the courts: A handbook for mental health professionals and lawyers* (3rd ed.). New York: Guilford Press.

Stern, R. (1988). *Law enforcement careers: A complete guide from application to employment*. Tarzana, CA: Lawman Press.

Weiner, I. B. & Hess, A. K. (2006). *The handbook of forensic psychology* (3rd ed.). New York: Wiley.

WEB RESOURCES

American Psychology-Law Society
http://www.unl.edu/ap-ls/

American Society of Trial Consultants
http://www.astcweb.org

Federal Bureau of Prisons
http://www.bop.gov/

Corrections Connection
http://www.corrections.com/

Law and Society Association
http://www.lawandsociety.org/

Mental Health in Corrections Consortium
http://www.forest.edu/mhcca/index.html

National Criminal Justice Reference Service
http://www.ncjrs.org/

National Institute of Corrections
http://www.nicic.org/

National Institute of Justice
http://www.ojp.usdoj.gov/nij/

Police stress
http://www.policefamilies.com/

Police Psychology Online
http://www.policepsych.com

CHECKLIST: IS LEGAL OR FORENSIC PSYCHOLOGY FOR YOU?

Do you:

- ☐ Enjoy shows like *Law and Order, CSI,* or *COPS*?
- ☐ Have an interest in politics?
- ☐ Think offenders have rights and should be treated justly and fairly?
- ☐ Think some people are so mentally ill that they shouldn't be punished for the bad things they do?
- ☐ Think you could try to help someone who murdered or raped someone?
- ☐ Think you could try to help someone who abused a child?
- ☐ Like solving puzzles?
- ☐ Like reading about criminal activity in your local newspaper?
- ☐ Like reading biographies about high profile criminals?
- ☐ Think you would like to work in a prison?
- ☐ Like studying about mental illness?
- ☐ Like a good debate?
- ☐ Like people to challenge your thoughts and opinions?
- ☐ Like to write?

Scoring: The more boxes you checked, the more likely it is that legal or forensic psychology is for you.

6 | HEALTH PSYCHOLOGY

In 2005, Hurricane Katrina devastated New Orleans and parts of Mississippi, generating feelings of chaos, anxiety, fear, and anger among those in these areas and in the country as a whole. These traumatic events raised health concerns of U.S. citizens effects not only those directly traumatized by the hurricane, but also those exposed to toxins and disease in relief efforts. How do people cope with such life-altering medical situations? What interventions are helpful for those suffering medical complications from disasters, injuries, or other medical hardships? Questions such as these are at the heart of health psychology.

HEALTH PSYCHOLOGY

Health psychology is the study of psychological influences on health, why people become ill, and how people respond when they become ill, as well as the application of preventive strategies and interventions aimed at helping people maintain or improve their health (Taylor, 1999). Health psychologists study the interactive influences of biological, behavioral, and social factors on health and illness (American Psychological Association Division 38, n.d.). In other words, health psychologists examine how our emotions, thoughts, behaviors, and social interactions influence our physical well-being (meaning, health and wellness) and response to illness. Health psychologists study ways to promote healthy behavior (for example help people stop smoking, urge use of sun block, and promote healthy eating). They also study how to prevent and treat illnesses through the use of behavioral management, stress management, and coping techniques. What are the effects of stress? Can stress lead to illness? Health psychologists study the role of psychological and social factors, like stress and social support, in the development of disease.

Before proceeding with our discussion of careers in health psychology, let's first clear up some potentially confusing terminology. Health psychology is a subfield of psychology and has frequently been referred to as *behavioral medicine*, *medical psychology*, and *psychosomatic medicine*; however, these terms are neither accurate nor appropriate (Belar & Deardorff, 1995). *Behavioral medicine* is the most commonly used alternative term, but it is an interdisciplinary term (including behavioral and biomedical science); psychologists practice psychology, not behavioral medicine (Belar & Deardorff, 1995). Thus, *health psychology* is the most appropriate term for this specialized field and it will be used throughout this chapter.

OPPORTUNITIES WITH A BACHELOR'S DEGREE

If you are interested in health psychology, you'll be glad to know that there are many opportunities for bachelor's degree holders to work in rewarding careers that challenge them to use their general training in psychology as well as specialized knowledge in health psychology. Examples of such careers include recreational therapist, occupational therapy assistant, physical therapy assistant, and health educator.

RECREATIONAL THERAPIST

Recreational therapists provide treatment and recreational activities to individuals with physical or emotional disabilities in a variety of settings, including medical settings, community-based programs (for example, parks and recreation, special education programs for students, adult living programs, community mental health centers), and prisons (Bureau of Labor Statistics, 2008). Recreational therapists are different from recreational workers. Recreational therapists provide treatment services to assist individuals with disabilities or problems and deficits, whereas recreational workers generally work with healthy and/or disabled individuals with emphasis on developing interests rather than treating problems.

Recreational therapists assess and treat individuals with physical or psychological problems. They use standardized assessments and observations, medical records, and collateral information to assess clients' problems and develop treatment strategies targeting physical, mental, or emotional well-being of clients (Bureau of Labor Statistics, 2008). Typical treatment activities include: arts and crafts, animals (meaning, pet therapy), gardening, sports, games, dance and movement, drama, music, and community outings, as well as specific strategies such as stress management and relaxation techniques (Bureau of Labor Statistics, 2008). Recreational therapists frequently are employed in hospitals, nursing homes, community-based programs such as assisted living and outpatient physical and psychiatric rehabilitation facilities, residential and correctional centers, adult daycare facilities, and social service agencies (Bureau of Labor Statistics, 2008).

The median salary for recreational therapists in 2006 was $34,990; however, growth in the field has slowed in recent years (Bureau of Labor Statistics, 2008). Employment opportunities may increase in the future given the rapidly increasing number of aging adults; thus, recreational therapy will remain a viable profession for many. Another benefit of this profession is the opportunity for advancement. Therapists may grow weary of the therapeutic contact and physical energy required to provide recreational therapy on a daily basis, particularly as they themselves age; however, there are opportunities within this profession to advance to supervisory positions or to pursue teaching interests in the field (Bureau of Labor Statistics, 2008). Recreational therapists typically have a bachelor's degree. Psychology's emphasis on understanding behavior, coupled with training in therapeutic recreation, will suit you well in this career.

OCCUPATIONAL THERAPY ASSISTANT

Occupational therapy assistants help occupational therapists provide rehabilitative services to patients with physical, developmental, or psychological impairments (Bureau of Labor Statistics, 2008). Occupational therapy assistants are not limited to working with patients who are attempting to re-enter the labor force; rather, this work is much broader and focuses on any aspect of a patient's life (for example, developing the skills necessary for independent living such as cooking, cleaning, and accessing transportation). Aides to occupational therapists are intimately involved with all aspects of a patient's rehabilitation from disabilities caused by injuries (for example, from an automobile accident); they also help individuals with developmental disabilities (such as mental retardation) to acquire skills for independent living.

Occupational therapy assistants may work with occupational therapists in hospitals, outpatient clinics, and offices. The hours may vary if working in a private medical office to include evenings or weekends in order to be flexible with client schedules; however, in clinics and hospital settings the hours tend to be more traditional (8 A.M. to 5 P.M.). The job outlook for occupational therapy assistants is outstanding with the market for occupational therapists expected to grow more rapidly than the average job over the next eight years (Bureau of Labor Statistics, 2008). Salaries of occupational therapy assistants are competitive, with a median salary of $42,060 (Bureau of Labor Statistics, 2008). One disadvantage of this career choice is the physical demand. Occupational therapy assistants must be strong enough to help lift patients (including overweight patients) as well as to stand, kneel, bend, stoop, and move from station to station for long periods.

Note that a bachelor's degree is not sufficient to be an occupational therapy assistant; the completion of a certificate in occupational therapy is also required (Bureau of Labor Statistics, 2008). It may be advisable to complete two years of college in a field such as psychology, and then work toward the completion of an occupational therapy assistance certificate program. Most states regulate this career option and occupational therapy assistants must pass a national certification examination before being appropriately credentialed to practice. (For more information, consult the American Occupational Therapy Association at http://www.aota.org.)

PHYSICAL THERAPY ASSISTANT

A career option that is related to occupational therapy assistant is the physical therapy assistant. Physical therapy assistants assist physical therapists in the provision of treatments and interventions for individuals suffering pain, loss of mobility, or other physical disabilities (Bureau of Labor Statistics, 2008). Although the work is demanding, including necessity of core body strength to assist or physically move patients with mobility issues, this career choice offers hands-on treatment that can be very rewarding. Like the occupational therapist assistant, this occupation may require the attainment of a license as a physical therapist; however, much of the training includes "on-the-job" training (Bureau of Labor Statistics, 2008); thus, a graduate with a major or minor in psychology, with an emphasis on health psychology-related coursework, will be very marketable with specialized training to meet the emotional and motivational needs of patients requiring physical therapy.

The occupational outlook for students interested in a career as a physical therapy assistant is promising as the field is expected to grow much more rapidly than the average job (Bureau of Labor Statistics, 2008). Additionally, income levels are very competitive, with a 2006 median income of $41,360, with the middle 50 percent of employees earning between $33,840 and $49,010 (Bureau of Labor Statistics, 2008).

HEALTH EDUCATOR

Health educators educate individuals and communities about healthy lifestyles and wellness (Bureau of Labor Statistics, 2008). In proving education and information, health educators work to prevent illnesses and increase healthy lifestyles. For example, health educators will share knowledge and information on health-related issues such as diet and nutrition, sleep and exercise hygiene, problem behaviors (for example, risky behaviors such as promiscuous sexual behavior, substance abuse), and general health hygiene (for example, dental care, self-examinations for breast or testicular cancer, medical check-ups). Health educators identify needs, with particular attention to cultural groups (Bureau of Labor Statistics, 2008) that may be lacking resources such as geriatric populations, low-income families, or

TABLE 6.1 | PREPARATION FOR BA–LEVEL CAREERS RELATED TO HEALTH PSYCHOLOGY

Coursework

    Abnormal Psychology or Psychopathology
    Anatomy
    Biology
    Epidemiology
    Health (courses in health and wellness at introductory and advanced levels)
    Health Education
    Health Psychology
    Interviewing, Counseling, or Helping Skills
    Mathematics
    Substance Abuse
    Writing

Applied Experiences: Volunteer, intern/practica, or paid part-time positions in any of the following settings

    Any medical setting
    Burn Unit
    Rehabilitation Unit
    University Wellness Center
    Health/Lifestyle Center
    Physical/Occupational Therapy Clinic

Research Experiences: Experiences studying and participating in research in any of the following areas*

    Health Psychology
    Wellness
    Health behaviors such as smoking, obesity
    At-risk behaviors such as unsafe sex, substance abuse
    Sleep disorders
    Behavioral decision making or health decision making

*Note that the content area of the research is less important than the experience itself, which enhances reasoning, quantitative, writing, and organizational skills.

minorities that may be lacking in resources. Health educators will then design and implement educational programs (for example, classes, promotional pamphlets, community activities) to meet the health-related informational need.

    A career as a health educator affords many exciting opportunities, including a diverse work setting as health educators typically transition between office and individual or group field placement settings (for example, individual home, community center). A career in health education can also be very rewarding, both professionally and personally, with an opportunity to reach and help marginalized and underserved populations. Additionally, a career in health education necessitates creativity in developing and implementing programs that will impact behavior. Although training and education in health education is likely a prerequisite for a career in health education, a dual major (or minor) in psychology can also make one very competitive. Understanding cultural differences, including attitudes and principles of behavior change, will serve one well when educating and confronting resistance to change that is inevitable when attempting to change behavior. Salary in health education is another benefit, with a median 2006 income of $41,330 (Bureau of Labor Statistics, 2008) and the middle 50 percent earning between $31,300 and $56,580. Finally, health education is a growing industry with a professional growth rate that is expected to be much higher than the average career/job.

Disadvantages to a career as a health educator include an unstable schedule, as many programs will need to be implemented during evening and weekend hours to avoid school and work demands. Additionally, given the nature of the work, some of the targeted clientele, and grassroots-level work, some of the homes and/or community centers encountered are impoverished and lacking in cleanliness; however, such settings offer opportunities for immediate progress.

CAREER AS A HEALTH PSYCHOLOGIST

The specialized nature of a career in health psychology requires training at the doctoral level (meaning, completion of a Ph.D. or Psy.D. program). Health psychologists earn a doctoral degree in psychology, typically clinical or counseling psychology (Belar, 1997), and specialize in health psychology during internship and postdoctoral training.

Because scientific knowledge in health psychology has experienced considerable growth in the past two decades, there are many career opportunities for health psychologists and the potential to expand clinical practice in this area is dramatic (Belar et al., 2001). In fact, the management of health and disease is one of the most rapidly growing research and practice specialties in professional psychology (Levant et al., 2001). Health psychologists are employed in a myriad of settings, and the professional activities in which they engage often are determined by the setting in which they work. Health psychologists may engage in applied activities (such as providing psychological services for the prevention or treatment of health-related problems and behaviors) or research and academic activities (such as conducting research to investigate health-related issues and behaviors or teaching at a university). Health psychologists are also found in medical settings, such as primary care programs, inpatient medical units, medical schools, and specialized healthcare programs (for example, pain management centers, long-term care facilities, or rehabilitation centers). Let's take a closer look at the settings and activities in which health psychologists engage.

ACADEMIC AND RESEARCH SETTINGS

In academia and research settings, health psychologists teach, conduct research to understand and treat illnesses, and develop preventive and treatment programs to avoid or reduce health-related problems and concerns. Like other professors, health psychologists in academia teach undergraduate and graduate students about the field, and conduct research to expand the field.

Although health psychologists engaged in research are not directly involved in client care, their work often holds profound implications for the care that clients receive. Research conducted by health psychologists provides practitioners with information about lifestyle and personality factors as well as the psychosocial factors that influence health (Sarafino, 2002). Researchers develop and evaluate therapeutic programs aimed at improving healthy functioning or reducing the likelihood of illness (for example, smoking cessation programs), as well as treating existing conditions (for example, stress-reduction programs for persons with coronary heart disease). Thus, researchers have a hand in influencing the health and care of today's medical patient.

Health psychologists who focus on program development actively work to create and assess the efficacy of wellness and health-related programs such as smoking cessation programs, healthy eating and exercising programs, and stress-management programs, to name just a few. The goals of these programs are to increase the well-being and health of individuals in high-risk groups (for example, patients with high blood pressure) or those actively engaged in risky behaviors (for example, smokers).

The benefits and pitfalls of an academic career as well as the credentials and job responsibilities of this career are covered in Chapter 13. We will note here that health psychologists tend to have specialized training which frequently includes postdoctoral experience, which can lead to slightly higher salaries than most other assistant professors.

SERVICE DELIVERY SETTINGS

Health psychology service providers are employed in hospitals, long-term care facilities, rehabilitation centers, medical schools, or private practice. In each of these settings, health psychologists provide assessment and intervention services and usually collaborate with other healthcare professionals such as physicians, dentists, nurses, physician's assistants, dietitians, social workers, pharmacists, physical and occupational therapists, and chaplains (Committee on Education and Training, Division 38, n.d.) in an effort to provide comprehensive and holistic healthcare. The clinical activities of health psychologists generally include assessment activities or prevention/intervention services.

Health psychologists often conduct assessments in conjunction with other medical professionals to determine the etiology (cause of) and correlates of healthy living and health-related problems (Taylor, 1999). Assessments conducted by health psychologists may include cognitive and/or behavioral assessments, psychophysical assessments, personality assessments, demographic surveys and clinical interviews, and other clinical protocols (Committee on Education and Training, Division 38, n.d.).

Treatment services, on the other hand, refers to prevention or intervention services. The goal of prevention is to help people improve their lifestyles and avoid major illnesses or health complications, whereas interventions target existing health-related problems with a focus on helping people cope with or adjust to health-related problems (Kaplan, Sallis, & Patterson, 1993). Examples of preventive care are programs aimed at educating at-risk populations (for example, the "Just Say No to Drugs" program) or the general population about the importance of lifestyle improvements (for example, programs advocating the health benefits of exercise and a proper nutritional diet). Examples of interventions include stress management for medical patients with high blood pressure and pain management for persons who have been injured in an accident. Health psychologists not only design and implement treatment strategies but also conduct research to assess the effectiveness of prevention and intervention programs.

The benefits of a career in health psychology service delivery may include a slightly elevated salary compared to other psychologists, especially when working in medical settings, as well as the opportunity to influence directly the quality of life and wellness of clients in a relatively short period of time (treatment gains in health psychology may be slightly more rapid than treatment gains by psychologists treating other problems or concerns such as severe mental illness). A benefit of becoming a health psychologist in private practice or developing a consulting career is the flexibility in scheduling clients. One limitation of a career choice in health psychology service delivery is the occasional experience of not being well-received by the medical community, where the M.D. is the preferred degree (compared to the Ph.D. or Psy.D. for psychologists). However, psychologists' contributions to wellness and healthy living are becoming increasingly recognized, particularly as the biopsychosocial model of health and illness becomes more widely accepted within the medical community (Sarafino, 2002).

PUBLIC HEALTH SETTINGS

Health psychologists also pursue careers in public health. Psychologists in public health settings will likely be involved in research of health issues, teaching and training future professionals, public health practice and service provision, or consulting with health organizations, professionals, and political leaders (Baskin, 2005). For example, psychologists in public health work may be involved in developing or evaluating programs for public health organizations, or may pursue involvement in social policy. Program developers, as we've discussed, are responsible for developing and implementing health-related programs in communities to promote wellness and healthy living or to treat health-related problems or concerns. Community-based AIDS education and support programs are an example of the type of work in which program developers may be involved. Health psychologists in social policy positions, on the other hand, spend their time developing and drafting legal statutes and proposals in an effort to create federal or state legislation that promotes wellness and health. An example of such legislation is the requirement that tobacco products carry warning labels on their packaging to warn customers of the health risks associated with tobacco products.

A primary benefit of seeking employment as a health psychologist in public health is the opportunity to influence directly the services available to communities and persons in need. Unfortunately, the time to develop and implement services can be extensive, and that can be very frustrating when there are people in need or there is an urgent problem to be addressed. Salaries in public health are comparable to other psychology-related positions discussed in this text. (For more information on policy-related careers, see Chapter 12.)

The field of health psychology offers knowledge and training that is relevant at both the bachelor's and graduate levels. At the bachelor's level, careers tend to be multi-disciplinary. If you are interested in pursuing a health-related position with your baccalaureate degree, supplement your academic training in psychology with courses in other health areas such as health education, nutrition, and safety. Careers at the doctoral level are more specialized. If you are considering a graduate-level career in health psychology, pursue generalist training during graduate school (meaning, clinical or counseling psychology programs), followed by specialized training in health psychology during internship and/or postdoctoral work.

SUGGESTED READINGS

Baskin, M. L. (2005). Public health: Career opportunities for psychologists in public health. In R. D. Morgan, T. L. Kuther, & C. J. Habben (Eds.), *Life after graduate school in psychology: Insider's advice from new psychologists*. New York: Psychology Press.

Belar, C. D., & Deardorff, W. W. (1995). *Clinical health psychology in medical settings: A practitioner's guidebook*. Washington, DC: American Psychological Association.

Boll, T. J., Johnson, S. B., Perry, N., & Rozensky, R. H. (2002). *Handbook of clinical health psychology: Volume 1. Medical disorders and behavioral applications*. Washington, DC: American Psychological Association.

Cohen, L., McChargue, D., & Collins, E. (2003). *The health psychology handbook: Practical issues for the behavioral medicine specialist*. Thousand Oaks, CA: Sage.

WEB RESOURCES

American Psychological Association, Division of Health Psychology (Division 38)
http://www.health-psych.org/

Society of Behavioral Medicine
http://www.sbm.org/

Health Psychology and Rehabilitation
http://www.healthpsych.com/

The Health Psychology Network
http://www.healthpsychology.net/

Careers in Health Psychology
http://www.wcupa.edu/_ACADEMICS/sch_cas.psy/Career_Paths/Health/Career02.htm

CHECKLIST: IS HEALTH PSYCHOLOGY FOR YOU?

Do you:

☐ Want to work in a medical setting?
☐ Want to better understand medical problems?
☐ Want to conduct research with the aim of helping people with health problems?
☐ Enjoy reading about health problems or concerns?
☐ Find satisfaction in the recent tobacco settlements?
☐ Want to help people live healthier lives?
☐ Want to understand the effects of stress and lifestyle choices on health?
☐ Have interest in the growing health concerns across the globe?
☐ Want to understand how the mind influences the body?

Scoring: The more boxes you checked, the more likely it is that health or sport psychology is a good match for you.

Sport Psychology | CHAPTER 7

The events of September 11, 2001 created chaos in New York City and Washington, D.C., as well as fear, anxiety, anger, and a myriad of other feelings and emotions for all citizens of the United States. Following the terrorist attacks on New York and Washington in 2001, all major sporting events were canceled in the days that followed, and debate ensued about the role of athletics for morale and patriotism of U.S. citizens (for example, do sports—watching and playing—help us deal with life-altering events and stressors?). Three days later the first Major League Baseball games were held. How did professional athletes remain focused on their sports while the

81

remainder of the country, and world, was focused on the devastation of New York and Washington? What psychological factors underlie the performance of expert athletes? Questions such as these are at the heart of sport psychology.

WHAT IS SPORT PSYCHOLOGY?

Sport psychology is the "study of the psychological aspects of sport" (Anderson, 2000, p. xiii); however, sport psychology isn't limited to sports and may include any type of physical activity or exercise (American Psychological Association Division 47, 2007). Thus, sport psychology services may address any aspect of athletes' or performers' lives, competitive or otherwise, to assist them in their performance and life endeavors (Anderson, 2000).

Sport psychologists examine topics such as the ways an athlete can use visualization techniques to improve performance, ways to manage performance anxiety, and ways athletes on sports teams can cooperate to work more effectively together. Like other psychologists, some sport psychologists conduct research in academic, clinical, government, and business settings. Others engage in clinical or consulting practice, helping individuals and teams improve their athletic performance, and training coaches to help them become more efficient and productive in leading athletic teams. It is easy to see why students are intrigued by sport psychology: the philosophy and principles of improving performance work for more than just athletes—they are effective beyond the field as well.

OPPORTUNITIES WITH A BACHELOR'S DEGREE

If you are interested in sport psychology, you'll be glad to know that there are many opportunities for bachelor's degree holders to work in rewarding careers that challenge them to use their general training in psychology as well as any specialized knowledge in sports. It should be noted that a history as an athlete is not a prerequisite for a career in the sport psychology arena; however, former athletes may find such careers highly rewarding as they are able to remain close to competitions and the athletes competing in sports. There are a wide variety of sports-related careers at the bachelor's degree level for which psychology majors will find themselves competitive, with just a few examples including careers as fitness instructors and recreational workers, physical education teachers, sport instructors and coaches, and sport reporters.

FITNESS INSTRUCTOR AND RECREATIONAL WORKER

Fitness instructors and recreational workers develop, plan, organize, and direct recreational activities (such as aerobics, arts and crafts, performing arts, camping, or recreational sports) for both healthy and disabled (physically or psychologically) persons (Bureau of Labor Statistics, 2008). In other words, fitness instructors and recreational workers are not limited to a specific clientele or persons with particular health-related issues. Fitness instructors and recreational workers are employed in educational and university settings, nursing homes, park and recreational centers, community activity centers, health clubs and fitness centers, and medical and rehabilitation centers. Although fitness instructors and recreational workers often major in recreational studies (such as leisure studies or parks and recreation) or related fields (for example, health sciences) (Bureau of Labor Statistics, 2008), psychology majors, particularly when accompanied by a dual major or minor in recreational studies or related fields, are highly competitive for this career because of psychology's broad based training in human development and motivation which are important skills in fitness and recreational work.

Typical activities of fitness and recreational workers will vary depending on agency type and clientele. For example, directors of parks and recreational programs spend the majority of their time developing and managing recreational programs in parks, playgrounds, and other child-oriented settings (Bureau of Labor Statistics, 2008). They may be responsible for park and recreational budgets, but also have an opportunity for direct involvement with program participants. Camp counselors, on the other hand, are recreational workers who "lead and instruct" children and adolescents in outdoor activities such as swimming and boating, horseback riding, camping, hiking, sports, music, drama, art, and computers (Bureau of Labor Statistics, 2008). Recreational workers may also assume more of a therapeutic role in residential camps where they provide assistance in skill building to individuals lacking daily living skills, social skills, and problem-solving skills. Fitness workers, on the other hand, coach groups or individuals in sporting or exercise activities with the goal of developing skills or promoting physical fitness and healthy living (Bureau of Labor Statistics, 2008).

Median salaries for recreational workers ($20,470) and fitness instructors ($25,910) are modest for entry-level positions (Bureau of Labor Statistics, 2008). However, one of the benefits of these careers is the opportunity to advance to supervisory positions or to pursue self-employment as a personal trainer, both of which offer salary increases. The job market for fitness instructors is very favorable; however, positions for recreational workers tend to be more competitive (Bureau of Labor Statistics, 2008). Advantages of these jobs include the employment setting; the nature of the work necessitates much time spent outdoors in parks, the wilderness, or near water, as well as other unique employment settings including tourist and vacation getaway spots. Imagine the enjoyment of working as a recreational worker on a cruise ship, on an island resort in the Bahamas, or at a secluded mountain spa. Although such positions remain highly coveted, and therefore competitive, such opportunities do exist. Another benefit is health-related—a fitness career will require you to maintain your fitness. As mentioned, the primary limitation of this career choice is the modest salary and the competition for entry-level positions for recreational workers; however, recognize that those with a bachelor's degree will most likely fare better, because many applicants for recreational positions will be applying with an associate degree or high-school diploma.

PHYSICAL EDUCATION TEACHER

Physical education (PE) teachers, employed in school settings, rarely major in psychology; however, training in psychology (for example, a double major or minor in psychology) may prove to be a great asset to PE teachers. A thorough review of the role of psychology in academic and school settings is discussed in Chapters 3 and 4, including discussion of the career choice of teacher. Here we focus on the benefit to PE teachers of specialized information in sport psychology. Course work in health and sport psychology at the undergraduate level is particularly beneficial to PE teachers in their roles as educators, trainers, and coaches. A foundation in psychology provides the necessary tools and principals to motivate students as well as to access the best learning strategies (for example, principles of reinforcement and overlearning for skill development). In addition, PE teachers are rarely restricted to the gym; thus, your degree in psychology, especially with a focus on sport psychology, may make you more competitive as you market yourself dually as a teacher of physical education as well as psychology-related classes. The salary, advantages, and disadvantages for a PE teacher are similar to those of other educators; we refer you to Chapter 4 for a review of this information.

SPORT INSTRUCTORS AND COACHES

With increased interest in youth sports, a growing field is sport instruction. Sport instructors work with individuals or a team of athletes to enhance skills. Sport instructors typically function in a consultant role, whereby they are hired to teach particular skills (for example, hitting coach for Little League baseball players, serving coach for youth tennis players, and so on). Coaches, on the other hand, are hired to lead a team (for example, baseball or football) or group of athletes (for example, golfers or cross-country runners) into competition. Whereas sport instructors work with people of all ages involved in sport, coaches are generally employed at the middle-school level and above. In middle and elementary schools, coaches are often dual-hires, meaning that they are hired both to teach a subject matter and to coach an athletic team (in the cases of smaller school districts, coaches may coach multiple team sports).

A bachelor's degree in psychology offers many advantages for sport instructors and coaches. The study of human behavior, including attitudes and motivation, will assist sport instructors and coaches trying to motivate athletes to improve. Additionally, studying psychology, including learning and motivation, will provide those in this field with the necessary knowledge to best teach athletes. Athletes of all ages and levels learn differently. The astute sport instructor or coach is able to modify his or her teaching style to best reach athletes. A bachelor's degree in psychology offers such a skill set and knowledge. Additionally, a bachelor's degree in psychology affords coaches the opportunity to teach diverse and interesting courses (for example, psychology, family studies, sociology) at the high-school level, a potential advantage in the hiring process in school districts that must juggle multiple demands with a hire—meaning, hire a coach that can also teach.

Sport instructor and coaching careers offer many benefits. First, the typical athlete is highly motivated and eager to improve; thus, resistance is generally minimal. Sport instructors and coaches frequently work outdoors, which is attractive for many, and the constant movement and teaching require some level of fitness, so opportunities for long-term fitness are good. Finally, sport instructors and coaches typically instruct or coach in sports of their choice, so interest remains high. Unfortunately, salaries in sport instruction and coaching are often low, especially in the early years of one's career, as it takes time to develop a reputation. The median annual income for coaches is $26,950; however, salaries will typically rise substantially as one moves up the athletic hierarchy (high-school coaches typically earn more than middle-school coaches; college coaches typically earn more than high-school coaches; professional coaches typically earn more than college coaches) (Bureau of Labor Statistics, 2008). Another disadvantage to a career in sport instruction or coaching is irregular work hours (Bureau of Labor Statistics, 2008). Sport instructors and coaches often can't begin their work day until after school hours, when athletes are available. Additionally, they must frequently attend events in the evenings and weekends. Lastly, coaches typically have small travel budgets.

SPORT REPORTER

Although a degree in journalism is often a prerequisite for a career as a sport reporter (including television or paper outlets), a minor in psychology is advantageous. Specifically, the writing, statistics, and analyzing of data that is required in the field of psychology affords excellent training for sport reporting. Sport reporters gather information (data), prepare stories (analogous to writing a research paper based on the obtained data), and publish or broadcast the information (similar to

TABLE 7.1 | PREPARATION FOR BA–LEVEL CAREERS RELATED TO SPORT PSYCHOLOGY

Coursework

Abnormal Psychology or Psychopathology
Biology
Communication
Exercise and Sport Science
Interviewing, Counseling, or Helping Skills
Physical Health
Principles of Sport Coaching
Psychology of Motivation (or Attitudes)
Sport Management
Sport Psychology

Applied Experiences: Volunteer, intern/practica, or paid part-time positions in any of the following settings

University Athletic Department
Youth/Adult Sports Programs (for example, Little League, Parks and Recreation)
University Recreational Center

Research Experiences: Experiences studying and participating in research in any of the following areas*

Sport Psychology
Exercise Psychology
Leadership
Goal setting
Performance enhancement
Motivation

*Note that the content area of the research is less important than the experience itself, which enhances reasoning, quantitative, writing, and organizational skills.

published psychological reports or professional presentations at a research conference). With increased media focus on celebrity-athlete behavior, a background in psychology, specifically social psychology with focus on group behavior, attitudes, and decision making, offers compelling insights into individual and team behavior. Thus, when editors request a special report on why a sport team engaged in a certain type of behavior or bonded better than other teams, a background in psychology may offer the advantage to get the special assignment.

Work hours vary by season (for example, the fall and winter include many weekend hours as collegiate and high-school football games, volleyball matches, basketball games, and wrestling matches, for example, typically occur on weekends). Additionally, the work schedule is frequently hectic (Bureau of Labor Statistics, 2008) as reporters struggle to meet deadlines for on-air reporting, often with minimal preparation, or for newspapers to go to press. A career as a sport reporter, however, offers the potential for great excitement as coverage of sporting events will often include highly contested and riveting games or competitions. Sport reporters are often very close to the action with a close-up of the stress and strain endured by the athletes. Income for sport reporters is respectable, with a median income in 2006 of $33,470, with the middle 50 percent earning between $24,370 and $51,700 (Bureau of Labor Statistics, 2008).

CAREER AS A SPORT PSYCHOLOGIST

Sport psychology is a "stimulating" field offering a variety of career opportunities (Carter, 2005). Educational requirements for sport psychology generally are more flexible than for other psychology careers. Academic degrees may be earned from departments of physical education, psychology, counseling, or sport science. In fact, sport psychology is a multi-disciplinary field, and course work should be taken in psychology and counseling, and also in courses such as exercise physiology, sport sociology, and biomechanics (Van Raalte & Williams, 1994). Although many employment opportunities for sport psychologists require the completion of a doctoral degree, some opportunities exist for individuals with a masters degree. (Note, however, that masters-level professionals will encounter a more limited and competitive job market.) Regardless of the educational track being pursued, specialized training (for example, internships) should be sought that provide training and experience in the field of sport psychology, yet such opportunities are limited.

Sport psychologists have three primary roles: practice, research, and teaching (Van Raalte & Williams, 1994). However, sport psychology is a highly specialized field which has lent itself to less career diversity than other areas of psychology. The vast majority of sport psychologists are employed in academic settings (47 percent) and private practice (37 percent) (Meyers, Coleman, Whelan, & Mehlenbeck, 2001). The following sections discuss the various settings in which sport psychologists work.

ACADEMIC AND RESEARCH SETTINGS

Within academia, sport psychologists may be affiliated with departments of psychology, sport exercise programs, and physical education programs. Not surprisingly, within academia the majority of their time is spent in teaching and research activities, with some time available for consulting or service delivery activities (Meyers et al., 2001). The aim of sport psychology research is to identify the effects of athletic participation (including exercise and other physical activities) on development, health, and overall well-being throughout the lifespan (Van Raalte & Williams, 1994). Much of this research focuses on strategies for improving athletic performance; however, sport psychologists also are interested in the overall life functioning of athletes and performers. Therefore, issues of life satisfaction, vocational plans for retired athletes, and relationship issues are a few examples of the varied research interests of sport psychologists.

As is true with other psychological specialties, academic careers in sport psychology afford the opportunity to collaborate with other professionals. Also of benefit is the potential for access to an athletic population via college sports teams, as well as flexibility of schedule to pursue practice or consultation interests. In fact, many collegiate athletic departments are moving to a model of hiring full-time sport psychologists, which affords great opportunity for research collaborations and the development of consultation relationships. The primary pitfall for academically inclined sport psychologists is the job demand, as there appear to be a limited number of available positions within higher-education settings during any given year, and competition is at a premium. However, this is true of most academic positions within and outside of psychology. Academic salaries of sport psychologists are consistent with other academic psychologists (Meyers et al., 2001).

PRACTICE SETTINGS

The goal of the practicing sport psychologist is to use psychological principles to help athletes and performers achieve optimal physical performance (American Psychological Association Division 47, 2007). This increased performance is accomplished through techniques such as relaxation, imagery, goal setting, and self-talk (Anderson, 2000). Relaxation strategies are taught to athletes and performers to reduce anxiety and stress in order to maximize performance (Sherman & Poczwardowski, 2000). Sport psychologists direct athletes to use imagery (Simmons, 2000) and self-talk (Perry & Marsh, 2000) before, during, and after an event to improve their focus and mental clarity with the expectation of improved performance. Goal setting is used with athletes and performers to increase their sense of self-control and to enhance performance over the long term (Marchant, 2000).

Sport psychologists tend to enjoy a flexible work environment. A sport psychologist may see an athlete in the office but may also travel to the relevant athletic arena for service delivery. For example, a sport psychologist may work with a golfer at the driving range or putting green to implement focusing strategies previously discussed in the office. A sport psychologist working with a basketball player may meet the client at the arena to implement relaxation strategies while the athlete shoots free throws. Thus, careers in sport psychology require flexibility and often creativity for service delivery. Sport psychologists who provide services are employed in university counseling centers, sports medicine clinics, consulting agencies, and in private practice.

Sport psychologists who work in private practice provide clients with performance enhancement, life-skills training, organizational consulting, psychotherapy and counseling interventions, and rehabilitation (Danish, Petit-pas, & Hale, 1993). Private practice, however, tends to be less financially successful and stable for sport psychologists than is academia; practitioners often must supplement their income (Meyers et al., 2001) by providing non-sports-related psychological services. Once supplemented however, the income of sport psychologists in private practice appears equivalent to other psychologists in private practice. Furthermore, sport psychologists who are fortunate enough to be affiliated with collegiate or professional teams and athletes are likely to have higher incomes than sport psychologists not working with elite athletes and their teams.

Throughout this chapter, we have seen that sport psychology offers knowledge and training that is relevant to many careers. If you are interested in pursuing a sports-related position with your baccalaureate degree, supplement your academic training in psychology with courses in other health- and recreation-related areas such as health education, nutrition, and safety. Careers at the doctoral level are more specialized. If you are considering a graduate-level career in sport psychology, recognize that there are few sport psychology programs. Most sport psychologists have degrees in clinical or counseling psychology and have specialized in sport psychology after graduate school. If a career as a sport psychologist appeals to you, pursue generalist training during graduate school (meaning, clinical or counseling psychology programs), followed by specialized training in health or sport psychology during internship or postdoctoral work.

SUGGESTED READINGS

Anderson, M. B. (Ed.) (2000). *Doing sport psychology*. Champaign, IL: Human Kinetics.
Carter, J. E. (2005). Sport psychology: Locker room confessions. In R. D. Morgan, T. L.Kuther, & C. J. Habben (Eds.), *Life after graduate school in psychology: Insider's advice from new psychologists*. New York: Psychology Press.
Cox, R. H. (2006). *Sport psychology: Concepts and applications*. New York: McGraw Hill.
Van Raalte, J. L., & Brewer, B. W. (2002). *Exploring sport and exercise psychology* (2nd ed.). Washington, DC: American Psychological Association.

WEB RESOURCES

Association for the Advancement of Applied Sport Psychology
http://www.aaasponline.org/

European Federation of Sport Psychology
http://www.fepsac.org

Sport Psychology OverSite
http://www-personal.umich.edu/~bing/oversite/sportpsych.html

Athletic Insight: The Online Journal of Sports Psychology
http://www.athleticinsight.com/

Sports and Performance Psychology
http://www.shpm.com/articles/sports/index.shtml

The International Society of Sport Psychology
http://www.issponline.org

CHECKLIST: IS SPORT PSYCHOLOGY FOR YOU?

Do you:

☐ Want to help people maximize their physical capabilities?
☐ Enjoy working with athletes? Want to help people live healthier lives?
☐ Enjoy sports?
☐ Want to work with athletes?
☐ Like conducting research?
☐ Want to learn more about athletic performance?
☐ Often wonder why some people succeed whereas others fail?
☐ Want to understand how the mind influences the body?

Scoring: The more boxes you checked, the more likely it is that sport psychology is a good match for you.

CHAPTER **8** | BIOPSYCHOLOGY, COGNITIVE NEUROPSYCHOLOGY, AND CLINICAL NEUROPSYCHOLOGY

CHAPTER GUIDE

Biopsychology, Cognitive Neuropsychology and Clinical Neuropsychology

Opportunities with a Bachelor's Degree

Science Technician

Psychiatric Technician

Clinical Laboratory Technologist or Technician

Pharmacy Technician

Opportunities with a Graduate Degree

Pharmaceutical and Biotechnology Research

Practice

Suggested Readings

Web Resources

Checklist: Is Biopsychology, Clinical Neuropsychology, or Cognitive Neuropsychology for You?

90

Do children act aggressively because they inherited an aggressive gene or do they learn aggressive behavior early in life? Are quiet people born shy or do they develop shyness in response to their early environment? You have undoubtedly been asked to think about such "nature versus nurture" issues by now in your college education and you've probably found it difficult to develop satisfactory answers. Don't worry, you're not alone! In fact, an entire field of psychology is devoted to one aspect of these questions—the study of the biological bases of behavior.

Technological breakthroughs are rapidly advancing scientific knowledge in the biological sciences (for example, DNA research, cloning, stem cell research). What do these advances mean for psychology? With increased technology and refined research methods we are able to identify more accurately the biological processes and neurological functioning that impacts human behavior. Thus, biopsychology, cognitive neuropsychology, and clinical neuropsychology have enormous potential for altering our understanding of human behavior, not only to increase our knowledge base but also to influence how psychology is applied in the real world. Before discussing applications of biopsychology, cognitive neuropsychology, and clinical neuropsychology, let's spend some time defining the fields.

BIOPSYCHOLOGY, COGNITIVE NEUROPSYCHOLOGY AND CLINICAL NEUROPSYCHOLOGY

Biopsychology, or physiological psychology, is the branch of psychology that studies the relationship between biology and behavior (Myers, 2004). Biopsychology integrates various areas of neuroscience (for example, neuroanatomy, the study of the structure of the nervous system; neurochemistry, the study of the chemical composition of neural activity; neuroendocrinology, the study of the interplay between the nervous system and endocrine system; neuropathology, the study of disorders that affect the nervous system; and neuropharmacology, the study of how drugs affect neural activity) to explain the biological bases of behavior. For example, a biopsychologist might study how genetics and experience interact to influence behavior. Others study the influence of hormones and other chemicals on behavior (for example, is there a "love" hormone? or does gambling or other risky behaviors release endorphins into the bloodstream?). Biopsychologists predominantly are researchers and academicians, employed by universities, government, research institutes, and pharmaceutical companies.

Cognitive neuropsychology is a branch of cognitive psychology that aims to understand cognition from the perspective of the brain—it represents the merge of cognitive psychology and biopsychology. Cognitive neuropsychologists study the brain to understand the neural bases of mental processes like thinking, memory, attention, and language (Carpenter, 2001). A cognitive neuropsychologist may use brain imaging techniques to study what happens in people's brains when they tackle math problems (see for example Murray, 2000). How does the brain of someone with dyslexia function differently from a typical brain? What areas of the brain are responsible for language, short-term memory, or decision making? Cognitive neuropsychologists conduct research to examine how neural activity translates into mental activity: How do collections of neurons communicate, and how do we interpret that communication as thought? As you might guess, cognitive neuropsychology is primarily a research-oriented field and cognitive neuropsychologists are found in a variety of research and academic settings.

Whereas cognitive neuropsychology represents the joining of cognitive psychology and biopsychology, *clinical neuropsychology* applies findings from biopsychology within clinical and counseling contexts. Clinical neuropsychology is the application of psychological assessments and interventions based upon the study of the central nervous system (American Psychological Association Division of Clinical Neuropsychology, 1989). In other words, clinical neuropsychology integrates biopsychology and clinical/counseling psychology to assist clients suffering from brain dysfunction (for example, a patient suffering memory loss following a traumatic brain injury).

Clinical neuropsychologists conduct neuropsychological assessments to identify the extent of brain damage or severity of impairment in clients. They also develop interventions to help clients adapt or regain function in order to maximize the potential for independent living and quality of life. Like other psychologists, clinical neuropsychologists are employed in applied settings such as medical hospitals, clinics, and private practice, and in academic positions within university settings or research positions in academia, government, or industry.

OPPORTUNITIES WITH A BACHELOR'S DEGREE

Although much training in biopsychology or neuropsychology occurs at the graduate level, students with interests at the baccalaureate level have many career options available to them, including science technician, psychiatric aide, psychiatric technician, clinical laboratory technician, and pharmacy technician. These positions provide students an opportunity to apply their knowledge of psychology along with their knowledge and interest in biopsychology.

SCIENCE TECHNICIAN

Science technicians are involved in laboratory research and "use the principles and theories of science and mathematics to solve problems in research and development" (Bureau of Labor Statistics, 2008). They are a scientist's "hands," so to speak. They maintain scientific laboratories, operate and maintain laboratory instruments and equipment, monitor experiments, make observations and record data, and work with scientists who are forming conclusions based on experiments and lab work. There are many different kinds of technicians, because many fields require technical assistance. Thus, professional titles are designated according to the specific field (for example, agricultural technician, forensic science technician, nuclear technician) (Bureau of Labor Statistics, 2008). Bachelor's degree holders in psychology with interests in biopsychology may choose positions as *biological technicians* or *research technicians*.

In collaboration with biologists, biological technicians study living organisms and may be involved in medical or pharmaceutical research, microbiological or biotechnological laboratories (Bureau of Labor Statistics, 2008). Examples of such research include studying cures for physiological diseases (for example, Alzheimer's or AIDS) or analyzing organic substances and the effects of chemicals on the treatment of mental illness. Other research technicians may assist biopsychologists with their research. Science technicians typically work in research laboratories; however, they may occasionally work in other settings (for example, the "laboratory" of a forensic science technician may be the crime scene under investigation) (Bureau of Labor Statistics, 2008).

The job outlook for science technicians is expected to remain steady through 2016 (Bureau of Labor Statistics, 2008). Competitive salaries are one of the advantages of a career as a science technician. For example, in 2006, biological technicians working in government settings earned an average salary of $40,629 for physical science technicians (Bureau of Labor Statistics, 2008). Similar to other career fields, science technician salaries fluctuate with employer (private employers tend to pay more than the government) and type of science work (forensic science technicians earn slightly more than biological technicians). In addition to salary, the perks of this job include a comfortable work environment (laboratories are typically made to be comfortable), casual dress codes (the laboratory can get messy, so most science technicians wear jeans and casual clothing to work), and a 40-hour work week with normal business hours. The primary disadvantage of this career is the limited opportunity to develop and design research projects of your own interest. Although science technicians may have input into the research on which they are working, the employer or agency being served will typically determine the focus of research studies. If you're interested in this career choice, supplement your biopsychology training with additional research and laboratory-related coursework, such as biology, chemistry, and physics. The more laboratory experience you have, the greater your marketability.

Psychiatric Technician

A career as a psychiatric technician involves assisting psychiatrists or other mental health professionals in their care of mentally ill or emotionally disturbed patients. A psychiatric technician follows both a physician's instructions and hospital procedures, monitors patients' physical and emotional well-being, reports to medical staff, and may also provide therapeutic services and administer medications. (Bureau of Labor Statistics, 2008). Psychiatric technicians may also develop specialized skills, such as providing biofeedback in a clinic or for a private practitioner or providing EEG services in a sleep disorders clinic.

Rewards of a career as a psychiatric technician include direct work with clients, the chance to make a difference in someone's life, and the opportunity to work with an interdisciplinary team (Jobprofiles, 2003). Unfortunately, this career can be stressful, with limited job opportunities and few opportunities for advancement. Compared to other healthcare professionals, salaries in this field are marginal; as a psychiatric technician, you can expect to earn an entry salary of approximately $27,865 (salary.com, 2008). If you're interested in becoming a psychiatric technician, supplement your psychology coursework with courses in nursing and seek certification as a psychiatric technician (available through many colleges and universities).

Clinical Laboratory Technologist or Technician

Graduates with biopsychology interests sometimes obtain positions within clinical laboratories, as clinical laboratory technicians or clinical laboratory technologists, where they play a vital role in detecting, diagnosing, and treating diseases through their work analyzing a patient's physical samples (for example, body fluids, tissues, and cells) (Bureau of Labor Statistics, 2008). Clinical laboratory technicians conduct work similar to science technicians. They work under the supervision of laboratory technologists or managers and assist in the medical process. Clinical laboratory technicians maintain the laboratory, prepare specimens, and conduct basic tests either manually or with automated analyzers (Bureau of Labor Statistics, 2008).

Clinical laboratory technologists supervise technicians and perform sophisticated medical testing, including "chemical, biological, hematological, immunological, microscopic, and bacteriological tests" (Bureau of Labor Statistics, 2008). In other words, clinical laboratory technologists conduct all of the sophisticated medical tests that your physician orders when you visit for a routine exam (for example, blood glucose and cholesterol levels) or if he or she suspects that you are ill (for example, searching for microscopic signs of pathology in blood and tissue samples). Clinical laboratory technologists "make cultures of body fluid and tissue samples to determine the presence of bacteria, fungi, parasites, or other microorganisms" (Bureau of Labor Statistics, 2008).

The job outlook for clinical laboratory workers over the next ten years is excellent, with more job openings than qualified professionals to fill them (Bureau of Labor Statistics, 2008). As a clinical laboratory technologist you can expect to earn approximately $49,700 per year (Bureau of Labor Statistics, 2008). Disadvantages to a clinical laboratory career include the physical hazards: as a clinical laboratory worker, you may handle infectious agents. In addition, clinical laboratory personnel often are exposed to fumes for significant time periods, and spend a significant portion of their work day on their feet.

If you're considering a position within a clinical laboratory setting, understand that your psychology degree will enable you to pursue a position as a technician. For a technologist position, take additional courses in biology, chemistry, and medical technology to be competitive for this career option. Understand that some states require laboratory personnel to be certified, registered, or licensed (Bureau of Labor Statistics, 2008), so contact your state department of health for more information.

PHARMACY TECHNICIAN

Pharmacy technicians often work in retail pharmacies, where they help pharmacists distribute medication and information to customers. Pharmacy technicians verify customer and prescription information, perform the many clerical duties that arise within a pharmacy, and prepare medications for patients, including counting medications and preparing bottle labels (Bureau of Labor Statistics, 2008).

Benefits of a career as a pharmacy technician include a very good job market, that is expected to increase more rapidly than average for both full-time and part-time work (Bureau of Labor Statistics, 2008), and an opportunity to work directly with the public (public relations are an important aspect of this career). A career as a pharmacy technician also typically offers a very comfortable work environment plus regular business hours. However, salaries for pharmacy technicians are modest, with a median salary in 2006 of approximately $25,625. Additionally, opportunities for job advancement are limited. Higher salaries are

TABLE 8.1	PREPARATION FOR BA–LEVEL CAREERS RELATED TO BIOPSYCHOLOGY, COGNITIVE NEUROPSYCHOLOGY, AND CLINICAL NEUROPSYCHOLOGY

Coursework
- Abnormal Psychology
- Anatomy
- Biopsychology
- Brain and Behavior
- Chemistry
- Cognitive Psychology
- Genetics
- Math
- Microbiology
- Neuropsychology
- Psychological Assessment
- Writing

Applied Experiences: Volunteer, intern, or paid part-time positions in any of the following settings
- Doctor's Office
- Hospital
- Mental Retardation Facility
- Pharmaceutical Company
- Pharmacy (as an aide behind the counter)

Research Experiences: Experiences studying and participating in research in any of the following areas*
- Biology
- Chemistry
- Cognitive Psychology
- Neuropsychology
- Psychopathology

*Note that the content area of the research is less important than the experience itself, which enhances reasoning, quantitative, writing, and organizational skills.

available for those employed in hospital and grocery store pharmacies (Bureau of Labor Statistics, 2008).

Although formal pharmacy technician programs and certification are available, and preferred by many employers, many pharmacy technicians are trained on the job (Bureau of Labor Statistics, 2008); thus, psychology graduates with emphasis in biopsychology should find themselves very marketable for this career. Nevertheless, supplemental course work in chemistry is likely to enhance your application. Once employed (or prior to employment if you're trying to maximize your credentials) you may want to pursue certification via the Pharmacy Technician Certification Board that administers a national exam for certification (Bureau of Labor Statistics, 2008, visit http://www.ptcb.org/). Although this examination and certification are voluntary in most states, some states require certification, and a particular pharmacy/pharmacist may prefer or require it.

OPPORTUNITIES WITH A GRADUATE DEGREE

A graduate degree in biopsychology, cognitive neuropsychology, or clinical neuropsychology is versatile, provides training for a career in teaching or research, and also enables the pursuit of applied interests. Although some opportunities are available to masters degree holders, if you're interested in applied work, a doctoral degree is preferred. You may obtain a doctoral degree in biopsychology, cognitive neuropsychology, or cognitive psychology within a program that specializes in cognitive neuropsychology, or in clinical/counseling psychology followed by specialized training in clinical neuropsychology during the yearlong internship and/or postdoctoral training.

As is true for all psychologists, biopsychologists, cognitive neuropsychologists, and clinical neuropsychologists often find employment in academic settings. We discuss academic careers in detail in Chapter 13, but biopsychologists, clinical neuropsychologists, and cognitive neuropsychologists in academia face a challenge that is often specific to their fields: They usually require expensive laboratory equipment to conduct their research. Thus, getting a laboratory established and functioning can be problematic because significant space and money are required. Although a university may provide funds to assist new faculty in developing a psychophysiological or neuroanatomy lab, additional funds are often required to fully establish and maintain the laboratory. These psychologists spend a great deal of time writing grants to find their work, yet grant writing is time consuming and detracts from the research and publication that new professors are expected to do. Once received, however, grants offer faculty many perks, including increased salary via summer pay, course release time, paid research assistants, and status within the department. For more on academic careers, see Chapter 13. Let's take a closer look at the work of biopsychologists, cognitive neuropsychologists, and clinical neuropsychologists outside of academia.

PHARMACEUTICAL AND BIOTECHNOLOGY RESEARCH

In addition to academia, biopsychologists, clinical neuropsychologists, and cognitive neuropsychologists may pursue research careers in pharmaceutical or biotechnology companies (as well as within government settings, as described in Chapter 13). Researchers with pharmaceutical companies work to develop medications and evaluate the effectiveness of existing medicines. Researchers in biotechnology manipulate biological organisms to make products (for example, food products and medicines) to benefit the human race (Levine, 2002). Psychologists employed in biotechnology agencies or companies may evaluate the effectiveness of a product or assist in developing new products.

A research career with a pharmaceutical or biotechnology company can be very rewarding because you'll have the opportunity to develop and evaluate products, whether food or medicine, designed to benefit people. Starting salaries for researchers with established pharmaceutical companies are typically well above other entry-level positions. You may expect to begin your first job earning more than $80,000 per year, with a rise to six figures expected in a short period of time (personal communication with Lee Cohen, July 29, 2008). On the other hand, research positions with pharmaceutical and biotechnology companies can be stressful because fluctuations in the stock market and product development continually push developers and evaluators to produce new and better products. In this career your work is never done, as you will always be looking for ways to improve current products or produce new, more effective products.

PRACTICE

Of the subfields discussed in this chapter, clinical neuropsychology most lends itself to an applied career. The most common practice of clinical neuropsychologists is neuropsychological diagnostic assessment to identify the extent of brain damage or severity of impairment. They may, for example, be asked to conduct an evaluation to discriminate between neurological and psychiatric symptoms, to identify a neurological disorder or help distinguish between different neurological conditions, or to assist in the localizing of a lesion site (Lezak, 2004). Other reasons for neuropsychological assessments include patient care and planning (including cognitive capacities), rehabilitation and treatment evaluations, and research purposes (Lezak, 2004).

The goals of clinical neuropsychological assessment are different from those of the general psychological evaluation. In the neuropsychological evaluation, four primary goals exist: (1) to locate and diagnose cortical damage or dysfunction; (2) to facilitate patient treatment and rehabilitation; (3) to identify the presence of mild disturbance that is unrecognized in other examination procedures; and (4) to examine brain dysfunction in clients with a preexisting condition (Kolb & Whishaw, 2003). Aside from these goals, the neuropsychological assessment serves four primary functions in the treatment of mental health patients and includes diagnosis, treatment planning, rehabilitational evaluations, and research (Lezak, 2004).

As psychologists, clinical neuropsychologists are interested in behavior; behavior in this career refers to cognition, emotionality, and executive functioning. According to Lezak (2004), cognition includes receptive functions (meaning, the ability to "select, acquire, classify, and integrate information") and includes expressive functions (for example, speaking), memory, constructional abilities (for example, building blocks), attention and concentration, consciousness, and mentation (speed of mental activities). *Emotionality* refers to personality or emotional changes that occur following a brain injury. Finally, Lezak (2004) refers to *executive functioning* as the abilities that contribute to the expression of behavior (meaning, functions that enable a person to engage in independent, goal-directed, and self-serving behavior). Referral questions may include one or any combination of these behaviors, and the type of neuropsychological evaluation conducted is determined by the referral question.

Examination procedures may include any or all of the following: a clinical interview, detailed case history, mental status examination, standardized neuropsychological assessments (e.g., Hallstead-Reitan Battery, Luria-Nebraska Neuropsychological Battery), standardized psychological instruments such as intelligence tests (for example, Wechsler Adult Intelligence Scale III, Wechsler Intelligence Scale for Children–IV, Stanford-Binet Intelligence Scale–Fifth Edition), memory tests (Wechsler Memory Scale–III), other brief examination instruments to assess specific deficits (for example, Rey Auditory-Verbal Learning Test, Rey-Osterrieth Complex Figure Test, Finger Tapping Test), personality assessment (Minnesota Multiphasic Personality

Inventory–2), and vocational/occupational assessments. A thorough clinical neuro-psychological assessment can be completed in as little as 4 to 6 hours, but may require as much as 8 to 12 hours of testing. Thus, neuropsychologists in full-time practice may spend the majority of their time conducting and reporting the results of their assessments.

Clinical neuropsychologists may also be involved in providing treatment and rehabilitation services. Thus, they can provide therapeutic services to help patients adapt to their injuries or develop new skills to compensate for lost abilities. Although psychotherapy or counseling is occasionally implemented to assist patients and their families struggling to cope with the life-altering effects of a brain injury, therapeutic services implemented by clinical neuropsychologists are typically cognitive in nature. In other words, the behaviors previously discussed as the targets of neuropsychological evaluations are the same behaviors that will be treated following a brain injury. For example, a patient suffering from short-term memory loss due to a cardiovascular accident (such as a stroke) may by presented with memory strategies (for example, developing chunking strategies where information is remembered in chunks rather than individual units of information). In addition, the patient may be encouraged to participate in a game (for example, "concentration" or the "memory" card game) that requires remembering information during the course of play.

Interventions, particularly rehabilitation, are becoming a primary role for clinical neuropsychologists (Golden, Zillmer, & Spiers, 1992). Rehabilitation psychology is the application of psychosocial principals to people with physical, sensory, cognitive, developmental, or emotional difficulties (American Psychological Association Division 22, n.d.) with a goal of helping clients "relearn" lost functions or develop new functions, or altering the environment to maximize quality of life (Golden et al., 1992).

An applied career as a clinical neuropsychologist has many benefits. First, clinical neuropsychology is a very specialized field that typically allows for hourly billing at a rate greater than general psychological billing; thus, salaries of clinical neuropsychologists are often greater those of nonspecialized psychologists (see Chapter 3 for a review of applied psychology salaries). In addition, clinical neuropsychologists are often afforded special status in medical settings because they work in conjunction with physicians and of all psychological professionals are the most closely aligned with the medical field. They may even be required to be present during brain surgery, for example, to map cognitive function, or to locate a lesion or a particular cognitive function. Finally, clinical neuropsychology training affords a psychologist flexibility with regard to employment settings, and clinical neuropsychologists are employed in medical settings (for example, hospitals, rehabilitation centers, specialty medical clinics, medical schools), private practice, private and public agencies, and other settings typical of the counseling and clinical psychologist without clinical neuropsychological training.

A primary drawback to an applied career as a clinical neuropsychologist is the amount of time spent writing reports. For every evaluation conducted, the clinical neuropsychologist must write a report, and these reports can be quite lengthy and time-intensive. For example, you may expect to spend anywhere from 1 to 6 hours for a single report (personal communication with Dan Johnson on October 27, 2005). Another disadvantage is the stress of continued work with severely injured people, including children. Automobile accidents, violent crime, and terrorism are a few examples of the types of incidents that lead to neurological damage, and clinical neuropsychologists must deal with these issues and their effects on an ongoing basis. On a positive note, clinical neuropsychology is one of the most rapidly growing fields in professional psychology, and it will continue to be as our society continues to age. In fact, many consider clinical neuropsychology to be one of the leading careers for psychologists in the twenty-first century.

SUGGESTED READINGS

Adams, R. L., Parsons, O. A., & Culbertson, J. L. (Eds.). (1996). *Neuropsychology for clinical practice: Etiology, assessment, and treatment*. Washington DC: American Psychological Association.

Frank, R. G., & Elliott, T. R. (Eds.). (2000). *Handbook of rehabilitation psychology*. Washington, DC: American Psychological Association.

Kolb, B. & Whishaw, I. Q. (2008). *Fundamentals of human neuropsychology* (5th ed.). New York: Bedford, Freeman, & Worth Publishers.

Lezak (2004). *Neuropsychological assessment* (4th ed.). New York: Oxford University Press.

Myers, D. G. (2004). *Psychology* (6th ed). New York: Worth.

Snyder, P. J. (2008). An interesting career in psychology: A neuropsychologist prospers in the pharmaceutical industry. Retrieved on July 29, 2008 from http://www.apa.org/science/ic-snyder.html.

Snyder, P. J., & Nassbaum, P. D. (Eds.). (2005). *Clinical neuropsychology: A pocket handbook for assessment*. Washington, DC: American Psychological Association.

WEB RESOURCES

Biopsychology.org
http://www.biopsychology.org/

American Board of Clinical Neuropsychology
http://www.theabcn.org/

American Academy of Clinical Neuropsychology
http://www.theaacn.org/

American Board of Professional Neuropsychology
http://abpn.net/

International Neuropsychological Society
http://www.the-ins.org/

National Academy of Neuropsychology
http://nanonline.org/

Behavioral Neuroscience and Comparative Psychology
http://www.apa.org/divisions/div6/

Rehabilitation Psychology
http://www.div22.org/

Clinical Neuropsychology
http://www.div40.org/

Neuropsychology Central
http://www.neuropsychologycentral.com/

Neuropsychology Homepage
http://www.tbidoc.com/

CHECKLIST: IS BIOPSYCHOLOGY, CLINICAL NEUROPSYCHOLOGY, OR COGNITIVE NEUROPSYCHOLOGY FOR YOU?

Do you:

☐ Enjoy biology classes?
☐ Remember dissecting frogs in biology class as a pleasant or non-aversive experience?
☐ Enjoy reading about the functions of the human brain?
☐ Get excited about human anatomy and biological functioning?
☐ Think you would enjoy conducting research aimed at identifying specific brain functioning?
☐ Want to work in a medical setting with brain-injured patients?
☐ Enjoy solving complex puzzles?
☐ Want to work in a hospital?
☐ Have an interest in technology?
☐ Believe that much of human behavior has a biological cause or component?
☐ Want to conduct neurological assessments?
☐ Want to help people overcome brain injuries and neurological problems?
☐ Like science?
☐ Want to go to graduate school?
☐ Do you want to conduct research (for example, psychosurgery) with animals?

Scoring: The more boxes you checked, the more likely it is that a career in biopsychology, neuropsychology, or cognitive neuropsychology is for you.

CAREERS FOR STUDENTS WITH INTERESTS IN INDUSTRIAL, ORGANIZATIONAL, AND HUMAN FACTORS PSYCHOLOGY

CHAPTER 9

CHAPTER GUIDE

Industrial Psychology

Selection and Placement of Employees

Training and Development of Employees

Performance Evaluation of Employees

Participation in Applying and Adhering to Laws and Litigation

Organizational Psychology

Improve Job Satisfaction and Quality of Work Life

Improve Leadership

Promote Organizational Development

Human Factors

Opportunities with a Bachelor's Degree

Human Resources Jobs

Commercial or Industrial Design Assistant

Administrative Assistant and Office Manager

Opportunities with a Graduate Degree

Human Resources

Consultant

Usability Specialist

Environmental Designer

Suggested Readings

Web Resources

Checklist: Is Work Psychology for You?

As you likely are aware by now, psychology—the study of human behavior—can inform all fields. Psychology offers important applications to business settings. Several subdisciplines of psychology address the needs of business and industry: industrial psychology, organizational psychology, and human factors psychology. Collectively, these areas are referred to as "work psychology" (Patterson, 2001). Degree holders in psychology work with owners, managers, and employees of business and industry to select, train, and manage employees, design and market products, and organize work environments. Those with interests in industrial and organizational psychology apply psychological principles to the workplace, and those with interests in human factors psychology apply psychological principles in the design of equipment, work spaces, and computer software. In this chapter, you'll learn about each of these areas of psychology and explore careers that combine psychology with business and industry.

INDUSTRIAL PSYCHOLOGY

Industrial psychology, sometimes called *personnel psychology*, is the study of individual behavior in work settings. A career as an industrial psychologist entails one or more of the following activities. Note that many of these activities may be conducted by persons with various levels of training, from a bachelor's degree with considerable work experience to a doctoral-trained industrial psychologist; however, the most advanced positions tend to be held by doctoral-level industrial psychologists.

Selection and Placement of Employees

Careful selection and appropriate placement of employees promotes their job satisfaction and productivity. An industrial psychologist employs a scientific approach toward selecting and placing employees. Degree holders with interest and experience in industrial psychology conduct job analyses to determine the specific tasks a job entails and the individual abilities and characteristics needed to be successful. With advanced training in industrial psychology, professionals create, validate, and choose tests and interviews that are administered to job applicants to determine whether they should be hired and where they should be placed (Kasserman, 2005; Kuther, 2005). Placing employees entails identifying what jobs are most compatible with an employee's skills and interests, as assessed through questionnaires and interviews (Muchinsky, 2006). After placing employees into jobs, the emphasis shifts to following up with employees to determine how well the assessment tests predict later job performance.

TRAINING AND DEVELOPMENT OF EMPLOYEES

Industrial psychology is applied in training and development of employees, specifically, in conducting needs analyses to determine the skills and technical needs of employees and developing training programs to impart those skills. Professionals with training in industrial psychology create assessment centers, collections of questionnaires, vignettes to assess problem-solving skills, and simulated work situations to determine an employee's skills and abilities (Aamodt, 2007; Tenopyr, 1997). Training needs may include assisting new employees during their transition to the workplace, updating current employees' technical skills, preparing employees for new responsibilities, and providing diversity training to retrain employees' attitudes, prejudices, and stereotypes (Muchinsky, 2006; Kasserman, 2005; Scrader, 2002). Training in industrial psychology also aids professionals in devising methods for evaluating the effectiveness of training programs.

PERFORMANCE EVALUATION OF EMPLOYEES

The first step in performance evaluation entails determining the criteria or standards by which employees will be evaluated. What defines employee success? Training in industrial psychology helps professionals choose, create, and validate methods for measuring the criteria that underlie employee success. They assess employees' abilities and performance, providing feedback and documentation about the quality and quantity of an employee's work to support pay increases and promotions (Aamodt, 2007; Muchinsky, 2006). Specialists in performance evaluation also train supervisors to evaluate employee performance and to communicate the results to employees.

PARTICIPATION IN APPLYING AND ADHERING TO LAWS AND LITIGATION

Industrial psychology examines how legal issues relate to the workplace (for example, selecting, hiring, and promoting employees). Professionals with training in industrial psychology create policies and conduct regular training workshops to promote a positive work environment and to prevent harassment and other issues that contribute to a hostile work environment. When companies are faced with layoffs they often seek advice from professionals with training in industrial psychology regarding how to act with fairness and sensitivity in order to avoid litigation from disgruntled former employees (Murray, 2002).

When devising employee selection, placement, and training procedures, industrial psychology professionals must learn a great deal about civil rights laws and build compliance with the laws into their efforts (Aamodt, 2007; Tenopyr, 1997). They must understand the legal context for personnel decisions and assist their employers in making personnel decisions that are legal. Individuals with training in industrial psychology may advise the company's attorneys and explain the science behind a company's hiring and promotion policies (meaning, the validity of the assessment tests and interviews). They often assist company attorneys in preparing for litigation in response to complaints from employees and former employees under the various federal, state, and local civil rights acts (Tenopyr, 1997). As expert court witnesses, professionals with advanced training and experience in industrial psychology persuade judges and juries that work was done correctly. Some might work as expert witnesses on employment-related cases, such as those concerning discrimination. In those cases the psychologist analyzes the information to determine whether discrimination has taken place and testifies concerning the results of the analysis (Weiner, 2001).

ORGANIZATIONAL PSYCHOLOGY

The distinction between industrial and organizational psychology is fuzzy because practicing industrial and organizational psychologists often share job descriptions and duties (and many graduate programs are labeled as Industrial-Organization Psychology); therefore, the two areas are often referred to as industrial/organizational psychology. As we've discussed, industrial psychologists traditionally focus on the individual worker: selection, placement, training, and evaluation. The organizational psychologist works at the organizational level to understand how workers function in the organization and how the organization functions as a whole. The following sections discuss activities typically ascribed to organizational psychologists. As with our discussion of industrial psychology, many of these activities may be conducted by persons with various levels of training, from a bachelor's degree with considerable work experience to a doctoral-trained organizational psychologist; however, the most advanced positions tend to be held by doctoral-level organizational psychologists.

IMPROVE JOB SATISFACTION AND QUALITY OF WORK LIFE

Professionals with interests in organizational psychology determine what factors contribute to a healthy and productive work force. They examine job satisfaction and study factors associated with it, such as employee turnover, absenteeism, age, pay, motivation, and attitudes toward the organization. They develop and evaluate systems to promote job satisfaction by rewarding good performance and redesigning jobs to make them more challenging, meaningful, and satisfying to employees (Muchinsky, 2006). Promoting job satisfaction entails understanding workers' needs and creating incentives that build job commitment and loyalty. For example, professionals with training in organizational psychology might attempt to understand how Generation Y workers are different from the generations that came before them and how companies can tailor employee incentives to maximize their satisfaction (Cohen, 2002). They also study how employee services (for example, office-based childcare, gym facilities) influence morale, job satisfaction, and productivity.

IMPROVE LEADERSHIP

Organizational psychologists study leadership: What makes a good leader? They identify characteristics of effective leaders and determine the types of leaders who are most effective in particular positions. People with training in organizational psychology create individual and group training programs to improve the leadership and communication skills of supervisors and managers (Williams, 2005). With advanced training in organizational psychology, some professionals act as executive coaches, working one-on-one with individuals to help them become better leaders and business people (Kilburg, 1996; Witherspoon & White, 1996).

PROMOTE ORGANIZATIONAL DEVELOPMENT

Professionals with training in organizational psychology help companies analyze the organization's functioning and determine when changes are needed. They help organizations make changes, transition to new ways of managing things, and accept change. Organizations grow and change over time. Organizational development entails studying growth, directing it, and facilitating it (Muchinsky, 2006).

Professionals in organizational psychology act as change agents who identify problems, study potential solutions, and make recommendations (Aamodt, 2004; Kasserman, 2005; Tenopyr, 1997). They might examine and refine business procedures, such as developing a paperwork processing plan that is concise, consistent, and without unnecessary steps. Professionals with training in organizational psychology help organizations manage and resolve interpersonal problems (Williams, 2005), such as using conflict-resolution skills to work out a solution for feuding departments or team members. Another task might entail examining the lines of authority or communication and redesigning them when necessary. Industrial and organizational psychology is applicable to all work settings—business, consulting firms, government, the military, and university.

HUMAN FACTORS

Human factors psychology, sometimes called engineering psychology, is concerned with the interaction between humans and their environments, and especially humans and machines. Human factors professionals design work environments to optimize productivity, employee satisfaction, and safety, and limit stress, fatigue, and error. Some specialize in human and computer interaction, or study how people interact with computers in order to improve computer applications and hardware designs (Chapman, 2005; Day, 1996). A human factors professional might study how to make Web sites more user-friendly (Clay, 2000), or engage in device testing, new product design, and developing warnings and labeling for products (Callan, 2004). Others may conduct research and develop programs in military command, aircraft and ship control systems, or Internet systems (Callan, 2004).

People with interests in human factors often study error prevention and management (the study of human error) in order to predict and prevent errors through excellent design. An understanding of how people use products and the common mistakes that people are likely to make aids in designing products that prevent error and misuse. For example, a professional might work to reduce human error in medicine by improving the accessibility of software for recording patient information, streamlining reporting procedures, or adding cross-checks before surgeries or other medical procedures are conducted (Kao & Thomas, 2008; Woods, 2002). Another area of work is in managing traffic, looking for ways to reduce accidents and injury, death, and property losses on highways. Human factors is also important in promoting aviation safety and preventing pilot error (Landwehr, 2001; Lauber, 1997; Tyler, 2000). Human factors professionals can play a role in improving national security by deterring future terrorist threats directed towards air travel because they analyze and have tools to evaluate proposed changes in equipment, procedures, and regulations, and study how they impact efficiency of people operating them and the system as a whole (Callan, 2004; Hart, 2002).

Ergonomics, the study of work environments and how to modify them to enhance productivity, is an important subarea of human factors. Ergonomic professionals adapt work environments, including computer interfaces and other equipment, to compensate for the limitations and qualities of people, increasing safety and reducing accidents. They study the effects of environmental factors such as light, noise, temperature, and work schedules (for example, night shifts or compressed work weeks) on worker safety, productivity, and satisfaction (Muchinsky, 2006). Others work to improve the safety and comfort of spaces. For example, investigating the capacity and comfort of aircraft seating and studying the user interface of anything with which an airline customer will interact (Landwehr, 2001).

OPPORTUNITIES WITH A BACHELOR'S DEGREE

A bachelor's degree prepares graduates for a variety of entry-level positions within business and industry. Because of the solid liberal arts background, psychology majors with interests in business are excellent matches for positions in human resource departments and can serve as assistants in other fields, as described in the following sections.

HUMAN RESOURCES JOBS

Human resources departments, also known as personnel departments, are responsible for managing an organization's employees: recruitment, placement, administering salaries and benefits, training, and conducting research on employee needs and satisfaction. Human resources personnel work to attract the most qualified employees, match them to the jobs for which they are best suited, help them to succeed in their jobs, and ensure that the organization complies with labor laws. Depending on your interests and experience, there are a variety of positions at all levels of education within human resource departments located in businesses, government, and private and nonprofit agencies. Recognize that the level of opportunities, responsibilities, and autonomy varies with expertise, experience, and education. Entry-level employees likely will not serve all functions described, but they will have the opportunity to learn and the potential to grow into positions with more responsibility.

HUMAN RESOURCE GENERALIST.   Human resource generalists engage in all aspects of managing personnel, including recruitment, placement, training, and development.

Often they also administer salary and benefits, and develop personnel policies that conform to labor laws. Entry-level generalist positions typically fall under the following titles: *human resource assistant, human resource specialist, personnel assistant, personnel specialist*, or *employee relations specialist*. They are more likely to be found in small businesses and organizations with few employees.

EMPLOYMENT, RECRUITMENT, AND PLACEMENT SPECIALIST. The job description of an employment, recruitment, and placement specialist includes recruiting personnel, collecting applications and résumés for jobs, assembling applicant files, performing background checks, interviewing applicants, administering pre-employment assessments and tests, and placing employees. In short, they are involved in hiring employees. They also orient new employees, educate employees about salary and benefits, and assess departmental needs for staffing. Entry-level positions for recent graduates will likely entail more paper-based activities such as filing, organizing applicant files, and so on. More advanced activities and responsibilities, such as interviewing, come with experience. Common titles for entry-level positions include *interviewer, recruiter, employment representative*, or *EEO (equal employment and opportunity) specialist*.

TRAINING AND DEVELOPMENT SPECIALIST. Training and development specialists conduct training sessions, provide on-the-job training, and maintain records of employee participation in training and development programs. They help employees improve their knowledge and skills (such as sales techniques, safety guidelines, and productivity), and assist supervisors and managers to improve their interpersonal skills in dealing with employees. More advanced training and development positions involve human resource planning and organizational development. For example, a training specialist might create a leadership development program to develop employees' leadership potential and prepare them for promotion and advancement. Entry-level positions in this area include *training specialist* and *orientation specialist*. Some might include the title of *assistant*.

COMPENSATION AND BENEFITS SPECIALIST. Compensation and benefits specialists engage in job analysis, write job descriptions, collect and organize information about an organization's benefits programs, administer benefits plans, and monitor costs. Typical titles include *benefits analyst, compensation specialist*, and *salary administrator*. Entry-level positions often include the title of *assistant* and generally include fewer responsibilities and entail providing support to supervisors.

EVALUATING CAREERS IN HUMAN RESOURCES. A career in human resources offers many advantages, including an office environment, a 40-hour work week, and opportunities for advancement with a bachelor's degree and job experience. As a human resources employee, you'll have the opportunity to directly help people, solve practical problems, and use your knowledge of psychology. You will interact with a wide range of people, which will require flexibility, patience, and excellent communication skills. Sometimes the "people" part of the job can be stressful and challenging. For example, you may deal with employees who are angry over changes in work conditions or who have been laid off. Human resources positions also entail

TABLE 9.1	SAMPLE HUMAN RESOURCE POSITIONS AND SALARIES (ADAPTED FROM SALARY.COM, 2008)

Title	Median 2008 Salary
Benefits Analyst	$45,946
Employee Relations Specialist	$45,750
Human Resources Assistant	$38,537
Human Resources Generalist	$46,590
Recruiter	$41,015
Training Specialist	$43,302

administrative work that requires attention to detail and can sometimes be tedious. Although entry-level positions in human resources are highly competitive, the field is expected to grow more rapidly than the average (16 percent) for all occupations through 2016 (Bureau of Labor Statistics, 2008) and human resources positions offer comfortable salaries, as shown in Table 9.1.

If you are interested in pursuing a career in human resources, psychology offers a solid background in communication skills, statistics, research methods, presentation skills, and human behavior. Additional courses in communication, writing, business administration, labor law, and accounting will enhance your employability. Seek an internship to obtain experience and make contacts that can help you find a human resources position after graduation.

COMMERCIAL OR INDUSTRIAL DESIGN ASSISTANT

An assistant to a commercial or industrial designer helps in designing products and equipment, such as airplanes, cars, children's toys, computer equipment, furniture, home appliances, and medical, office, and recreational equipment. A designer combines artistic talent with research on customer needs, ways products are used, the consumer market, and production materials and methods to create a design that is functional, appealing, and competitive with others in the marketplace. An assistant to a designer conducts research and engages in support functions related to the designer's needs. Depending on the particular field or industry, design assistants may help designers in planning packaging and containers for products such as foods, beverages, toiletries, or medicine, or might assist in creating and designing packaging, illustrations, or advertising for manufactured materials. Design assistants help the designer to coordinate design concepts among engineering, marketing, production, and sales departments in order to produce a product that is safe, well-designed, and marketable.

Designers and design assistants are employed by manufacturers, corporations, and design firms. They tend to work regular 40-hour weeks in an office setting. At the entry level, design assistants often provide administrative support including clerical tasks; as they demonstrate competence, assistants will take on more design-related tasks.

The market for design assistants is expected to grow as rapidly as the average through the year 2016; however, competition is keen (Bureau of Labor Statistics,

2008). In 2008, the median entry-level salary in design was $35,000 (American Institute of Graphic Arts, 2003). If you're interested in becoming a design assistant, creativity is essential and sketching ability will help you to advance to design positions. Psychology's emphasis on research methods and problem solving will suit you well in this field. In addition, take courses in merchandising, business administration, and marketing, and seek training in art—especially a course in computer-aided design (CAD).

ADMINISTRATIVE ASSISTANT AND OFFICE MANAGER

Traditionally the administrative assistant was a secretary who spent her (as the majority were women) days typing memos on an old-fashioned typewriter (the machine in which you roll the paper in and each letter is stamped onto the page as you press the keys). Today's administrative assistants (also known as *executive assistants* or *executive secretaries*) tend to engage in office management functions and support executive staff. Increasingly, office automatization and executives' use of word processing software has relieved administrative assistants from typing. In addition to coordinating administrative and information management activities within an office, many administrative assistants train and orient new staff, and conduct research on the Internet. Administrative assistants schedule meetings and appointments, maintain files, conduct research, manage databases, create reports, and manage projects.

Office managers, sometimes titled *administrative services managers*, oversee various components of an office, varying from administrative assistance and reception services to data processing, conference planning, payroll, and other office functions. The responsibilities will vary with the position and organization, but the role is to oversee office functions.

Employment of administrative assistants and administrative services managers is expected to grow about as rapidly as the average for all occupations through 2016 (Bureau of Labor Statistics, 2008). An administrative assistant position offers several advantages, including an office environment, a 40-hour work week, and the opportunity to help others solve practical problems. Administrative services manager positions have similar advantages as well as the opportunity to lead others, have relative autonomy, and the ability to show creativity in solving office problems. Salaries for administrative assistants and administrative services managers are competitive. In 2008, the median salary for administrative assistants was $39,568; half of administrative assistants earn between $34,985 and $44,152 (Salary.com, 2008). In 2008, the median salary for all administrative services managers, regardless of education or experience, was $71,922; half earn between $60,965 and $82,880 (Salary.com, 2008). Salaries rise with experience. Administrative positions can entail stress, especially when the office is trying to meet a deadline or if a boss expects the assistant to run personal errands. Managing administrative staff can be particularly stressful because it entails coordinating the activities of several employees in order to achieve goals, and requires excellent interpersonal and planning skills. Skills in organization, communication, research, and stress management, as well as understanding of human behavior, leadership, and groups, make the psychology major competitive for administrative assistant and manager positions.

TABLE 9.2	PREPARATION FOR BA–LEVEL CAREERS RELATED TO INDUSTRIAL, ORGANIZATIONAL, AND HUMAN FACTORS PSYCHOLOGY

Coursework

Human Resources Positions
    Accounting
    Business Administration
    Communication
    Economics
    Human Resources Management
    Labor Economics
    Labor Law
    Management Information Systems or Database Applications in Business
    Organizational Behavior
    Writing

Commercial or Industrial Design Assistant Positions
    Advertising
    Architecture
    Art: Sketching, Design, and Computer-Aided Design (CAD)
    Business Administration
    Engineering
    Industrial Design
    Marketing
    Mathematics
    Product/Brand Management
    Certification in art and design from the National Association of Schools of Art and Design is available at some institutions (about 250 in the U.S.)

Administrative Assistant and Office Manager Positions
    Accounting
    Business Administration
    Business Law
    Communication
    Finance
    Human Resources Management
    Management Information Systems or Database Applications in Business
    Purchasing and Sales
    Writing

Applied Experiences: Volunteer, intern, or paid part-time positions in any of the following settings
    Advertising Department
    Any Office Setting
    Architect
    Human Resources Department
    Leadership programs
    Product design firm
    Engineering firm

Research Experiences: Experiences studying and participating in research in any of the following areas*
    Human factors
    Industrial psychology
    Management and leadership
    Organizational behavior
    Social psychology

*Note that the content area of the research is less important than the experience itself, which enhances reasoning, quantitative, writing, and organizational skills.

OPPORTUNITIES WITH A GRADUATE DEGREE

Although a bachelor's degree in psychology prepares graduates for entry-level jobs, graduate degree holders have more opportunities for advancement. A masters degree can serve as the basis for supervisory and advanced opportunities in human resources, usability, and market research fields. Doctoral degrees offer additional opportunities, especially in upper management, consulting, and product design and development careers. Masters degree holders who have extensive experience often obtain positions comparable to those of doctoral degree holders.

HUMAN RESOURCES

Graduate degree holders may work in any of the human resources career tracks that we have discussed, with additional responsibilities and compensation. A graduate degree enables the employee to engage in management and executive functions within human resources departments.

Human resource generalists with graduate degrees are involved with all human resource activities, including designing and administering human resources policies, collecting and analyzing data, making recommendations to management, and taking leadership roles on projects. Similarly, graduates who specialize in *employment, recruitment, and placement* design assessment techniques to select and place employees, collect data on the effectiveness of the assessments, and supervise other workers. Graduate degree holders specialized in *training and development* create training programs, conduct research on the effectiveness of those programs, and supervise other workers. Other human resources professionals specialize in the training and development needs of the organization as a whole; these professionals often are called *organizational development specialists*. With additional experience, graduate degree holders move on to managerial positions, as well as more advanced positions that entail overseeing all human resources functions within an organization, such as human resources manager or human resources director. Salaries for human resources positions for graduate degree holders are shown in Table 9.3.

CONSULTANT

Consultant is an umbrella term for a variety of individuals who engage in problem solving within organizations. Consultants specialize in a variety of areas, including management of employees or an organization's resources, strategy development and long range planning, training, organizational development, and recruitment. Consultants in each of these areas engage in the same basic task: they advise organizations on how to solve problems, such as researching a new market, reorganizing a company's structure, hiring top executives, or improving productivity. Consultants offer their clients perspective and insight (an understanding of the big picture and the problem at hand), analysis (an examination of potential solutions), and recommendations (a strategic plan to address the problem) (Boulakia, 1998; Kasserman, 2005). In other words, consultants solve business problems by applying a scientific approach through testing hypotheses and analyzing data (McCracken, 1998).

TABLE 9.3 | SAMPLE HUMAN RESOURCE POSITIONS AND SALARIES FOR
GRADUATE DEGREE HOLDERS (ADAPTED FROM SALARY.COM, 2008)

Title	Median 2008 Salary
Advanced Human Resources Positions	
Employee Relations Specialist	$71,188
Human Resources Generalist	$68,848
Organizational Development Specialist	$76,263
Executive Recruiter	$75,124
Training Specialist	$64,575
Managerial Positions	
Employee Relations Manager	$82,768
Human Resources Manager	$81,100
Organizational Development Manager	$97,627
Recruiting Manager	$83,650
Training Manager	$78,712

There are many different types of consultants. *Management consultants* analyze ways to make an organization more competitive and efficient (Bureau of Labor Statistics, 2008). *Search consultants* are high-level recruiters, often called "head hunters," who use their knowledge of industrial psychology to recruit, assess, and place employees in top positions. *Organizational development consultants* help companies with team building, training, dealing with change, and professional development. Marketing consultants help companies advertise and market products and services. *Mediation consultants* help organizations to solve interpersonal conflicts in the workplace (meaning, conflicts among individuals, and within and between departments and teams) and teach communication and conflict management skills. Some consultants emphasize developing leadership skills in executives; recently, these consultants have been referred to as *executive coaches* (Kilburg, 1996). An executive coach helps an executive identify personal strengths and weaknesses, and works to enhance an executive's skills and promote growth (Witherspoon & White, 1996).

Advanced analytical skills developed in graduate school make graduate degree holders well suited to careers in consulting. They understand how to analyze data, manage databases, and present data simply and elegantly through the use of tables and graphs. Their knowledge of computer software and statistics is an asset to any organization, and their communication skills, honed through writing papers, theses, and dissertations, as well as making conference presentations, are valuable in the office setting (Sebestyen, 2000).

There are many advantages to a career in consulting. It is a great way to learn about business because most firms offer plenty of opportunities for professional development through training workshops, seminars, and mentoring programs. (McCracken, 1998; Montell, 1999). As a consultant you'll collaborate with talented colleagues from a variety of educational and experiential backgrounds. You'll be challenged to devise and implement useful solutions to real problems (Smith, 1997). As a recent graduate, you likely will find that your lack of experience is an important challenge to doing your job, so you will find yourself working hard to catch up (Hedge & Borman, 2008). The pace is quick and the problems constantly change: One day you might analyze the potential market for a new product and the next day consider reorganizing the management structure of an organization. The main disadvantage of a career in consulting is that it often requires long hours and travel; however, the salary makes up for the long hours. In 2008, the median annual salary for consultants to businesses and organizations, across all education levels, was $82,658, with 25 percent earning less than $71,068 and 75 percent earning more than $94,249 (Salary.com, 2008).

Among doctoral-level industrial/organizational psychologists sampled who work at consulting firms, the median salary for consultants with 5 to 9 years of experience in 2007 was $110,000, with 50 percent earning between $96,500 and $148,500 (American Psychological Association, 2008). The median starting salary for psychologists from other subfields who work at consulting firms was $85,000 for those with 2 to 4 years of experience and $120,000 for those with 5 to 10 years of experience, with 50 percent earning between $75,000 and $125,000 and $100,000 and $130,000, respectively (American Psychological Association 2008). Finally, consulting careers are expected to grow much more rapidly than the average for all occupations through 2016 (Bureau of Labor Statistics, 2008); the field is expected to grow by 78 percent, making consulting the most rapidly growing industry.

Usability Specialist

Many professionals with graduate degrees in industrial/organizational or human factors psychology obtain positions in product design and development, often specializing in promoting product usability, or ease and pleasure of use. Usable, or user-friendly, products are easy for users to learn how to use, are efficient and memorable, minimize errors, and are pleasing or satisfying to use (Aamodt, 2004). Usability specialists ensure that product designs fit users. They work with all kinds of products: toys, computer hardware and software, electronic equipment, cars, and more.

The understanding of human capacities and limitations that comes with a graduate degree in psychology is excellent preparation for a career in usability applied to product design and production (Day, 1996). Usability specialists serve as user advocates in that their goal is to create products that meet the needs of the user. They research a product, create product prototypes, and test and modify them based on input from potential users. For example, in designing the interior of an automobile, they might create a life-size prototype in which all of the instruments and controls can be moved (for example, by attaching them with Velcro). Potential users then provide feedback on the best location for each of the instruments and controls, moving them as necessary. Other usability specialists conduct usability studies to create aircraft that meet pilots' needs and thereby reduce pilot error (Lauber, 1997; Tyler, 2000). Psychologists are also employed by NASA and contribute to the operation of the space shuttle by applying information about how people think and perceive sensory stimuli into the design of equipment and controls used to pilot space craft (McCann, 2001).

Usability research also takes place in the computer software industry. Knowledge of cognitive psychology can be applied to explain why a particular software interface design is confusing for users (Chapman, 2005; Diddams, 1998). Psychologists record and analyze users' behaviors when they try to accomplish a task using a computer software product, such as a spreadsheet program or computer game. For example, how easily can consumers navigate software programs designed to manage pictures? How do they manage their digital photos, and is there a way to improve the ease and speed with which the user can access photographs (Czerwinski, 2002)? Psychologists interview users about their experience with the product: Was it easy to use? What confused them about the interface? The resulting knowledge is used to improve the software design. This problem-solving technique is applied in many contexts. For example, human factors psychologists might assess the credibility of a computer program that simulates medical surgeries, permitting medical students and doctors to practice surgical techniques (Haluck, 2005).

Psychologists who choose careers in product design and development have the opportunity to engage in research that improves people's experiences with products. Their research has practical implications and they get to see the results of their work. A regular 40-hour work week, excellent opportunities for masters-level psychologists, and high rates of compensation are other advantages. The design and development industry is expected to grow as rapidly as the average through 2016 (Bureau of Labor Statistics, 2008). In 2008, the average entry salary for usability practitioners was about $60,000; the average for those with 5 years of experience was about $90,000 (Nielson, 2008).

ENVIRONMENTAL DESIGNER

Professionals trained in industrial/organizational psychology or human factors often work in environmental design. They study the interactive relationship between environments and human behavior and seek to understand why people find some spaces comfortable and others threatening, as well as why some spaces are easier to navigate than others. They then apply this information to design and enhance environments, such as the layout of offices, the design of office buildings and shopping malls, and even the design of neighborhoods and communities, to reduce stress, create more efficiency, and minimize accidents (Winerman, 2004).

Environmental design professionals work for corporations, local and federal governments, and consulting firms. Some participate in city and community planning, designing buildings, and enhancing the interior layout of existing structures. A career in environmental design requires good communication skills and the ability to work as part of a team. Environmental designers who are assigned to large projects will work closely with professionals from many fields, including politicians, architects, urban planners, economists, and engineers, to complete projects. Working with many disciplines can be interesting, but challenging. Good listening and research skills are essential to success in this field, because environmental designers spend lots of time interacting with people—consumers, community members, and other professionals. For example, when a city plans to rebuild a run-down neighborhood, an environmental design professional may interview people who live in the neighborhood to obtain their ideas and perspectives about how to improve the area.

An important advantage of a career in environmental design is the opportunity to be part of a large project and to make a difference. An environmental designer who participates in designing a new community housing project, for example, will find that the work influences residents' day-to-day lives. The teamwork needed to complete large-scale projects can sometimes lead to frustration, because when many people are involved, decisions can take a long time. Also, projects generally take a long time to implement, which can be challenging for someone who is looking for more immediate results from their work. Environmental designers who can take criticism well and deal with pressure without becoming burned out are at a distinct advantage in this stressful field.

Careers in environmental design are expected to increase about as rapidly as average through the year 2016 (Bureau of Labor Statistics, 2008), and salaries are competitive. In 1999, the average salary for a doctoral-level psychologist in environmental design was over $65,000 ($83,506 adjusted for 2008; Conaway, 2000). If you're interested in a career in environmental design, seek additional training in communications, research design and statistics, and related fields such as economics, urban planning, and architecture. Also, seek an internship with an environmental design firm, city planning office, or related placement to obtain hands-on experience in this exciting field.

As we've seen, there are many career opportunities for psychology students with business interests. Many entry-level positions are open to bachelor's degree holders in psychology who have taken coursework and obtained experience in relevant areas. Opportunities expand for graduate degree holders. Remember that these are just a sampling of possible careers; more await your exploration. Finally, note that many other careers described in this book are pertinent to students with interests in industrial, organizational, and human factors psychology. See Chapter 13 to learn about careers in research, publishing, and academia, as well as Chapter 10 for other career options for graduates with quantitative skills.

SUGGESTED READINGS

Aamodt, M. G. (2007). *Applied industrial/organizational psychology*. Pacific Grove, CA: Wadsworth.

Chapman, C. N. (2005). Software user research: Psychologist in the software industry. In R. D. Morgan, T. L. Kuther, & C. J. Habben (Eds.), *Life after graduate school in psychology: Insider's advice from new psychologists* (pp. 211–224). New York: Psychology Press.

Kasserman, J. (2005). Management consultation: Improving organizations. In R. D. Morgan, T. L. Kuther, & C. J. Habben (Eds.), *Life after graduate school in psychology: Insider's advice from new psychologists* (pp. 183–196). New York: Psychology Press.

Kuther, T. L. (2005). *Your career in psychology: Industrial/organizational psychology*. Belmont: Wadsworth.

McKenzie, J. S., Drinan, H. G., & Traynow, W. J. (2001). *Opportunities in human resource management careers*. New York: McGraw-Hill.

Muchinsky, P. M. (2006). *Psychology applied to work.* Pacific Grove, CA: Wadsworth.

Pass, J. (2006). Industrial/Organizational (I/O) psychology as a career: Improving workforce performance and retention. In Sternberg, R. J. *Career paths in psychology: Where your degree can take you*, 2nd ed. Washington, DC: APA.

Pond, S. B. (1999). Industrial-organizational psychology: The psychology of people working together. *Eye on Psi Chi, 3*(3), 34–37.

Salvendy, G. (2006). *Handbook of human factors and ergonomics.* Hoboken, NJ: Wiley.

Tenopyr, M. L. (1997). Improving the workplace: Industrial/organizational psychology as a career. In R. Sternberg (Ed.), *Career paths in psychology: Where your degree can take you* (pp. 185–196). Washington, DC: American Psychological Association.

Wetfeet (2008). *Careers in management consulting.* New York: Wetfeet.com

Williams, S. (2005). Executive management: Helping executives manage their organizations through organizational and market research. In R. D. Morgan, T. L. Kuther, & C. J. Habben (Eds.), *Life after graduate school in psychology: Insider's advice from new psychologists* (pp. 225–238). New York: Psychology Press.

Wolgalter, M. S., & Rogers, W. A. (1998). Human factors/ergonomics: Using psychology to make a better and world. *Eye on Psi Chi, 3*(1), 23–26.

WEB RESOURCES

An Interesting Career in Psychology: Collection of Career Articles
http://www.apa.org/science/nonacad_careers.html

Society for Industrial and Organizational Psychology
http://siop.org/

Professional Industrial Organizational Psychologist Network
http://www.piop.net

Academy of Management
http://www.aomonline.org/

Society for Human Resource Management
http://www.shrm.org/

Human Factors and Ergonomics Society
http://hfes.org/

Getting an Industrial Design Job
http://new.idsa.org/webmodules/articles/articlefiles/GETIDJOB.pdf

Current Trends in Environmental Psychology
http://www.ucm.es/info/Psyap/iaap/evans.htm

Careers in Industrial/Organizational Psychology
http://www.wcupa.edu/_ACADEMICS/sch_cas.psy/Career_Paths/Industrial/Career06.htm

Careers in Consulting
http://jobsearch.about.com/cs/businessjobs/a/consulting.htm

Consulting Career, Job, and Training Information
http://www.careeroverview.com/consulting-careers.html

CHECKLIST: IS WORK PSYCHOLOGY FOR YOU?

Do you:

☐ Have an interest in business?
☐ Want to understand how psychological methods can improve employee selection and placement?
☐ Want to help others gain skills?
☐ Want to devise methods to evaluate employees?
☐ Want to advise businesses and corporations on personnel policies?
☐ Want to promote teamwork in an office environment?
☐ Want to study leadership, understand the qualities of an effective leader, and help supervisors and managers to improve their leadership skills?
☐ Have an interest in helping organizations make transitions and changes?
☐ Have an interest in the way the environment shapes our behavior?
☐ Want to design and organize work environments to maximize efficiency?
☐ Have good communication skills?
☐ Feel comfortable working in groups?
☐ Enjoy conducting research?
☐ Have the ability to be flexible and deal with ambiguity?

Scoring: The more boxes you checked, the more likely it is that you're a good match for a career in work psychology.

CHAPTER **10** | EXPERIMENTAL, COGNITIVE, AND QUANTITATIVE PSYCHOLOGY AND PSYCHOMETRICS

CHAPTER GUIDE

118

Suggested Readings

Web Resources

Checklist: Are Experimental, Cognitive or Quantitative Areas of Psychology for You?

Number crunching, pocket protectors, lab rats, and IQ tests are just some of the things that come to mind when most psychology students think of experimental, cognitive, and quantitative psychology, and psychometrics. Expertise in statistics and research methodology is valuable, offering graduates some of the most flexible career paths in psychology.

EXPERIMENTAL PSYCHOLOGY

All psychologists learn how to conduct and interpret research, but experimental psychologists specialize in conducting research. Experimental psychologists tend to study research methodology in greater detail than do other psychologists and they apply these methods to study a variety of topics including learning, sensation, perception, human performance, motivation, memory, language, thinking, and communication. Some experimental psychologists study animals to apply what they learn to humans, or simply because animal behavior is interesting.

We usually identify experimental psychologists by the area in which they conduct research (such as perception psychologist or learning psychologist). For example, a sensation and perception psychologist studies the way we use our senses to become aware of the world around us; he or she might study vision, hearing, taste, smell, touch, or all of the senses. A learning psychologist studies processes of learning, such as classical and operant conditioning. There are a wide variety of experimental psychologists, because there are many areas in which to conduct research.

COGNITIVE PSYCHOLOGY

Cognitive psychologists study human cognition: how we take in, store, retrieve, and apply knowledge. They attempt to understand the nature of human thought. How do we attend to the world around us? How do we take in, learn, understand, remember, and use information to make decisions? Cognitive psychologists are interested in topics like attention, visual and auditory perception, memory, reasoning, retrieval and forgetting, and problem solving. They conduct research to extend our knowledge about the mind and to construct theories that explain why our minds work the way they do. Some cognitive psychologists conduct applied research to develop products that people find easy to use (for example, computer software, handheld computer, or remote control, similar to the work of human factors psychologists). Other cognitive psychologists study how people learn in order to develop effective teaching methods. Given the wide range of activities in which humans engage, cognitive psychologists have a great many kinds of decisions and cognitive activities to explain and improve—and a wide range of potential research topics.

QUANTITATIVE PSYCHOLOGY

Quantitative psychology, sometimes called *mathematical psychology*, is the study of research methodology, or methods and techniques for acquiring, analyzing, and applying information. Quantitative psychologists are specialists in designing, conducting, and interpreting experiments. Quantitative psychologists create new methods for analyzing data (for example, statistical tests) and work to develop and test quantitative theories of cognition and behavior (for example, equations and formulas that can account for the range of behavioral phenomena that we see). Today there are mathematical theories of cognition, perception, social interactions, memory, decision making, abnormal behavior, and many other psychological phenomena.

PSYCHOMETRICS

Psychometrics is the science of measuring human characteristics. Psychometricians measure people's behavior, abilities, and potential in the intellectual, emotional, and social realms of functioning. Like quantitative psychologists, psychometricians are well versed in statistics; however, they specialize in measurement (meaning, how do you design a survey that captures the behavior that you intend to study?). Psychometricians create and revise personality tests, intelligence tests, and aptitude tests. They also use these tests to assess people's abilities and level of functioning to assist other psychologists who develop interventions, treatment plans, and diagnostic schemes.

OPPORTUNITIES WITH A BACHELOR'S DEGREE

If you're interested in experimental, cognitive, and quantitative psychology, or psychometrics, there are a variety of career options at the undergraduate level. However, remember that most bachelor's degree holders will begin in entry-level positions that generally entail fewer responsibilities and more clerical, data entry, and supervised work. With experience comes greater autonomy and responsibility, such as that entailed in jobs discussed in the following sections. As with all areas of psychology, graduate degrees open doors to additional career opportunities. Note that the following sections present national data on job growth and salaries; however, availability of jobs and the typical salary that you can expect for each varies by geographic region. Seek advice and do your homework when considering potential careers.

INSURANCE UNDERWRITER

Before an insurance company takes on a new client, whether individual or organizational, an insurance underwriter evaluates the risk of loss, determines the appropriate premium rate, and writes the insurance policy to cover the individuals or organization's risks of loss. An underwriter analyzes information that potential clients provide in insurance applications and supplements the analyses with information from loss control reports, medical reports, and other data to determine if a client is an acceptable risk. The underwriter then determines the appropriate insurance premium to charge. Entry-level positions as underwriters carry the titles of *assistant underwriter* or *underwriter trainee*, with duties and salaries commensurate with experience.

A career as an underwriter offers several advantages: a standard 40-hour work week, quiet office environment, competitive salary, and a measure of job security. Insurance underwriting is not a growth field; employment of underwriters is expected to grow more slowly than average through 2016, but is expected to increase as a growing economy and population expands the insurance needs of businesses and individuals (Bureau of Labor Statistics, 2008). However, insurance is a necessity for both individuals and organizations, so it is a profession that is less vulnerable to economic recessions and layoffs than other fields (Bureau of Labor Statistics, 2008). Finally, underwriting provides a comfortable salary. In 2008, the median salary for an assistant underwriter was $36,082 and median entry-level underwriter salary for life insurance plans was $42,272 and property and casualty plans earned a median salary was $44,430 (Salary.com, 2008). According to the Occupational Outlook Handbook, the median salary for all insurance underwriters was $53,350 in 2006 (Bureau of Labor Statistics, 2008).

Psychology majors have a solid liberal arts background, computer skills, and quantitative abilities that are useful for careers as insurance underwriters. If you're interested in this career, supplement your psychology major with additional courses in statistics, business administration, finance, or accounting. Consider a minor in business administration. Also, consider seeking an internship with an insurance company to learn more about the field.

COMPUTER PROGRAMMER

Computer programmers write the programs, or detailed instructions, that computers follow in performing their functions. They install, test, and debug programs to keep an organization's server and computer systems functional. For example, they might write programs to maintain and control computer systems and networks that permit an organization's computers to communicate with each other and enable an organization's website to function. Computer programmers use technology to solve problems. For example, they may write a new program or adjust existing software in order to assist an organization in performing its mission (for example, write a program to handle a specific job, such tracking inventory). If you are interested in computer programming and understand programming languages like C++, COBOL, or JAVA, a programming career might be for you.

An important advantage of a career in programming is the opportunity for life-long learning. New computer programs and languages rapidly emerge; programmers continually must reevaluate their skills and know the latest technologies. On the other side of the equation, long hours or weekends sometimes are required to meet deadlines or to fix bugs in computer programs. Through 2016, employment of programmers is expected to decline slowly (Bureau of Labor Statistics, 2008). Although overall employment of computer programers is expected to decline, numerous job openings will result from the need to replace programmers who leave the labor force or transfer to other occupations. A typical entry-level programmer earned a median salary of $49,928 in 2007. Median annual earnings of computer programmers were $65,510 in 2006, with the middle 50 percent earning between $49,580 and $85,080 (Bureau of Labor Statistics, 2008).

Psychology students' experience with computers and critical thinking are useful in this field. The analytical approach that cognitive psychologists take towards understanding human problem solving is similar to the methodical step-by-step approach that computer programmers take toward writing computer programs and solving bugs and glitches in programs. Helpful courses to take include mathematics, computer programming, and management information systems. A minor in computer science or management information systems will help you develop proficiency and courses in various programming languages, including C++ and Java, and will demonstrate breadth of knowledge. Employers primarily are interested in programming knowledge, so a degree in computer science isn't necessary if you understand programming languages and have hands-on experience. Seek internship or summer employment opportunities in the field to gain experience and contacts.

COMPUTER SUPPORT SPECIALIST

A computer support specialist provides technical assistance to users of hardware, software, and computer systems, acting as a troubleshooter who interpret problems and provide technical support for hardware, software, and systems. Computer support specialists work in at least two capacities: *technical support specialists* and *help-desk technicians*. Technical support specialists are employed by companies to help employees solve computer-related problems. They respond to inquiries from users, diagnose and solve problems, and may install, modify, clean, and repair computer hardware and software. Help desk technicians answer telephone calls and email inquiries from customers seeking technical assistance for a given hardware or software product. They help users by listening, asking questions to diagnose the problem, and walking the user through steps to solve the problem. Many companies consult help-desk technicians about customers' experiences with the product, what gives them the most trouble, and other customer concerns.

Advantages to careers in computer support include an office environment, excellent job outlook, and high starting salaries. Computer support specialists are projected to increase much more rapidly than the average through 2016 (Bureau of Labor Statistics, 2004). In 2008, a typical help desk technician earned a median salary of $43,319 (Salary.com, 2008); a technical support analyst earned a median salary of $50,586. Psychology majors have computer knowledge, interpersonal skills, and communication skills that are useful for careers in computer support. Completing additional computer classes may increase your marketability.

BUDGET ANALYST

Budget analysts provide data to an organization's management that help them to decide how to allocate an organization's financial resources. Budget analysts develop and analyze an organization's budgets. They analyze spending to determine ways of improving efficiency and increasing an organization's profits. Budget analysts provide advice and technical assistance to managers and department heads in preparing their annual budgets. They examine budgets for accuracy, completeness, and conformance with organizational procedures, objectives, and budgetary limits (Bureau of Labor Statistics, 2004). Throughout the year, budget analysts

TABLE 10.1	PREPARATION FOR BA-LEVEL CAREERS RELATED TO EXPERIMENTAL, COGNITIVE, AND QUANTITATIVE PSYCHOLOGY, AND PSYCHOMETRICS

Coursework

Insurance Underwriter Positions

>   Accounting
>   Business Administration
>   Business Law
>   Communication
>   Finance
>   Statistics
>   Math
>   Writing

Computer Programmer Positions

>   Computer Science
>   Database Systems such as DB2, Oracle, or Sybase
>   Management Information Systems
>   Mathematics
>   Programming Languages, including C++ and Java

Computer Support Positions

>   Communication
>   Computer Science
>   Computer Software Applications
>   Information Systems
>   Writing

Budget Analyst Positions

>   Accounting
>   Business Administration
>   Communication
>   Economics
>   Finance
>   Statistics
>   Mathematics

Applied Experiences: Volunteer, intern, or paid part-time positions in any of the following settings

>   Accounting Firm
>   Evaluation, Measurement, or Assessment Department or Company
>   Finance Firm
>   Information Technology Department
>   Insurance Company

Research Experiences: Experiences studying and participating in research in any of the following areas*

>   Cognitive Psychology
>   Experimental Psychology

continued

TABLE 10.1 | CONTINUED

Human Factors
Program Assessment
Psychometrics
Quantitative Psychology
Test Development

*Note that the content area of the research is less important than the experience itself, which enhances reasoning, quantitative, writing, and organizational skills.

monitor the budget to alert management to risks of overspending and avoid financial deficits.

Advantages of a career in budget analysis are the comfortable office setting, relative independence, and comfortable salary. However, long hours and tight, stressful deadlines are common. A bachelor's degree in psychology is sufficient for entry-level positions in budget analysis because psychology majors are skilled in communication, quantitative analysis, and computer use. Additional courses in business, accounting, economics, finance, and statistics are helpful. In 2008, a typical entry-level budget analyst earned a median base salary of $46,926 (Salary.com, 2008). Median annual salary for all budget analysts was $61,430 in 2006 (Bureau of Labor Statistics, 2008). Employment of budget analysts is expected to grow as rapidly as the average rate for all occupations through 2016 (Bureau of Labor Statistics, 2008).

OPPORTUNITIES WITH A GRADUATE DEGREE

The undergraduate psychology degree offers useful preparation to entry-level positions in a variety of areas. As is often the case, a graduate degree serves as preparation for additional and more advanced positions. A graduate degree in experimental psychology, cognitive psychology, quantitative psychology, or psychometrics opens doors to a variety of careers in business settings.

OPERATIONS RESEARCH ANALYST

Operations research (sometimes called *management science*) is a scientific approach to analyzing problems and making decisions. It entails using mathematics, statistics, and computer science to quantify situations and make decisions. Operations research analysts examine how to make products more efficiently, solve problems, and control inventory and distribution of products. They engage in problem solving by studying the problem, gathering data, analyzing it, and coming up with practical solutions. For example, operations research analysts might conduct research to determine the most efficient amount of inventory a business must keep on hand by talking with engineers about production levels, discussing purchasing levels and arrangements, and examining data on storage costs. If you choose a career in operations research analysis, you'll use mathematical modeling on computers to predict the potential outcomes of alternative solutions to a problem in order to determine which is best.

Operations research analysts are found in all work settings (military, government, business, and industry) and under various titles (*operations analyst, management analyst, policy analyst*). As an operations research analyst, you can expect an office environment and high salary, but also stressful deadlines and long hours. Employment of operations research analysts are expected to grow as rapidly as the average (Bureau of Labor Statistics, 2004). The median annual salary of operations research analysts was $64,650 in 2006; 50 percent earned between $48,820 and $85,760 (Bureau of Labor statistics, 2008).

A graduate degree in the quantitative areas of psychology (experimental, quantitative, psychometrics, and even cognitive psychology) offers the mathematical, statistical, and analytical expertise needed for a career in operations research. In addition to quantitative skills, operations research analysts need excellent communication and computer skills, including statistical software packages and programming. Courses in computer science, business, information systems, and management science are useful. An understanding of how the human mind works (for example, thinking and problem solving) is always useful for operations research analysts who want to minimize the effects of human error on their work (meaning, understanding the kinds of mistakes that workers might make can help operations research analysts make useful decisions).

COMPUTER SYSTEMS ANALYST

A computer systems analyst helps a company or organization use its technology resources effectively to achieve its goals, for example, organization by incorporating new technology into existing systems. An organization typically uses a variety of software applications; systems analysts work to make the computer systems within an organization compatible in order to share information. *Systems architects* are computer system analysts who specialize in helping organizations select the software and infrastructure that are the basis for the organization's computing and information management resources. *Systems designers* specialize in designing a system to meet an organization's computing needs by a variety of quantitative and mathematical techniques, such as data modeling, mathematical model building, and information engineering. Some computer systems analysts engage in both architectural and design functions.

Systems analysts work in offices with a standard 40-hour work week, but evening and weekend work is sometimes needed to meet deadlines or resolve problems. Graduate degree holders in experimental, quantitative, and cognitive psychology typically gain experience in computer programming, understand the use of databases, think analytically, work on a number of tasks simultaneously, and can concentrate and pay attention to detail, which are valued by employers of systems analysts. Interpersonal and communication skills, particularly the ability to work as part of a team to tackle large projects, are required. Additional courses in computer science, management information systems, or the use of specific computer software, such as C++, are recommended. Employment of systems analysts is expected to increase much more rapidly than the average for all occupations through 2016; systems analysis is one of the most rapidly growing occupations (Bureau of Labor Statistics, 2008). Salaries for systems analysts are competitive, with a 2005 median annual entry-level salary of $52,528 (Salary.com, 2008). Graduate degree holders are likely to be hired at a higher level. In 2006, the median annual salary for all systems analysts, regardless of experience, was $69,760; the middle 50 percent earned between $54,320 and $87,600 a year (Bureau of Labor Statistics, 2008).

DATABASE ADMINISTRATOR

A database administrator determines how to organize, store, and retrieve data using database management systems. They determine the needs of organizations and users and design, implement, update, test, and repair computer databases. Database administrators are responsible for ensuring database performance, backing up and archiving information, and, increasingly important as computer networks become more interconnected, ensuring database security.

Graduate degrees in quantitative and cognitive areas of psychology offer experience with computer systems and analytic skills that are in demand by employers. If you're interested in a career in database administration, seek experience with popular programs, such as Oracle, SQL, or Sybase. Most colleges and universities offer courses in these programs, but if yours does not, you can seek certification from courses that are developed by software manufacturers, or purchase the software and related books to explore on your own. Also take additional courses in computer science, information science, or management information systems. Employers look for excellent problem solving skills and interpersonal skills, skills that graduate study in psychology imparts.

Advantages of a career in database administration include intellectual challenge and never-ending learning, because technology is constantly changing. Like computer systems analysts, database administrator's work in an office environment, but they often put in long hours to solve problems and debug databases. Database administration is a hot growth field. Employment of database administrators is expected to increase much more rapidly than the average for all occupations through 2016 (Bureau of Labor Statistics, 2008). It also offers a high salary. In 2008, database administrators earned a median salary of $82,594 (Salary.com, 2008).

ACTUARY

Actuaries use statistics and mathematical models to estimate the statistical probability of particular types of risk, such as death, injury, property loss, or financial risk. Most actuaries are employed by insurance companies. They gather and analyze data to determine who will and will not receive insurance coverage, as well as the price to charge for insurance that will cover claims and ensure profitability. Some actuaries are employed in finance industries to help organizations manage credit or plan new investment tools to help their company compete against others. Actuaries are also employed as consultants, engaging in similar functions, but usually on a contractual basis.

The strong background in mathematics and statistics that graduate degree holders in psychometrics or experimental, cognitive, and quantitative psychology obtain is excellent for a career as an actuary. Actuaries also require strong communication and computer skills, including spreadsheets, databases, and statistical analysis software. Knowledge of computer programming languages, such as

Visual Basic for Applications, SAS, or SQL, is useful. Additional courses in business, economics, and finances will improve your application. If you seek a career as an actuary, be prepared to pass a series of examinations to become certified by Society of Actuaries (SOA), which certifies in the fields of life insurance, health benefits systems, retirement systems, and finance and investment, or the Casualty Actuarial Society (CAS), which certifies actuaries in the property and casualty field, which includes automobile, homeowners, medical malpractice, workers compensation, and personal injury liability. Most actuaries complete licensure exams and become certified while they work and most employers pay some or all of the costs of licensure.

A career as an actuary offers a comfortable office environment, a standard 40-hour work week, and the ability to work autonomously. The employment of actuaries is expected to grow much more rapidly (24 percent) than the average for all occupations through 2016 (Bureau of Labor Statistics, 2008). Actuarial careers have been rated among the top ten careers by *The Wall Street Journal* because they offer high salaries, pleasant working environments, a reasonable job outlook, job security, and reasonable levels of stress (Lee, 2002). According to Salary.com (2008), the typical entry-level actuary earned a median base salary of $55,061 in 2008, with the middle 50 percent earning between $41,976 and $50,796. Median annual earnings of all actuaries were $82,800 in 2006; 50 percent earned between $58,710 and $114,570 (Bureau of Labor Statistics, 2008).

FINANCIAL ANALYST

Financial analysts (also called *security analysts* and *investment analysts*) provide organizations (typically banks, insurance companies, mutual and pension funds, and securities firms) with guidance in making investments. They synthesize financial information by combining data from financial statements, commodity prices, sales, costs, expenses, and tax rates to determine a company's value. They then make recommendations on how to best manage an organization's financial assets and avoid risk.

The broad background in statistics that graduate education in experimental psychology, quantitative psychology, cognitive psychology, or psychometrics provides is an asset to a career in financial analysis. Psychologists in these areas understand how to use mathematics and statistics as a means to an end: to arrive at a practical solution. As a financial analyst, your knowledge of the scientific method will come in handy, because financial analysis entails developing hypotheses and designing tests to validate them using available data, and drawing conclusions (Attfield, 1999). Graduate training offers other benefits to this career, such as experience in giving presentations, strong communication skills, and the ability to work independently. Courses in finance, business administration, accounting, economics, financial analysis methods, or risk management will broaden your knowledge base and demonstrate your interest in applying your statistical skills to financial analysis. Some financial analysts are required to be licensed by the Financial Industry Regulatory Authority (FINRA). Licensure must be sponsored by an employer, so individuals are not expected to be licensed before starting a job.

Advantages of a career in financial analysis include intellectual challenge, comfortable offices, and high salaries. Financial analysts also face long hours, stressful deadlines, and sometimes frequent travel (Attfield, 1999). Financial analysis is a growth occupation; employment of financial analysts is expected to grow much more rapidly (34 percent) than the average for all occupations through 2016 (Bureau of Labor Statistics, 2008). Despite this growth, financial analysis remains a very competitive field. In 2006, the median annual earnings of financial analysts were $66,590 (Bureau of Labor Statistics, 2008). In 2008, a typical entry-level financial analyst earned $46,565 (Salary.com, 2008). A graduate degree may result in a more advanced title and higher entering salary. Annual bonuses increase the salary substantially as they can amount from one-half of to well over the annual salary; however, bonuses fluctuate with the organization's profits.

DATA MINING

Graduate degree holders in quantitative and experimental psychology and psychometrics are especially prepared for careers in data mining. Data mining is the extraction of useful information, or "nuggets," from large databases of information with the use of statistical methods and computational algorithms. It is akin to finding a needle in a haystack, where the needle is critical information that an organization needs and the haystack is the large database with information stored over a long period of time. Data mining entails using statistical analysis to examine large databases for patterns and trends that shed light on consumer habits and potential marketing strategies.

Data mining is used in all industries. For example, discovering new patterns and trends through data mining can help banking executives to "predict with increasing precision how customers will react to interest rate adjustments, which customers will be most receptive to new product offers, which customers present the highest risk for defaulting on a loan, and how to make each customer relationship more profitable" (Fabris, 1998). Data mining professionals, sometimes called *data warehousing professionals* or *database analysts*, are in high demand to develop highly targeted marketing programs, analyze economic trends, detect credit fraud, and forecast financial markets. It is a challenging career that requires analytic thinking and problem-solving skills. If you're interested in a career in data mining, learn about the most popular databases, like SQL, DB2, and Oracle. The main challenges of a career in data mining and data warehousing are the stresses of meeting goals, rolling out database upgrades, learning new analysis techniques, long hours, and analyzing data and drawing conclusions on tight deadlines and with limited budgets and staffs (Smith, 2002). According to *Information Week* (2007) a typical person working in the data mining and warehousing field earned a median base salary of $88,000 in 2007. An entry-level database analyst earned $52,439 in 2008 (Salary.com, 2008). The statistic and research basis of a graduate degree in psychology is likely to result in a higher entry-level salary and title.

As you can see, there are a variety of careers for undergraduate and graduate degree holders that require the statistical expertise of experimental, cognitive, and quantitative psychology and psychometrics. In addition to the careers discussed in this chapter, remember that many individuals with these interests seek careers in research (Chapter 13), teaching (Chapter 4), consulting (Chapter 9), human factors and business (also in Chapter 9), and marketing research (Chapter 11). Quantitative skill is one of the most highly sought skills in the workplace today. Regardless of your career interests, the statistical and methodological knowledge provided by a degree in psychology is excellent preparation for entry-level (for undergraduate degree holders) and more advanced (for masters and doctoral degree holders) quantitative careers.

SUGGESTED READINGS

Bramer, M. (2007). *Principles of data mining.* New York: Springer.

Fitch, T. (2007). *Career opportunities in banking, finance, and insurance.* New York: Checkmark Books.

Henderson, H. (2004). *Career opportunities in computers and cyberspace.* New York: Facts on File.

Hillier, F. S., & Lieberman, G. L. (2005). *Introduction to operation research.* New York: McGraw-Hill.

Liberty, J. (1999). *Complete idiot's guide to a career in computer programming.* New York: Alpha Books.

Schrayer, R. M. (2007). *Opportunities in insurance careers.* New York: McGraw-Hill.

Stair, L., & Stair, L. B. (2002). *Careers in computers.* New York: McGraw-Hill.

Wise, S. (2002). The assessment professional: Making a difference in the 21st century. *Eye on Psi Chi, 6*(3), 20–21.

WEB RESOURCES

Insurance: Overview
http://www.careers-in-finance.com/in.htm

Is a Career in Operations Research/Management Science Right for You?
http://www.informs.org/Edu/Career/booklet.html

Be an Actuary
http://www.beanactuary.org

Data Mining: What Is Data Mining?
http://www.anderson.ucla.edu/faculty/jason.frand/teacher/technologies/palace/datamining.htm

The Data Warehousing Information Center
http://www.dwinfocenter.org/

Budget Analysis as a Career: Information and Opinion from the Budget Analyst
http://www.budgetanalyst.com/careers.htm

Insurance Information Institute
http://www.iii.org/

Institute for Operations Research and the Management Sciences

http://www.informs.org/

CHECKLIST: ARE EXPERIMENTAL, COGNITIVE, OR QUANTITATIVE AREAS OF PSYCHOLOGY FOR YOU?

Do you:

☐   Enjoy conducting research?
☐   Like working with numbers?

☐ Enjoy problem solving?
☐ Like science?
☐ Find computers fun to work with?
☐ Take an analytical approach towards understanding problems?
☐ Know how to use a computer programming language?
☐ Pay attention to detail?
☐ Enjoy writing research reports?
☐ Enjoy intellectual challenges?
☐ Like "fixing" computer problems?
☐ Like math?
☐ Find research methodology courses fun?
☐ Like statistics?
☐ Enjoy using new computer programs?

Scoring: The more boxes you checked, the more likely it is that you're a good match for a career in the experimental or quantitative areas of psychology.

SOCIAL AND CONSUMER PSYCHOLOGY

CHAPTER **11**

CHAPTER GUIDE

What causes social problems like interpersonal violence, prejudice, and stereotyping? How do we change people's attitudes? What influences purchasing patterns? Why do people buy what they buy? Social and consumer psychology address a variety of interesting and important questions. Whereas consumer psychology is an applied discipline, social psychologists traditionally find careers in academia, teaching, and

131

conducting research; however, the increasing emphasis on application within social psychology has translated into a variety of new career options.

SOCIAL PSYCHOLOGY

Social psychology is the study of how people interact with each other and the social environment. Social psychologists study personality (for example, why do we act the way that we do?), attitude formation and change, and interpersonal relations such as attraction, prejudice, group dynamics, and aggression. Like many of the other psychologists you've read about, social psychologists engage in both basic and applied research. Basic research advances knowledge about fundamental questions, such as: How does culture and our social environment shape us? The goal of basic research is to advance scientific knowledge; its application value is not inherent to its worth. In other words, basic research results in knowledge for its own sake. Applied research, on the other hand, is conducted to gain insight and solve real world problems. For example, applied social psychologists conduct research on practical questions, such as: How can we reduce aggression among school children? How can we reduce the effects of prejudice in the classroom or office environment? Social psychologists who emphasize basic research are found in academic and research settings, as described in Chapter 13. Social psychologists who are interested in applied questions can be found in the settings described in this chapter as well as in social policy settings (Chapter 12), and business and organizational settings (Chapters 9 and 10).

CONSUMER PSYCHOLOGY

If you're interested in understanding subliminal suggestions and why some commercials and marketing campaigns are more successful than others, consumer psychology may be for you. Consumer psychologists study how we process information and make decisions about purchasing products and services (Beall & Allen, 1997). They use this information to help businesses and organizations improve their marketing and sales strategies (Carpenter, 2000). A consumer psychologist might design a study to evaluate which type of ketchup container (for example, glass or squeezable plastic) consumers are more likely to purchase. They study consumer behavior to aid companies in their marketing strategies. For example, a consumer psychologist might study factors that contribute to the effectiveness of fast-food commercials, conclude that we are more receptive to such commercials when we are hungry, and therefore suggest that fast-food companies place their commercials in the late afternoon, before dinnertime. Consumer psychologists study the effectiveness of different types of sales techniques and provide advice to businesses based on their research. They train salespeople, conduct consumer satisfaction surveys, and study the growth of consumers' emotional attachments to products.

In other words, consumer psychologists attempt "to understand the processes by which consumers search for goods and services, decide which goods and services to purchase, and consume the items they purchase" (Beall & Allen, 1997, p. 199). They try to understand changing needs of consumers and help companies adapt their products and services accordingly. Consumer psychologists are found in business, government, and nonprofit environments, where they work as consultants and employees in departments of marketing research.

OPPORTUNITIES WITH A BACHELOR'S DEGREE

Persuasion is an important topic of study in social and consumer psychology. Perhaps it shouldn't be surprising that bachelor's degree holders with interests in these areas often find work in advertising, real estate, retail, and public relations.

ADVERTISING

Advertising is a broad field that is concerned with helping companies to market their products. There is a variety of positions in this field, at each rank, from entry level to senior executives. Entry-level positions in advertising are typically in the account management and media departments.

The account management department serves as the link between agency and client; it brings the client to the agency and is responsible for ensuring that the various components of the agency work smoothly to ensure that the client's advertising needs are met. The *assistant account manager* (also called an *account coordinator*), an entry-level position, assists the account manager in completing these tasks. Account managers identify and solicit new clients, determining client needs and communicating them to those who create advertisements. Account managers create schedules, enforce deadlines, and help creative staff and management to understand client needs (Wetfeet, 2005a). Social psychological principles underlie much of their work because account managers must have good interpersonal and sales skills, and understand persuasion and attitude formation, in order to attract new clients and assist them in developing marketing plans to advertise their products.

The media department places ads and is responsible for placing the right ad at the right time in order to reach the appropriate audience cheaply and effectively. Entry-level positions in media departments include *assistant media planners* and *assistant media buyers*. Assistant media planners help media planners examine the public's reading and viewing preferences, study the demographics of various types of media (what consumers read and watch), and evaluate the content of newspapers, magazines, and television programs to determine where to place advertising. Assistant media buyers help media buyers buy ad time and space, make sure that ads appear as planned, and create ad budgets. Psychology students bring a host of useful skills to media planning, including a firm grasp of research methods and statistical analysis, plus an understanding of attitude formation and change, which are all essential to studying the public's preferences and designing effective advertisements. The median salary in media planning in 2007 was $47,052 (Salary.com, 2008).

Careers in advertising are fast-paced and exciting. They offer opportunities to exercise creativity, solve problems, engage in research, and advance in the field. To prepare for a career in advertising, take classes in social psychology, consumer psychology, marketing, accounting, advertising, business management, communications, and design. Hone your communication, creative, and organizational skills. The ability to handle stress, work in a team environment, and use technology (for example, Internet research, Web design, computer skills) are essential to this career path.

Seek an advertising internship to gain hands-on experience as well as contacts in the field, because entry-level positions in advertising are competitive (Bureau of Labor Statistics, 2008). Despite the competitive nature of entry-level positions, there is plenty of room for growth. Employment in advertising is expected to remain steady through 2016 (Bureau of Labor Statistics, 2008). Finally, careers in advertising offer comfortable salaries. In 2007, the average starting salary for advertising positions was $33,831 (Bureau of Labor Statistics, 2008).

REAL ESTATE

How does psychology relate to a career in real estate? Believe it or not, psychological principles underlie much of the work. Real estate agents bring buyers and sellers together and act as intermediaries in the sale of land and residential and commercial properties. They generate lists of available properties, learn as much as possible about them, market them through open houses and advertisements, show them to clients, and assist clients in obtaining financing and drawing up contracts to purchase properties. Real estate agents earn a commission on each property that is sold.

Sales techniques, persuasion, and attitude formation and change are important social psychological principles used daily by real estate agents in their marketing, advertising, and client activities. An effective real estate agent can "read" clients to determine which homes are an appropriate fit. Persuasive techniques are used in describing the home and its benefits (for example, the home is "cozy," rather than "cramped and tiny," or "lively," instead of "next to a late-night pub").

Real estate agents must understand the neighborhoods and surrounding communities in which they sell properties. They must be both interpersonally skilled and competent at number crunching, because they must be able to assess which neighborhoods best fit clients' needs and budgets. Real estate agents spend much of their time obtaining listings (agreements from property owners to sell their properties through a particular real estate agency). When a property is sold, both the agents who sold the property and obtained the listing receive a commission.

An advantage to a career in real estate is the flexibility. Much of the administrative work can be completed out of a home office. However, a great deal of time will be spent showing properties to clients. Real estate agents often work long hours, often more than 40 hours per week (Bureau of Labor Statistics, 2008). In addition to long hours, real estate agents must be available to meet clients on evenings and weekends. As agents gain experience, they may earn higher commission rates as well as become more efficient, and thus can handle more business. With experience, some agents are promoted to supervisory positions or open their own businesses. The primary disadvantage to a career in real estate is the reliance on commission income. Income is irregular and there are often months without income, especially for beginning agents (Evans, 1998). Real estate agents earned a median salary of $39,760 in 2006 (Bureau of Labor Statistics, 2008). Employment of real estate brokers and sales agents is expected to grow about the same as all occupations through 2016 (Bureau of Labor Statistics, 2008).

If you are considering a career in real estate, recognize that all real estate agents must be licensed. Each state has different requirements, but all include a written test with questions on basic real estate transactions and laws about the sale of property.

Many states require 30 to 90 hours of classroom instruction. Licenses must be renewed every 1 or 2 years (without an exam) and continuing education is often required because zoning restrictions and laws change (Bureau of Labor, 2008). For more information about obtaining a real estate license, contact the Association of Real Estate License Law Officials (http://www.arello.org/). Classes in real estate, finance, business administration, economics, or law will provide a helpful background for a career in real estate.

RETAIL

Approximately 15 percent of all workers in the United States are employed by retail establishments (Wetfeet.com, 2005b). Retail sales personnel sell goods, provide customer service, and help buyers make informed purchases. They must understand consumer behavior, sales techniques, and their products, because a high level of service and expertise is essential for success in retail. Many large retail stores have management training programs in which an employee learns about all aspects of the business and, after training, is placed as an assistant manager or store manager (Bureau of Labor Statistics, 2008). *Store managers* are responsible for operation and activity of a store. They manage sales staff, order and track inventory, market products, design techniques to attract customers, and promote sales and good customer relations (Wetfeet.com, 2005b). *Sales representatives* are employed directly by a manufacturer or wholesaler. Sales representatives travel often to visit clients. They develop relationships with clients, discuss the client needs, suggest how their merchandise can meet those needs, and show samples and catalogs of the products they sell (Bureau of Labor Statistics, 2008).

Retail careers are busy, people-oriented, and exciting, and provide opportunities for advancement. If you choose a career in retail, you'll meet many people from different walks of life, use your psychology skills every day, and even travel (if you become a sales representative). Retail careers usually require unusual work hours (often during evenings and weekends). Psychology majors' understanding of human behavior, motivation, and attitudes suit this career well. Strong communication skills, friendliness, decisiveness, enthusiasm, and the ability to manage stress are essential. Management careers also require leadership skills, self-direction, and interpersonal skills (for example, the ability to soothe angered customers). Prepare for a career in retail by taking additional courses in business, marketing, accounting, and communications. Retail positions are expected to grow about as rapidly as the average for all occupations through the year 2016 (Bureau of Labor Statistics, 2008). As shown in Table 11.1, retail careers offer a range of salaries, depending on the position.

PUBLIC RELATIONS SPECIALIST

Public relations specialists work to improve an organization's communication with the community, with consumer, employee, and public interest groups, and with the media. They build and maintain positive relationships with the public by informing the community and media about an organization's policies, activities, and accomplishments (Bureau of Labor Statistics, 2008). Public relations specialists write and distribute press releases to media contacts, who print or broadcast the releases.

TABLE 11.1　|　SALARIES IN RETAIL (ADAPTED FROM SALARY.COM. 2008)

Title	Median salary
Assistant retail store manager	$37,001
Retail store manager	$46,178
Retail sales person	$21,724
Sales representative	$31,588

They keep organization representatives in contact with the community by arranging speaking engagements and often prepare and edit speeches for company leaders.

Public relations specialists anticipate, analyze, and interpret public opinions about organizations to influence an organization's future decisions and business practices (Public Relations Society of America, n.d.). They keep an organization's management and administrative personnel aware of the attitudes and concerns of the public and special interest groups. They give advice to management about the public ramifications of policy decisions and communications and how to build good public relations, which are critical to an organization's success (Public Relations Society of America, n.d.). Public relations also entails research on the public's attitudes and opinions, as well as evaluating the effectiveness of an organization's fundraising, marketing, community relations, and other programs. Public relations specialists are found in a variety of settings, including businesses, government, universities, hospitals, schools, and other organizations. Titles include *public relations specialist, information officer, press secretary, communications specialist, public affairs specialist*, and others.

A career in public relations offers exciting and varied work. Psychology majors are well suited to careers in public relations because of their background in survey research, interpersonal skills, writing skills, and understanding of human behavior, attitude formation, and attitude change. Some of the disadvantages of a career in public relations include long hours, irregular work schedules that are frequently interrupted, and stress (resulting from high-pressure deadlines). Sometimes public relations can be frustrating because, unlike advertising, which pays for media coverage and therefore controls the advertisement message and its distribution, public relations professionals must earn their media coverage and have little control over how the ultimate message is conveyed (Bergen, n.d.).

Entry-level positions in public relations are competitive; therefore, preparation is important. Take courses in communication, journalism, and business to enhance your marketability. Perhaps most important is hands-on experience, through internships with public relations firms, corporate departments, or nonprofit organizations (Public Relations Society of America, n.d.). Despite the competitive nature of entry-level positions, overall employment of public relations specialists is expected to increase much more rapidly than the average for all occupations through 2016 (Bureau of Labor Statistics, 2008). A final advantage of a career in public relations is the salary. In 2006, the median salary for a public relations specialist was $47,350, with half of the people employed as public relations specialists earning between $35,600 and $65,310 (Bureau of Labor Statistics, 2008).

TABLE 11.2 | PREPARATION FOR BA–LEVEL CAREERS RELATED TO SOCIAL AND CONSUMER PSYCHOLOGY

Coursework

    Accounting

    Advertising

    Business Administration

    Business Law

    Consumer Psychology/Psychology of Decision Making

    Economics

    Finance

    Industrial-Organizational Psychology

    Marketing

    Math

    Social Psychology

    Statistics

    Statistics

    Writing

Applied Experiences: Volunteer, intern, or paid part-time positions in any of the following settings

    Advertising Department or Firm

    Business Settings

    Marketing Department or Firm

    Real Estate Firm

    Retail

Research Experiences: Experiences studying and participating in research in any of the following areas*

    Consumer Behavior

    Decision Making

    Group Behavior

    Social Psychology

*Note that the content area of the research is less important than the experience itself, which enhances reasoning, quantitative, writing, and organizational skills.

OPPORTUNITIES WITH A GRADUATE DEGREE

Graduate degree holders in psychology with interests in social and consumer psychology are employed in many of the fields discussed, but at more advanced levels. They also apply their skills to solve real-world problems in a number of other fields.

MARKET RESEARCH

Market researchers are found in a variety of organizations, including public relations firms, advertising agencies, and corporations. They gather data on what people think. They conduct research on the sale of a product or service. Market researchers design methods of gathering information on products or services, as well as consumers' needs, tastes, purchasing power, and buying habits. They examine consumer reactions to products and services. Through research, they identify advertising needs, measure the effectiveness of advertising and other promotional techniques, gather data on competitors' products, services, and locations, and analyze their marketing methods and strategies (Bureau of Labor Statistics, 2008). Market researchers who work for public relations firms or in government positions often conduct opinion research to determine public attitudes on various issues, which may help political and business leaders evaluate public support for their positions or advertising policies (Bureau of Labor Statistics, 2008).

Careers in market research are fast-paced and exciting. Market researchers work on a variety of projects, and project turnover is fast. In addition to conducting research with practical implications, another advantage of a career in market research is that it is a growth field. Employment of market researchers is expected to grow more rapidly than the average for all occupations through 2016, with job opportunities being strongest for those with a masters degree or Ph.D. (Bureau of Labor Statistics, 2008). Finally, salaries in market research are very competitive. In 2006, a typical market research analyst earned a median base salary of $58,820; half of the people in this job earn between $42,190 and $84,070 (Bureau of Labor Statistics, 2008). Market research managers, on the other hand, earn an average of $88,383 (Salary.com, 2008).

PRODUCT DEVELOPMENT CONSULTANT

Psychologists use their knowledge about human development, interpersonal relations, and attitude formation and change to provide organizations with research-based information to assist them in providing goods and services that meet people's needs. Psychologists often work as consultants in product development. They examine people's reactions to particular products, as well as their needs, tastes, purchasing power, and buying habits. The resulting knowledge is used to improve the product, and develop the advertising and promotional campaigns that are used to sell the product.

Product development consultants work for companies and consulting firms, and in private practice. An important reward of a career as a consultant in product development is that you'll engage in work with practical implications and then get to see the results of your work. You will work on a variety of projects, and project turnover is fast. A regular 40-hour work week and high rates of compensation are other advantages. For example, the median salary for product development managers, who oversee the development of specific products, was $75,984 in 2008, and for product development directors, who oversee all product development activities for an organization, was $144,230 (Salary.com, 2008).

MANAGEMENT

A degree in social or consumer psychology prepares graduates for management careers in advertising, marketing, public relations, and sales. Managers in these fields coordinate the market research, marketing strategy, sales, advertising, promotion, pricing, product development, and public relations activities of large companies.

Advertising managers oversee advertising and promotional activities within a firm. If a firm contracts an advertising agency to handle promotions, then the advertising manager may serve as a liaison between the firm and the advertising agency (Bureau of Labor Statistics, 2008). Larger companies have their own advertising staff, overseen by advertising managers.

Marketing managers coordinate the work of market researchers to determine the demand for products and services offered by the firm and develop a marketing strategy (Bureau of Labor Statistics, 2008). They also develop pricing strategies that maximize profits while ensuring customer satisfaction. Marketing managers confer with advertising managers and market researchers to promote products and services and devise strategies to attract new customers.

Public relations managers supervise the work of public relations specialists and direct publicity programs. They determine the target of publicity programs and evaluate their effectiveness. In a large company, public relations managers may examine the compatibility of the advertising and public relations programs and suggest changes, when needed, to the company's top management. Public relations managers keep abreast of social, economic, and political trends, and make recommendations on how to enhance the company's visibility and positive image in light of current trends (Bureau of Labor Statistics, 2008).

Sales managers direct a company's sales program. They hire sales representatives, devise programs to train sales representatives, assign sales territories, set sales goals, and oversee the work of sales representatives (Bureau of Labor Statistics, 2008). They determine the sales potential of products, assess inventory requirements, monitor customer preferences, and communicate this information to other departments to help develop and modify or maximize products.

Like other careers, there are a variety of benefits and challenges to careers such as advertising, marketing, public relations, and sales. Long hours, including evenings and weekends, are common. For example, approximately 44 percent of advertising, marketing, and public relations managers worked more than 40 hours per week in 2002 (Bureau of Labor Statistics, 2008). Managerial careers often entail substantial travel (for example, attendance at meetings sponsored by associations or industries, meetings at national, regional, and local offices, and meetings with dealers, distributors, and clients). In addition, tight deadlines can make for stressful work.

According to the Bureau of Labor Statistics (2008), management positions in advertising, marketing, public relations, and sales are expected to remain steady through 2016; however, such positions will remain competitive. Finally, management careers pay well. In 2002, the median base salary for advertising managers was $73,060, $98,720 for marketing managers, and $91,560 for sales managers (Bureau of Labor Statistics, 2008).

If you're interested in a career as an advertising, marketing, public relations, or sales manager, take additional courses in business administration, marketing, business law, advertising, accounting, public speaking, and finance. Graduate degree holders' expertise with statistics is especially valuable. Finally, managerial careers require maturity, creativity, motivation, resistance to stress, flexibility, and the ability to communicate persuasively—all skills that are developed with graduate study in psychology.

Graduate degrees in social and consumer psychology are among the most marketable of psychology degrees. This chapter presented just a few of the opportunities for graduate degree holders in these areas. If you are interested in other alternatives to the traditional academic career as professor, consider writing and publishing careers (Chapter 13), trial consulting (Chapter 5), consulting (Chapter 9), or social policy careers (Chapter 12). With creative thinking and innovation, you'll design and achieve the career of your dreams.

SUGGESTED READINGS

Beall, A. E., & Allen, T. W. (1997). Why we buy what we buy: Consulting in consumer psychology. In R. Sternberg (Ed.), *Career paths in psychology: Where your degree can take you* (pp. 197–212). Washington, DC: American Psychological Association.

Branscombe, N. R. & Spears, R. (2001). Social psychology: Past, present, and some predictions for the future. In J. S. Halonen & S. F. Davis (Eds.), *The many faces of psychological research in the 21st century*. Retrieved July 29, 2008 at http://teachpsych.org/ resources/ e-books/faces/script/Ch07.htm

Edwards, K. W. (2006). *Your successful real estate career*. New York: Amacom.

Field, S. (2001). *Career opportunities in the retail and wholesale industry*. New York: Facts on File.

Field, S., & Rubenstein, H. J. (2005). *Career opportunities in advertising and public relations*. New York: Checkmark.

Friestad, M. (2001). What is consumer psychology? *Eye on Psi Chi*, 6(1), 28–29.

Neidle, A. (2002). *How to get into advertising: A guide to careers in advertising, media, and marketing communications*. London: Cassell Academic.

Wagner, R. (2001). A hot market for social scientists in market research. *Chronicle of Higher Education*. Retrieved on June 1, 2002 at http://chronicle.com/jobs/2001/01/ 2001011901c.htm

Wetfeet (2008). *Careers in advertising and public relations*. Wetfeet.

WEB RESOURCES

What Is a Personality/Social Psychologist?
http://www.spsp.org/what.htm

Social Psychology
http://www.trinity.edu/~mkearl/socpsy.html

Realty Times
http://realtytimes.com

Association of Real Estate License Law Officials
http://www.arello.org/

Consumer Behavior: The Psychology of Marketing
http://www.consumerpsychologist.com/

A Guide to Public Relations Education and Training
http://www.martex.co.uk/prcareerdevelopment/index.htm

About Advertising
http://advertising.about.com/

About Retail Careers
http://retailindustry.about.com/

CHECKLIST: IS SOCIAL OR CONSUMER PSYCHOLOGY FOR YOU?

Do you:

Like shopping and spending time in stores?
Wonder what influences people's purchases?
Have an interest in attitude formation and change?
Like solving problems?
Enjoy persuading others?
Like watching the Super Bowl for the commercials?
Like "reading" people?
Find research enjoyable?
Think quickly on your feet?
Like working with numbers?

Scoring: Add up your checkmarks; the greater the score the more likely a career in social or consumer psychology is for you.

CHAPTER 12 | DEVELOPMENTAL PSYCHOLOGY

Babies, children, teenagers. That's what most people think of when they hear the phrase *developmental psychology*. Yes, developmental psychologists are interested in how vision changes over the first year of life or the ways in which the media influences children's behavior, but they are also interested in adults. Is there a midlife crisis? What is the role of social support in health and well-being in older adulthood? Developmental psychologists examine questions pertinent to our everyday lives. Historically, graduate training in developmental psychology led to academic

142

careers; however, today more developmental psychologists are entering applied careers. In this chapter we'll explore careers for students who are interested in developmental psychology.

DEVELOPMENTAL PSYCHOLOGY

Developmental psychology is the study of how people grow, develop, and change across the lifespan. Developmental psychologists are concerned with the emotional, intellectual, and physical development of children, adolescents, and adults. Many developmental psychologists specialize with particular age groups, such as infants and young children, adolescents, young adults, or older adults. Perhaps the most rapidly growing field within developmental psychology is gerontology, or the study of the aging process from middle age through later life. Gerontologists study physical, emotional, social, and psychological changes that older adults experience as they age, how our society is changing as the population of the United States ages, and how knowledge about development can be applied to create and modify policies and programs to assist older adults and their families. Developmental psychologists conduct research on a diverse array of topics, such as the effects of divorce on adults and how they parent, how infants learn language, and influences on anti-social activity during adolescence.

A growing number of psychologists are concerned with the application of developmental science, or applied developmental psychology (part of the larger, multi-disciplinary field of applied developmental science). Applied developmental psychologists conduct research on practical problems in real-world settings, such as the scope and nature of children's exposure to violence and how to promote resilience in children and adolescents reared in disenfranchised neighborhoods. Applied developmental psychologists develop and evaluate interventions that promote optimal cognitive, emotional, and social development. They disseminate knowledge about developmental processes to policymakers, businesses, industry, healthcare professionals, and parents. Applied developmental psychologists also engage in direct service delivery by constructing, administering, and interpreting assessments of developmental strengths and vulnerabilities, developing behavioral management programs for individuals and groups, and delivering psychological services in various mental health settings (Fisher & Osofsky, 1997; Kuther, 1996; Toth, Manly, & Nilsen, 2008).

OPPORTUNITIES WITH A BACHELOR'S DEGREE

Many students who earn bachelor's degrees in psychology would like to work with people and many are interested in specific age groups, such as children or older adults. Students who are interested in developmental psychology might consider jobs as gerontology aide, child life specialists, or among the many that are found in nonprofit organizations.

Gerontology Aide

Gerontology aides are human services workers (also known as social and human services assistants) who specialize in working with older adults and provide direct and indirect services to clients. They develop programs such as health promotion, senior theater groups, and intergenerational activities for older people in senior centers, community agencies, and retirement communities. Gerontology aides also provide direct care to older adults in hospitals, clinics, and nursing homes, or through adult daycare or home care programs. They monitor and keep records on clients' progress and report to supervisors and case managers. Gerontology aides may accompany clients to group meal sites, adult daycare centers, or doctors' offices, telephone or visit clients' homes to make sure services are being received, and help some with daily living needs. Most gerontology aides work under the direction of professionals such as psychologists, nurses, counselors, or social workers, depending on the setting. Gerontology aides are found in offices, clinics, hospitals, group homes, clay programs, and clients' homes.

An important advantage to obtaining a position as a gerontology aide is the ability to help others and contribute to their welfare. Other advantages include a fairly standard 40-hour work week—but weekends and evenings may be necessary depending on the setting. Social and human services assistant positions, including gerontology aides, are projected to grow much more rapidly than the average for all occupations through 2016 (Bureau of Labor Statistics, 2008), ranking among the most rapidly growing occupations, so psychology students will have many career choices in this field. If you're interested in becoming a gerontology aide, your psychology curriculum will prepare you well. Additional courses in communication, gerontology, and social work will round out your skills.

Helping others is very rewarding, but a position as a gerontology aide can be emotionally draining. It can be difficult to work with clients you cannot help, such as clients who are dying. Human services careers are not for everyone and turnover among staff tends to be high. Finally, gerontology aides earn a relatively low salary. In 2006, the median annual earnings of social and human service assistants, such as gerontology aides, were $25,580, and 50 percent earned between $20,350 and $32,440 (Bureau of Labor Statistics, 2008).

CHILD LIFE SPECIALIST

Child life specialists help children and families adjust to a child's hospitalization. They typically are found in hospital settings and implement pediatric programs, therapies, and activities with children. Child life specialists educate and assist families in the physically and emotionally demanding process of caring for hospitalized or disabled children. They help children cope by engaging them in activities that permit children free expression and opportunities to engage in normal play that promotes social and emotional development and feelings of competence.

Helping families in crisis can be very rewarding, but it is also challenging and some child life specialists burn out. Child life specialists are found in children's hospitals across North America, but are less common in small hospitals. There are geographic restrictions on this career as hospitals that hire child life specialists tend to be located in urban areas. If you are interested in a career as a child life specialist, take courses in child and family studies, human development, and early childhood education, and obtain knowledge of common medical terms and familiarity of some of the most common serious illnesses of children.

Child life specialists must obtain certification which, in addition to a bachelor's degree, requires an internship or employment experience of at least 480 hours and completion of the certification exam offered by the Child Life Council (visit http://www.childlife.org). In 2008, a bachelor's-level child life specialist earned a median salary of $38,000; 50 percent earned between $35,000 and $43,134. A child life specialist who has earned supervision responsibilities, such as mentoring colleagues, organizing and supervising programs, and grant writing, earned a median salary of $41,196 in 2008 (50 percent earned between $36,058 and $47,382) (Child Life Council, 2008).

Careers in Nonprofit Organizations

The nonprofit sector offers new graduates a broad range of job opportunities. In the last 20 years, the nonprofit sector has grown at a rate surpassing both government and private business. What is a nonprofit organization? Nonprofit organizations do not operate to earn a profit; in other words, their income is not used to benefit or gain stockholders, directors, or any other persons with interests in the organization. Instead, income is funneled back into the organization to assist it in meeting its goals. There are a variety of nonprofit organizations, and most work to advance a cause or interest. For example, some nonprofits promote educational, scientific, cultural, civic, or social welfare causes. Many psychology graduates are hired by nonprofit organizations that work to improve the lives of individuals, families, and children.

Nonprofit organizations offer opportunities for both program and administrative positions. Students who are interested in applied developmental psychology often seek program positions within organizations that focus on the needs of children, youth, and families. If you seek a program position, you might assist in providing health services, counseling, crisis intervention, therapy, education, and research activities (Rowh & Suchorski, 2000). As a *program assistant*, you'll help the program director and work on analyzing issues and implementing programs. Tasks might include data entry and analysis, report writing, and office work. The typical salary range for such a position is $20,000 to $35,000 (Wetfeet.com, 2008). With several years of experience a program assistant might be eligible for a job as *program director*, which is often a mid-level management position. Duties tend to include overseeing and managing specific program, including hiring, fundraising, and administrative and management functions. The typical salary range for program directors is $45,000 to $65,000 (Wetfeet.com, 2008).

Other psychology graduates with applied developmental psychology interests are hired in direct service positions in which they work with an organization's clients by leading support groups for children, youth, and parents, conducting education and training sessions for parents, or providing education and support to families in their homes. In 2004, the typical *direct service outreach worker* earned a median salary of $25,580 (Bureau of Labor statistics, 2008). With experience a psychology graduate may be promoted to *case worker*, responsible for providing services to clients and their families, ensuring a healthy living and social environment. The median salary for case workers is $43,063 and the middle 50 percent of case workers earn between $39,746 and $46,380 (Salary.com, 2008). For more

TABLE 12.1	PREPARATION FOR BA–LEVEL CAREERS RELATED TO DEVELOPMENTAL PSYCHOLOGY

Coursework

Gerontology Aide Positions
    Gerontology
    Communication
    Social Work
    Health and Wellness
    Family Studies
    Developmental Psychology or Human Development

Child Life Specialist
    Child Development
    Family Studies
    Human Development
    Early Childhood Education
    Communication
    Health and Wellness
    Child Psychopathology
    Seek Certification by The Child Life Council (Visit http://www.childlife.org)

Nonprofit Positions
    Communication
    Social Work
    Mathematics
    Writing
    Family Systems
    Child Development
    Marketing
    Accounting
    Business Administration

Applied Experiences: Volunteer, intern, or paid part-time positions in any of the following settings
    Boys and Girls Clubs
    Children's Hospitals or Pediatric Units
    Day Care
    Geriatric Facility
    Mental Retardation Facility
    Nonprofit Organizations, such as shelters, women's centers, advocacy centers
    School

Research Experiences: Experiences studying and participating in research in any of the following areas*
    Aging
    Child Development
    Child Psychopathology
    Developmental Assessment
    Developmental Psychology
    Program Development and Evaluation
    Geriatric Psychology

*Note that the content area of the research is less important than the experience itself, which enhances reasoning, quantitative, writing, and organizational skills.

information about direct service positions for baccalaureate degree holders in psychology, see Chapter 3.

Nonprofit organizations rely heavily on contributions and grants to fund their organizations. Fundraising is a critical activity and an important opportunity for psychology students. As a *fundraiser* for a nonprofit organization, you will be involved in planning and organizing programs to raise money to support the organization and its work. You will design programs and activities to encourage contributions and financial support, solicit donations from individuals, foundations, and corporations, and work to achieve and maintain positive relationships with donors. Fundraising positions also entail writing proposals for grants or donations, conducting research on prospective donors, and coordinating special fundraising events. Salaries in fundraising typically range from $30,000 to $50,000 (Wetfeet.com, 2008).

Fundraising positions require strong communication, public relations, and organizational skills in order to mobilize public support, as well as an appreciation for how people respond to solicitations and requests for help. Psychology clearly holds implications for fundraising because an understanding of interpersonal behavior, principles of persuasion, and attitude formation and change underlies successful fundraising attempts. The psychology major's people skills, problem-solving ability, understanding of social psychological principles, and critical analysis skills are very useful to a career in fundraising. Courses in marketing, accounting, communication, and business administration will broaden your skills.

An important advantage to a career in a nonprofit organization is the opportunity to help others and to improve the health and welfare of people. The work is interesting and you'll be able to influence pressing social issues. With experience, there are opportunities for advancement within an organization, taking on additional supervisory and administrative tasks, and to move from small to larger nonprofit organizations. Disadvantages to a career in the nonprofit sector include low pay relative to skills and education. In addition, most nonprofits depend on a variety of unstable funding activities including grants, public donations, and fundraising events. The financial stability of many nonprofits is uncertain, so workers are sometimes subject to layoffs. The overall lack of funding can contribute to a stressful work environment because of inadequate resources for staff development, quality equipment, and office space. Administrative positions within nonprofit organizations include public relations specialists (Chapter 11), administrative assistants (Chapter 9), computer staff (Chapter 10), and other office support workers.

Careers in childcare, gerontology services, and nonprofit organizations are just some of the opportunities available for students who are interested in developmental psychology. Also consider careers in teaching (Chapter 4), corrections (Chapter 5), and public relations (Chapter 11).

OPPORTUNITIES WITH A GRADUATE DEGREE

As with most fields, a graduate degree in developmental psychology opens up a number of career doors. The following sections explore a range of new opportunities for graduate degree holders in developmental psychology who are interested in applying their skills to solve real-world problems.

SCIENTIST-PRACTITIONER CAREERS

Applied developmental psychologists merge science with practice. They are found in medical facilities, schools, social service agencies, and private practice. Some serve as consultants who provide teachers with information about behavioral management and instructional techniques appropriate for individuals with a wide range of developmental needs, including those with developmental disabilities (Fisher & Osofsky, 1997). Others conduct developmental assessments of children who have suffered injuries or who are suspected of having a developmental delay. After diagnosing a developmental delay or learning disability, an applied developmental psychologist discusses treatment and intervention alternatives with parents, and provides teachers and parents with information about the child's condition and how to promote development. In cases of severe developmental delays, applied developmental psychologists in hospital and service settings work with a multidisciplinary team of physicians, social workers, physical therapists, and other professionals to determine the best course of treatment or intervention. As you can see, applied developmental psychologists engage in activities similar to clinical and counseling psychologists, but the applied developmental psychologist differs from other clinicians in at least two important ways: (1) applied developmental psychologists do not conduct individual therapy; and (2) applied developmental psychologists are oriented toward promoting development across the lifespan by helping individuals to develop skills to optimize their capacities.

Applied developmental psychologists design and empirically evaluate programs provided by hospitals, social service agencies, mental health clinics, and schools (Bruzzese, 2005). For example, an applied developmental psychologist might evaluate the impact of a behaviorally oriented program administered in a hospital or clinic setting, such as the effect of maternal prenatal care and education on infant health outcomes. In school settings, they might design and evaluate remedial education programs, or determine the effectiveness of mainstreaming practices. Applied developmental psychologists who work in residential care settings might evaluate the effectiveness of a program to help improve feelings of self-efficacy (or control) in older adults.

Applied developmental psychologists are also found in social services agencies and court settings, where they evaluate families who wish to provide foster parenting, determine parental fitness for regaining child custody after loss of parental rights, or participate as part of a multidisciplinary team to assist children who have suffered abuse during the subsequent investigation and court process. Applied developmental psychologists conduct evaluations of children and families during divorce and child custody cases, determine the developmental status of adolescents in criminal cases in which they might be tried as adults, and serve as expert witnesses in child abuse, custody, and trials in which the defendants are children and adolescents.

If you are interested in a career in applied developmental psychology, recognize that a masters degree will prepare you for engaging in developmental assessment activities under the supervision of a licensed psychologist. A masters degree will also prepare you for many positions in program design and evaluation. Doctoral degrees enable graduates to engage in more advanced activities, but also hold additional responsibilities, including seeking licensure.

Applied developmental psychologists who plan careers as scientist-practitioners must seek state licensure in order to offer psychological services to the public (Goldstein, Wilson, & Gerstein, 1983; Kuther, 1996). State licensure was developed to provide a measure of assurance as to the minimum competency of practitioners. Licensure provides a standard of professionalism in psychology and protects consumers from the consequences of unprofessional conduct by licensed professionals. Licensure has personal, professional, and economic implications for applied developmental psychologists. By providing statutory recognition, licensure has a legitimizing and enhancing effect on any profession. A license offers public recognition that a psychologist is competent to offer services to the public, and it is required for psychologists who wish to be reimbursed by health insurers for providing mental health services. Typically, licensure eligibility requires two years of supervised field experience, with at least one year postdoctoral, passing a written national examination and a written examination covering ethical and legal issues within a particular state, as well as an oral examination in some states. It should be noted that the requirements for licensure vary from state to state. Licensure offers scientist-practitioners additional employment and professional advancement opportunities. In 2003, licensed scientist-practitioner psychologists working in direct human services positions, regardless of experience, earned a median salary of $75,500 (Pate, Finkel, and Kohout, 2005).

Although this discussion has emphasized the applied and practice activities of applied developmental psychologists, recognize that many of these professionals conduct applied research in university, hospital, government, and private settings. For example, a researcher in a university might study risk factors for adolescent delinquency and then develop a prevention and intervention program to help at-risk adolescents. For more information about research careers in a variety of settings, see Chapter 13.

PRODUCT DEVELOPMENT AND MEDIA CONSULTANT

Psychologists use their knowledge about human development, interpersonal relations, and attitude formation and change to provide organizations with research-based information to assist them in providing goods and services that meet people's needs. Developmental psychologists offer organizations special assistance in designing and marketing developmentally appropriate toys, learning products, television programs, and more.

Psychologists often work as consultants in product development and marketing. They determine the developmental appropriateness of toys and provide insight into children's abilities and play styles. They test prototypes of toys with children and modify them based on their input. Consultants conduct focus groups with parents and children to determine their views about specific products and to get feedback on toy designs. The resulting knowledge is used to improve the product. They also conduct market research by examining children's and parents' reactions to particular toys, advertising, and promotional techniques, as well as their needs, tastes, purchasing power, and buying habits. The next time you're in a toy store and pick up a particular toy, notice the label describing the toy's age-appropriateness; that's probably the work of a developmental psychologist.

Other developmental psychologists assist companies in developing and marketing products that are appropriate for older adults. They apply developmental knowledge to improve the design of products and environments (such as a residential home). For example, a consultant might suggest modifying the design of product packaging by using contrasting colors and larger print that's easier for older adults to read. Through focus groups and research, consultants determine older adults' needs and preferences, and provide organizations with the information needed to design better products and marketing techniques.

The media offers additional marketing research opportunities for developmental psychologists. Psychologists provide developmental and educational advice to creators of children's programs. For example, they conduct and interpret research on children's attention spans that inform creative guidelines for television programs such as Sesame Street. Similar to product development, focus groups and market research forms the information base that is used to target viewers of television programs and radio shows.

Product development and marketing consultants work for companies, consulting firms, and in private practice. An important reward of a career as a consultant in product development and marketing is that you'll engage in work with practical implications and they get to see the results of your work. You'll work on a variety of projects and project turnover is fast. The research often is needed quickly as clients must make swift business decisions. A regular 40-hour per week work schedule and high rates of compensation are other advantages. In 2008, a typical market research analyst earned a median base salary of $68,574; 50 percent earn between $59,509 and $77,639 (Salary.com, 2008).

SOCIAL POLICY RESEARCH

Developmental psychologists often find satisfying careers in social policy. Social policy work typically is conducted within government positions (for example, National Institute of Mental Health, National Institute on Drug Abuse) and at think tanks or policy-oriented organizations that resemble academia. We will discuss the nature of research positions in Chapter 13; however, research careers in social policy–oriented organizations deserve special mention within this chapter because many social and developmental psychologists are interested in applying the psychological knowledge base to promote public welfare by educating legislators and lobbying for social change. If you choose a career in social policy, much of your time will be spent writing grants, conducting research, analyzing the impact of various policies, and writing, presenting, and publishing your work in various formats to ensure that your findings are accessible to the public and to policymakers.

Perhaps the best way to gain perspective on research careers in think tanks is to explore three prominent policy-oriented organizations. Remember that these are just a small sampling of the policy centers that abound.

- RAND (the acronym is a contraction of the term "research and development") is the oldest think tank, created in 1946. The mission of RAND, like other think tanks, is to apply research and analysis to improve policy and decision making.

RAND, a very large think tank, conducts policy research in a variety of areas. Projects have included creating a nationwide drug prevention program for school children, evaluating the quality of health care for older adults, and assessing the impact of Indonesia's economic crisis on its citizens. For more information about RAND, see http://www.rand.org.

- The Families and Work Institute (http://www.familiesandwork.org) is a research center that provides data about the interaction of work and family to inform decision making. Researchers at the Families and Work Institute conduct research on "work-life issues and concerns confronting workers and employers in order to inform decision-makers in government, business, communities, and families" (Families and Work Institute, n.d.). Sample projects include longitudinal studies with nationally representative samples of U.S. workers to learn about the changing nature of work, longitudinal studies of employers to understand how U.S. employers are responding to employee work-life needs, and interviews with children to understand how they make sense of their world and the implications for schools, programs, and policies.
- Manpower Demonstration Research Corporation (MDRC) is dedicated to learning what works to improve the well-being of low-income people and actively communicating findings to enhance the effectiveness of public policies and programs. Researchers at MDRC conduct evaluations of welfare reforms and other supports for the working poor as well as research on how programs affect children's development and their families' well-being. Other projects examine the effectiveness of school reform policies designed to improve academic achievement and access to college, and community approaches to increasing employment in low-income neighborhoods. For more information about MDRC, visit http://www.mdrc.org.

How do you prepare for a career in policy research? Although graduate training provides a knowledge base about research methodology, students who are interested in conducting policy-related research must learn how to formulate research questions in ways that can inform policy and must learn how to communicate findings with a wide and varied audience (Susman-Stillman et al., 1996; Weinberg & Susman-Stillman, 1999). Seek a policy-related undergraduate, predoctoral, or postdoctoral fellowship and get hands-on learning to supplement your graduate training. Researchers in think tanks and policy-oriented organizations earn salaries similar to those in academia. In 2007, doctoral degree holders with 5 to 9 years of experience earned a median salary of $76,000 in nonprofit research settings, with 50 percent earning between $66,000 and $96,000 (APA, 2008).

An interest in development across the lifespan can support a variety of careers. In addition to those discussed in this chapter, as well as Chapters 3, 4, and 5.

SUGGESTED READINGS

Acuff, D. S., & Reiher, R. H. (1999). *What kids buy and why: The psychology of marketing to kids.* New York: Free Press.

Berk. L. (2001). Trends in human development. In J. S. Halonen & S. F. Davis (Eds.), *The many faces of psychological research in the 21st century.* Retrieved June 5, 2002 at http://teachpsych.org/resources/e-books/faces/index_faces.php

Bruzzese, J.M. (2005). Medical schools and centers: The merger of developmental psycho-
     logy and pediatric asthma education. In R. D. Morgan, T. L. Kuther, & C. J. Habben
     (Eds.), *Life after graduate school in psychology: Insider's advice from new psychologists.*
     New York: Psychology Press.

Burns, J. B. (2006). *Career opportunities in the nonprofit sector.* Checkmark Books.

Coffey, T. & Livingston, G. (2005). *Marketing to the new super consumer: Mom & kid.*
     Paramount Marketing Publishing.

Eberts, M., & Gisler, M. (2006). *Careers for kids at heart & others who adore children.*
     New York: McGraw-Hill.

Giacobello, J. (2001). *Choosing a career in the toy industry.* New York: Rosen.

Grabinsky, C. J. (2007). *101 careers in gerontology.* Springer.

King. R. M. (2000). *From making a profit to making a difference: How to launch your new
     career in nonprofits.* Planning/Communications.

Kuther, T. L. (1996). Doctoral training in applied developmental psychology: Matching
     graduate education and accreditation standards to student needs, career opportunity,
     and licensure requirements. In C. B. Fisher, J. P. Murray, & I. E. Sigel (Eds.), *Applied
     developmental science: Graduate training for diverse disciplines and educational settings.*
     (pp. 53–74). Norwood, NJ: Able.

Rowh, M., & Suchorski, J. (2000). *Opportunities in fund-raising careers.* New York:
     McGraw-Hill.

Susman-Stillman, A. R., Brown, J. L., Adam, E. K., Blair, C., Gaines, R., Gordon, R. A.,
     et al. (1996). Building research and policy connections: Training and career options for
     developmental scientists. *Social Policy Report, 10*(4), 1–19.

Wagner, L. (2001). *Careers in fund raising.* Wiley.

Web Resources

National Child Care Association
http://www.nccanet.org/

National Association for the Education of Young Children
http://www.naeyc.org

National Network for Child Care
http://www.nncc.org

Society for Research in Child Development
http://www.srcd.org

Careers in Aging
http://www.careersinaging.com/

Careers in Gerontology
http://www.geron.org/StudentOrg/careers.htm

Toy Inventor Designer Guide
http://www.toy-tia.org/industry/publications/inventor.html

Sesame Workshop
http://www.sesameworkshop.org/

Children's Advertising Review Unit
http://www.caru.org

Society for Research on Adolescence
http://www.s-r-a.org

Families and Work Institute
http://www.familiesandwork.org

American Geriatrics Society
http://www.americangeriatrics.org

American Association of Fund-Raising Executives
http://www.afpnet.org/

Association for Gerontology in Higher Education
http://www.aghe.org

RAND
http://www.rand.org/about/

MDRC
http://www.mdrc.org/

CHECKLIST: IS DEVELOPEMENTAL PSYCHOLOGY FOR YOU?

Do you:

☐ Want to know how people change as they age?
☐ Like solving problems?
☐ Like learning about older adulthood?
☐ Have the ability to consider multiple perspectives?
☐ Like working with theories?
☐ Find infants interesting?
☐ Have the ability to tolerate ambiguity?
☐ Want to do work that helps people?
☐ Like children?
☐ Not want to be a clinician?
☐ Have interests in social policy?
☐ Think adolescents are interesting?
☐ Wonder how we change as we progress through adulthood?
☐ Enjoy conducting research?
☐ Find all ages interesting?
☐ Enjoy reading books about developmental issues (for example, What to expect the first year, What to expect during the toddler years)?

Scoring: Count the number of checkmarks; the higher the number, the more likely a career in developmental psychology is for you.

CHAPTER 13

GRADUATE-LEVEL CAREERS IN PSYCHOLOGY

CHAPTER GUIDE

In each chapter in this book we have discussed career options for psychologists in specific disciplines, such as social, experimental, and developmental psychology. Some career options are appropriate for psychologists of all subdisciplines. In this chapter, we examine career options available to all graduate degree holders in psychology. As you know, many psychologists work as professors. However, did you know that, in addition to staffing psychology departments, psychologists are also professors in schools of business, medicine, and education? Similarly, research training in psychology prepares graduate degree holders for careers as researchers outside of academia, including the government, foundations, business, and research groups. Some psychologists seek careers in the military and engage in a variety of activities ranging from assessment and counseling to research and human factors. Others pursue publishing, journalism, and writing careers. Our goal in this chapter is to highlight these careers as a sample of the diversity a graduate degree in psychology offers; however, as you will learn throughout this book, you are by no means limited to the careers we summarize here.

THE IVORY TOWER: PSYCHOLOGISTS AS PROFESSORS

Aside from the therapist, perhaps the most familiar career path for those with graduate degrees in psychology is that of the college professor. Professors have the opportunity to share information they find fascinating with their students. Psychologists work as professors in a variety of academic departments of psychology and schools of education; however, some psychologists are professors outside of psychology departments, sometimes in places you might never have imagined. Psychologists who are trained in industrial/organizational psychology, human factors psychology, or social psychology might work in business schools and within departments of engineering. Psychologists trained in clinical or health psychology sometimes work as professors in medical schools.

Expectations and activities of professors vary by institution. There are several types of colleges and universities. For example, two-year community colleges tend to focus heavily on teaching with few requirements for engage in research. In these settings, faculty often teach five courses per semester, leaving little time to conduct research or engage in scholarly writing. Performance evaluations of faculty in community colleges are based on teaching and service to the community. Liberal arts colleges also emphasize teaching and contact with students. Faculty often teach three to four classes each semester and are expected to have scholarly contacts with students in and out of the classroom. Expectations for faculty research are that faculty incorporate students into their research programs. Faculty are expected to work closely with students on research projects, publishing jointly when appropriate. Teaching, however, is the top priority. and therefore research is viewed as pedagogy. At the other extreme of community and liberal arts colleges are research universities. Research universities are large schools with prestigious graduate programs; at these universities faculty teach only one to two courses per semester. Instead, they focus heavily on research because they are judged on their reputations as scholars, and teaching contributes less to their professional advancement (Vesilind, 2000). Many four-year universities fall somewhere between the two extremes and encourage faculty to engage in both research and teaching. As you can see, even within academia there are several career tracks for psychologist-professors.

Despite the different types of institutions, all academic careers share certain features. As you consider a career as a professor, recognize that there is more to the professorate than lecturing in front of a classroom. Before a professor steps into the classroom, a great deal of time and effort has gone into preparation. Each lecture requires background reading of chapters and journal articles in addition to the text, note taking, and preparation of overheads, activities, and discussion questions. This work is never complete, because even experienced professors must update their notes to remain current with the ever-changing field. Professors who teach three, four, or even five courses per semester may find that preparation takes all of their time, especially in the early years of a career (Roediger, 2006). A professor's teaching activities extend beyond the classroom to include grading, writing letters of recommendation for students, meeting with students to answer questions and discuss course content and professional issues, and advising students on career choices.

In addition to teaching, professorial careers entail many roles, usually including research and service to the campus and community (such as advising, committee work, or administrative work). During a typical week, professors often divide their time among multiple research tasks, including writing an article or book, conducting statistical analyses, planning research, writing grant proposals, searching the literature, reading research articles, meeting with student research assistants, advising students on their research, and preparing or giving talks at professional meetings. Professors also must spend time on service to the university and community. They participate in faculty meetings as well as some of the many committees that administer and run the university. Some faculty engage in consulting work, or serve as consultants and advisors for community agencies.

Many students seek a graduate degree in order to teach in a college or university setting. With a masters degree, it is possible to become a community college professor. However, faculty positions at community colleges have become more competitive in recent years; many are held by psychologists with doctoral degrees (Lloyd, 2000; Peters, 1992). Similarly, although masters degree holders may be hired to teach at four-year colleges on a part-time basis, they are unlikely to be hired for full-time positions. If your goal is to teach at the college level, it's in your best interest to pursue a doctoral degree that will provide you with the most opportunities for employment, mobility, and advancement as a faculty member (Lloyd, 2000; Roediger, 2006). Graduates with doctoral degrees may teach undergraduate, masters, and doctoral students in a variety of educational settings, including universities, professional schools, and medical schools.

An additional aspect of training that may not be covered in graduate school, but is necessary for success as a professor, and often for winning a faculty position in the first place, is training in pedagogy (Kuther, 2002). Pedagogy refers to the art of teaching. Successful professors master the techniques of their trade and learn how to compose lectures; lead discussions; create syllabi; enhance student learning through effective use of the blackboard, overheads, or PowerPoint presentations; and model best practices for interacting with students and handling disagreements. We hope you have experienced a professor who made the course material "come to life" and whose class you looked forward to attending. Such skill comes with work and effort; good teachers are made, not born.

If you're interested in becoming a professor, seek a graduate program that helps to prepare students for the teaching aspects of the professorate. Many graduate programs present seminars or courses in how to teach. The Preparing Future Faculty program, a program designed to prepare aspiring academics for the variety of teaching, research, and service roles entailed in the professorate, has also created a wealth of resources and a Web site available at http://www.preparing-faculty.org. Seek practical experience as a teaching assistant or adjunct professor at your university or a nearby college. You can also volunteer to teach a class or two for your primary instructors or for instructors teaching courses in your area of interest. Most important, find a mentor in graduate school who can help you with these essential aspects of training.

There are many advantages to the professorate, but perhaps the greatest advantages are academic freedom and the autonomy and flexibility of academic life. Academic freedom means that professors are intellectually free; they may conduct whatever research interests them and may "teach the truth as they see it" (Vesilind, 2000, p. 10). In other words, professors decide on the best methods to teach their courses. Texts, reading assignments, grading, and evaluation procedures are often up to the professor. Aside from class time, professors' schedules tend to be flexible. Most develop work habits that fit their lives, allowing time to pick up children from school, spend time with their families, and complete preparation and writing in the late evenings or early mornings. Another advantage is tenure, a permanent job contract, typically offered after a probationary period of six or seven years. Tenure provides complete academic freedom because it prevents professors from being fired for airing unpopular views or pursuing controversial research. Professors with documented teaching histories, excellent student evaluations, publications, campus committee work, and outreach to the community earn tenure and its associated job security. The professorate also offers intangible benefits, such as the excitement of discovery and innovation, as well as the rewards of imparting knowledge and introducing students to a life of the mind (Roediger, 2006; Vesilind, 2000).

The disadvantages of the academic life are related to the scarcity of academic positions. The academic job market is very competitive; there aren't a lot of positions available. Some applicants spend several years on the job market, working in postdoctoral research, in one-year instructor appointments, or in adjunct positions (teaching part-time, often at several colleges at once). Applicants must be prepared to seek faculty positions in a variety of geographic locations; applicants cannot limit themselves to searching in only one place. Applicants also cannot afford to limit themselves to positions in psychology departments, but must consider academic positions in other departments, medical schools, and business schools. Once a position is obtained, new professors juggle many demands. In addition to teaching loads and service responsibilities, most new faculty are expected to begin a research program, because research has increased in importance as well—even for those in "teaching" colleges (Salzinger, 1995). Faculty in research universities experience pressure to win large competitive research grants and publish in the best journals. Finally, as shown in Table 13.1, professors' salaries allow them to live comfortably, but certainly will not make them rich.

TABLE 13.1 | MEAN SALARIES FOR PROFESSORS (ADAPTED FROM AMERICAN ASSOCIATION OF UNIVERSITY PROFESSORS, 2008)

Institution and Position	Average Salary
Doctoral institutions	
Professor	$118,444
Associate Professor	$80,043
Assistant Professor	$68,112
Comprehensive Institutions (masters level)	
Professor	$87,272
Associate Professor	$68,637
Assistant Professor	$57,549
Baccalaureate Institutions	
Professor	$83,560
Associate Professor	$64,277
Assistant Professor	$53,351
2-Year institutions	
Professor	$71,779
Associate Professor	$58,492
Assistant Professor	$51,183

RESEARCH IN AND OUT OF THE IVORY TOWER

A graduate degree in psychology offers many opportunities for careers in research. Research psychologists conduct basic and applied studies of human and animal behavior. They conduct their research in universities, government agencies, private organizations, and businesses and corporations. Some psychologists conduct their research in military settings, while others work in research and development departments at pharmaceutical companies and businesses. Let's take a look at the variety of settings in which psychologists conduct research.

ACADEMIA

Many psychologists work in university settings as research scientists, conducting basic and applied research. For example, a research scientist might study how neurotransmitters affect learning in rats. Another research psychologist might design a research program to examine smoking cessation. Her basic research might explore the environmental factors that help or hinder quitting smoking. She might conduct applied research as well, developing and evaluating school-based programs to prevent smoking in children. Medical schools are emerging as an important employment setting for research psychologists, who work on multidisciplinary teams addressing health problems in people of all ages. Interdisciplinary study and the merging of scientific fields such as anatomy, biochemistry, physiology, pharmacology, and microbiology are leading to more research opportunities for psychologists outside of psychology departments (Balster, 1995).

A research career in academia offers a flexible schedule and is prestigious. Research scientists gain independence and autonomy as they progress in their careers.

By writing and winning research grants, research scientists are able to fund and study problems of their choosing. With advancement, research scientists take on supervisory roles, run their own labs, and train graduate and postdoctoral students. There are also opportunities for travel and contact with the public through speaking at conferences, consulting, and writing for the popular press (Bartholomew, 2001a). A disadvantage of a research career in academia is the competition. Generally, academic positions that don't require teaching can be difficult to obtain. Applicants may need to be geographically mobile and able to relocate for available positions.

Research and professorial careers in academia entail long hours, especially in institutions that maintain the "publish or perish" mantra. Publish or perish means just that: publish many articles in prestigious journals, or lose your job! As you might imagine, psychologists in research and professorial positions can experience a great deal of stress. Publishing is a tenuous and lengthy process; therefore, professors, particularly new professors, may spend many evenings in the lab or at the computer completing or writing research results for publication. Once completed, however, the sense of accomplishment, contribution to the field, and seeing one's name in print are primary benefits of this research track.

INDUSTRY

Some psychologists conduct research in business and industry. Psychologists in business might conduct surveys of consumer opinion, for example. Others who work for pharmaceutical companies might test the effectiveness of drugs or work as statisticians, analyzing the data from a variety of research projects. Psychologists in industry design and test products for human use. For example, a psychologist might design a car's dashboard to allow drivers the ability to easily and reach the displays and knobs while viewing the road. Or a psychologist might design a computer monitor to reduce glare and eyestrain.

A career in industry is different from academia because in industry the focus is on promoting the success of the company. The goal is to create products that benefit the company, employees, and shareholders (Bartholomew, 2001b). Research takes place at a faster pace in industry than in academia because information must be gathered quickly to help create and sell products. Teams conduct the research, enabling greater productivity. In addition, psychologists in business and industry settings tend to have access to more funding than do those in academia, meaning that they tend to work with newer and more sophisticated equipment. The primary drawback of conducting research in business and industry is that your research questions are assigned based on the needs of the company, not necessarily on your interests. An important benefit of working in industry is the contact with people of diverse fields and educational backgrounds. Other benefits are the high salaries and regular work schedule; in business and industry, your weekends generally are your own.

GOVERNMENT

Although research psychologists engage in similar activities regardless of work setting, whether universities, industry, or government, the three settings differ in terms of the autonomy afforded researchers. As with researchers in industry, those employed by the government and military usually examine research questions not conceived by them (Bornstein, 2006; Herrman, 1997). Instead, researchers in government examine questions that are created by politicians and policy makers, designed to promote the security and well being of the American people. As Copper (1997) points out, "The critical aspect of working in a public-policy environment is that many people can be directly affected by decisions over a very long period of time. Therefore, the research questions and hypotheses are often more complex, sensitive, and require much broader data collection efforts and greater coordination with staff from federal branch agencies and the private sector."

An advantage of a research career in government is that you'll be exposed to many different projects. Unlike academia, where researchers spend a career focused on a particular research problem or area, research psychologists in government work on a diverse range of projects and become generalists. Most research projects initiated by the government are short in duration (about one year to complete) because the research is intended to help resolve practical problems. Also, shifts in public opinion and interest lead political leaders to eliminate some projects and initiate new ones; whether this is an advantage or disadvantage perhaps depends on your interest in the project. If you're interested in a research career in government, be prepared to engage in lots of supervisory work because contractors conduct much of the hands-on work under supervision by government researchers. This enables government researchers to work on multiple projects at once and not become overly involved in any one project. Like industry, government research involves working on a team, because the research topics that the government is interested in are applied in nature, requiring creativity and planning by an interdisciplinary team of researchers consisting of psychologists, sociologists, statisticians, computer scientists, economists, and others.

SOCIAL SERVICE AGENCIES AND NONPROFITS

Research psychologists employed at social service or nonprofit agencies conduct research to assess and improve the agency's programs and often write grants to help fund the agency. Social service and nonprofit agencies often are contracted by the government to conduct policy analyses, literature reviews, and research to improve decision making by political leaders and consumers. A psychologist at such an agency might examine the effectiveness of new drug-control interventions like mandatory minimum sanctions, residential and group home treatments for youthful offenders identified as drug users, and school-based prevention programs.

The primary benefit of working in a nonprofit or social service agency is that your time is focused on research that may lead to social change rather than teaching or academic curriculum meetings. Such agencies tend to conduct interdisciplinary research, enabling research psychologists to work with a diverse range of specialists from other fields. Though the salaries at nonprofit and social service agencies tend to be lower than in other research settings, the research often directly benefits consumers and families.

Bachelor's degree holders may obtain research assistant positions in any of these research environments discussed. Opportunities for advancement, however, come with graduate degrees. Many research positions are available to masters degree holders, especially in industry, government, and nonprofit and social service

TABLE 13.2 | MEDIAN SALARIES FOR DOCTORAL PSYCHOLOGISTS WITH 2 TO 4 YEARS OF EXPERIENCE IN RESEARCH SETTINGS (ADAPTED FROM APA, 2007; PATE, FRINCKE, & KOHOUT, 2005)

	Median Salary
University Psychology Department	$68,000
Medical School Psychiatry Department	$50,000
Medical School (not Psychiatry)	$78,500*
Private Research Organization	$85,000
Government Research Organization	$77,000
Nonprofit Organization	$76,000*
University Research Center	$59,000
Consulting/Industry	$76,500**

*Psychologists with 5–9 years experience.
**2003 data.

agencies. In academic settings, the doctoral degree offers the most flexibility, opportunities for advancement, and opportunities to serve as the primary investigator of federal grants (Lloyd, 2000). Research psychologists in academia often obtain two to three years of postdoctoral training after obtaining the doctoral degree. To be competitive for research positions within academic and nonacademic settings, hone your skills in research methods and statistics (Copper, 1997). As shown in Table 13.2, salaries for research positions vary by setting.

THE MILITARY

The military offers a range of opportunities for psychologists in all disciplines. Psychologists work in the military as enlisted military personnel and as civilian consultants. They practice and conduct research in a variety of areas, including personnel selection and classification, training, human factors, leadership and team effectiveness, as well as clinical settings (Dunivin & Ingram, 2006; Wisckoff, 1997).

PSYCHOLOGISTS IN THE MILITARY

Some military psychologists engage in personnel selection and classification. They screen, select, and place recruits, and select personnel for jobs requiring special skills such as piloting aircraft, air traffic control, and special operations personnel. They create procedures for evaluating the performance of enlisted and officer personnel, and conduct research on how to use simulators to evaluate special abilities. Psychologists in the military also train personnel. They conduct research examining the most effective techniques of training personnel in basic skills, military skills, and technical skills, as well as increasing operational readiness. They conduct research on how to design effective instructional systems, measure training performance, and best use computer-simulated scenarios and technology such as virtual reality.

Other psychologists in the military work in human factors and engineering to design the human-machine interfaces that improve the functioning of military systems and equipment. For example, how can artificial intelligence and the use of sophisticated computer systems enhance human decision making? Psychologists study how to help military personnel operate most efficiently, maintain health, enhance performance, and reduce human error under adverse circumstances, such as sleep deprivation, in extreme environmental conditions, and hazardous conditions.

Some psychologists study team effectiveness and ways to improve communication in multinational forces. Psychologists study how to promote effective leadership, as well as how to select, train, and evaluate leaders. Some psychologists might get involved in political-psychological issues such as the study of the behavior of world leaders. Others examine team processes such as structure, communication, subordinate-supervisor relations, team cohesion, the functioning of small groups, and tactical decision making.

Clinical and counseling psychologists in the military often work in counseling or mental health clinics providing mental health services and counseling to improve the lives of military personnel and their families. They focus on how to help personnel acclimate to military life, deal with stress, and cope with serious psychological reactions in the aftermath of combat. Counseling and clinical psychologists serve in a wide variety of settings, such as military hospitals, outpatient clinics, mental health centers, daycare centers, military prisons, and onboard ships.

ADVANTAGES, DISADVANTAGES, AND SALARY

Psychologists in the military often spend significant amounts of time overseas, which, depending on your inclination and family situation, may be an advantage or disadvantage. Clinical and counseling psychologists go wherever there are concentrations of troops, in peacetime and war, and to hostile environments. A uniformed psychologist can count on a change of geographical location every two to three years (Wiskoff, 1997). Thus, in spite of potential familial conflicts, military psychologists' opportunities to see the world are unmatched by nonmilitary psychology positions.

A significant limitation for practicing psychologists is the absence of the traditional confidential therapeutic relationship. Members of the military who seek or are referred for mental health services do not have the same rights and privileges to confidentiality that nonmilitary clients enjoy. Rather, higher-ranking personnel may and do request information regarding the functioning of a military client, and psychologists must become comfortable with the military process and the limits and professional dilemmas this presents. Furthermore, research psychologists will experience many of the same limitations as their colleagues in government and industry, because their research is directed by practical problems and questions rather than by their own intellectual curiosity.

A final potential limitation for psychologists in the military is the issue of enlistment. Some psychologists work as civilians in military environments; others enlist and "join the ranks." Once you have enlisted, working for the military is no longer optional; rather, you become an officer and must serve for the duration of your commitment. Psychologists in academia, business and industry, or other branches of the government have the option of leaving their jobs if they decide they no longer want to do them, but enlisted military psychologists do not have this option. Thus, it is important to consider your own level of satisfaction and comfort with the military lifestyle, because once you are sworn in as an officer, you cannot change your mind and simply go do something else. Other important benefits of military service include job security, opportunities for additional education, and an excellent benefits and retirement system. Few professional positions offer the opportunity to retire after as few as twenty years of service, and to do so with a pension. The salary scale for military psychologists is aligned with the government pay scales (Wiskoff, 1997). In 2001, government starting salary for masters-level psychologists was $33,300; starting salary for doctoral-level psychologists was $40,200 (Bureau of Labor Statistics, 2002). In addition to base pay, all military receive subsistence and housing allowances, which are not taxable, which substantially increases income.

PUBLISHING AND WRITING

Publishing and the media offer new career opportunities for students of psychology. Some psychologists pursue careers in publishing as acquisitions editors and developmental editors. Others become science writers for print, Internet, radio, and television.

BOOK PUBLISHING

Publishing generally is an apprenticeship field, so most successful editors begin in entry-level positions and work their way up. Many begin as assistants to acquisitions editors (we'll talk more about acquisitions editors in a moment) or sales representatives who ensure that every customer (for example, professor or bookstore) is informed of the publisher's book offerings. Sales representatives are often on the road, traveling to their customers, sales conferences, and professional conferences, where they market books. With time, some sales representatives gain the experience and contacts to become acquisitions editors.

An *acquisitions editor* is responsible for acquiring books for a publishing company. The job entails a variety of tasks, including reading book proposals, making decisions about the financial viability of proposals and whether to offer book contracts to authors, ensuring the quality of proposals and completed manuscripts by getting reviews from specialists in the field, interpreting reviews, approaching potential authors with book ideas, attending conferences to meet potential authors and reviewers, and discussing works-in-progress with authors. The acquisitions editor often oversees all stages of the publication process, including contract negotiation, promotional planning, manuscript delivery, and financial planning. The position is appropriate for individuals who like the messiness of problem solving in the real world and have broad interests, because acquisitions editors often oversee manuscripts in multiple sub-fields, not just the ones in which they have extensive training (Ansel, 1996).

With a graduate degree in psychology and writing experience, you might consider a position as a *developmental editor*. A developmental editor handles the day-to-day work of coordinating and editing manuscripts for large publishing projects such as psychology textbooks. The developmental editor is involved in all aspects of developing a textbook, beginning with the early stages of conceptual and structural planning before the author writes. Developmental editors often nurture authors through the writing process and coordinate the artwork, writing style, and preparation of supplements or ancillaries (large textbooks may include instructor's manuals, student study guides, test banks, Web sites, and more; Hart, 1996).

Positions in publishing offer opportunities for psychology degree holders at all levels who have interests in writing and the ability to think critically and problem solve effectively. Bachelor's degree holders usually begin in entry-level positions such as editorial assistants or sales representatives, whereas applicants with graduate degrees and editorial skill may be hired to mid-level editorial positions. More advanced positions in publishing come with extensive experience. Individuals who seek careers in publishing must be able to juggle multiple tasks, meet budgets, and cope with the pressure of deadlines.

WRITING

Scientific writing careers come in many shapes and forms. Some science writers engage in technical writing. Others work in public relations and traditional or new media venues. A *technical writer* translates large amounts of information into useful and easily digested forms for specialized readers. Technical writers create user guides, repair manuals, online help files, and reference manuals for new products, computer software, hardware, and toys (Randall, 2006). Technical writers must be able to explain complex phenomena for general readers. Other science writing positions are found in public relations or public information. Universities, medical centers, hospitals, and other institutions where research is conducted have staffs of reporters who keep track of research findings and events at the institution (Goetnick Ambrose, 2006). *Public information officers* write press releases to distribute to the media. They also contribute to institutional publications and alumni magazines, monitor news and media trends to determine which institutional staff might have something notable to contribute, and act as liaisons between journalists and the institution's staff. Some writers work in research or human services settings as grant writers, assembling the pieces of a grant proposal prepared by a group of researchers and checking for style, accuracy, formatting, grammar, and spelling.

Science writers and journalists also write as staff members and freelancers for newspapers, magazines, Internet, radio, and television. They learn about scientific findings and translate them accurately into a form that will interest the general reader. By teasing out details and anecdotes, they write to draw casual readers, listeners, or viewers into topics that they ordinarily might not care much about. Science writing requires omnivorous reading of newspapers, books, reports, journals, and Internet news groups to look for story ideas. Writers attend scientific conventions, interview scientists, and regularly check in with laboratories, factories, hospitals, universities, and government agencies for breaking news and interesting stories.

Science writing offers an opportunity to write about science without becoming immersed in the lab, focusing on one minute area of research, or being confined to the stilted and formal academic style of writing. It offers a chance to be in the real world, explore a variety of topics, interview great thinkers, share psychological findings with the rest of the world, and see your writing in print quickly

TABLE 13.3	MEDIAN SALARIES FOR CAREERS IN WRITING AND PUBLISHING (ADAPTED FROM ABBOTT, LANGER, AND ASSOCIATES, 2006, SALARY.COM, 2008).

	Median Salary
Grants/proposal writer	$51,363
Technical writer	$65,626
Web writer	$61,882
Acquisitions editor	$70,377
Developmental editor	$50,000
Marketing specialist	$43,125
Reporter/correspondent	$26,506
Speech writer	$60,745

(Augenbraun & Vergoth, 1998; Carpenter, 2002). Individuals with broad scientific interests who love learning, are fluent writers, and like challenges, are well suited to careers in science writing. However, science writing is a highly competitive field. Writers must be able to juggle multiple stories at once, meet deadlines, and deal well with criticism (no thin skins allowed!). Freelancers must be prepared to pay for their own benefits, save for retirement, and weather ups and downs in work.

If you're interested in a science-writing career, seek opportunities to publish in nonscientific publications. Write for the university newspaper, local organizations, or any other sources to earn writing clips. Clips, or clippings of your published articles, are your ticket to a writing career. Understand that science writing is very different from the academic writing that you learned in college or graduate school. Aspiring science writers should seek training opportunities such as media fellowships, internships (often unpaid), and science journalism programs to gain excellent training, sources of networking contacts, and clips (Randall, 2006). Table 13.3 illustrates salaries for careers in writing and publishing.

A graduate degree in psychology opens doors to a variety of careers for individuals with diverse interests ranging from therapy to research, teaching to publishing, and more. Remember that the advice in this chapter is offered as a first step. Seek assistance from your advisor and the career center at your university to help you learn more so that you can choose career goals that match your interests and aspirations.

SUGGESTED READINGS

Bly, R. W. (2003). *Careers for writers and others who have a way with words.* New York: McGraw Hill. Education.

Hancock, E. (2003). *Ideas into words: Mastering the craft of science writing.* Baltimore.

Hayes, W. (2003). *So you want to be a college professor?* Lanham, MD: Scarecrow Education.

Robbins-Roth, C. (2006). *Alternative careers in science: Leaving the ivory tower* (second edition). San Diego, CA: Academic Press.

Sternberg, R. J. (2006). *Career paths in psychology: Where your degree can take you (second edition)*. Washington, D.C.: American Psychological Association.

U.S. Department of Defense. (2003). *America's top military careers: Official guide to occupations in the armed forces*. Indianapolis, IN: Jist Publishing.

Vesilind, P. A. (2000). *So you want to be a professor? A handbook for graduate students*. Thousand Oaks, CA: Sage.

Yager, F. & Yager, J. (2005). *Career opportunities in the publishing industry*. New York: Facts on File.

WEB RESOURCES

Career Path Less Traveled
http://www.apa.org/monitor/feb01/careerpath.html

Society for the Teaching of Psychology
http://teachpsych.org/

Office of Teaching Resources in Psychology
http://teachpsych.org/otrp/index.php

Preparing Future Faculty
http://www.preparing-faculty.org/

Military Career Guide Online
http://www.todaysmilitary.com/careers

About the U.S. Military
http://usmilitary.about.com/

So You Want to Be an Editor
http://www.editors.ca/join_eac/be_an_editor/so.html

A Guide to Careers in Science Writing
http://casw.org/booklet.htm

Career Development Center for Postdocs and Junior Faculty
http://nextwave.sciencemag.org/career_development

Science, Math, and Engineering Career Resources
http://www.phds.org/

So You Want to Be a Science Writer?
http://www.absw.org.uk/So_you_want_to_be_a_science_writer.htm

Advice for Beginning Science Writers
http://www.nasw.org/resource/beginning/archives/000145.htm

How Do I Become a Science Journalist?
http://www.scidev.net/en/practical-guides/how-do-i-become-a-science-journalist-.html

CHECKLIST: IS AN ADVANCED CAREER IN PSYCHOLOGY FOR YOU?

Do you:

☐ Want to teach college?
☐ Think you would enjoy a career interacting with students?
☐ Like to challenge others to think?

- ☐ Think broadly and have a unique ability to apply psychology to many different fields?
- ☐ Have an interest in applying psychology to a non-psychology career?
- ☐ Like to write?
- ☐ Think quickly on your feet?
- ☐ Enjoy giving presentations and speeches?
- ☐ Enjoy research?
- ☐ Think analytically?
- ☐ Want to work for an agency or the government?
- ☐ Want to have a career with flexible hours?
- ☐ Want to attend graduate school?

Scoring: The more boxes you checked, the more likely it is a graduate-level career in psychology is for you.

CHAPTER 14

GETTING INTO GRADUATE SCHOOL IN PSYCHOLOGY

CHAPTER GUIDE

Throughout this book, we have discussed some of the job opportunities available to bachelor's degree holders in psychology. If you're like most psychology students, the possibility of attending graduate school has probably crossed your mind.

Most students, however, enter the workforce after graduating college. Whereas each year about 88,000 students graduate with a bachelor's degree in psychology, about 15,000 (17 percent) enroll in psychology doctoral programs (National Center for Education Statistics, 2008; Pate, 2001). A graduate degree in psychology opens up new opportunities for students—we have discussed some of the opportunities in this book. Why do some students seek jobs after graduation and others enter graduate school? Is graduate study right for you and your goals? The following section will help you answer these questions.

IS GRADUATE SCHOOL FOR YOU?

Is graduate school really necessary to get a good job? If you want a job that permits you to help people, use your research skills, or apply your understanding of psychology—no, you don't need to go to graduate school. So why do students attend graduate school?

The primary reason students *should* attend graduate school is to fulfill a thirst for knowledge about human behavior. Successful graduate students have a love of learning and thrive on discovery. Graduate study provides a unique opportunity to discover and to apply knowledge of the causes and correlates of human behavior. Many students pursue graduate study in order to contribute to society, help others in need, and improve the quality of life for others.

Students also pursue graduate study in order to qualify for a career that requires specialized study, such as teaching in colleges, universities, or medical schools, conducting research in academia, industry, or business, practicing psychology in applied settings, and engaging in a variety of consulting and applied roles. What kind of career do you want? Is it really necessary for you to go to grad school to achieve your goals? Are there alternative ways of achieving them? As we have discussed throughout this book, if your main goal is to work with people, there are many alternatives to a doctoral degree in psychology.

Is graduate school for you? If so, why? Why do you want to go to graduate school? Is it for the right reasons? Some of the reasons that students pursue graduate degrees include intellectual curiosity, career advancement, a desire to help others, and simply the prestige associated with a doctoral degree. What are your reasons? What degree will help you obtain your goals? A doctoral degree often is not the answer. Discuss your decision—your reasons for graduate study and your career goals—with your advisor, other faculty, family, and friends. Be honest about your goals and what it truly takes to meet them. Choose the level of education, whether masters or doctoral degree, that offers the training and coursework to prepare you for the career to which you aspire. Why focus on whether graduate school is the right thing for you?

Questioning your intentions is important because you're making a decision that you will live with for the next two to seven years, or longer. Graduate school is a full-time commitment and a long-term investment. It is not college. Grad students frequently spend 50 to 60 hours each week on studies and research. Graduate school can also be very expensive, with student loan debt rising to alarming levels. In 2003, doctoral graduates reported a median of $50,000 in debt, with Psy.D. degree holders reporting a mean debt level of $90,000, clinical Ph.D. degree holders a median debt of $55,000, and Ph.D. degree holders in the research fields a median debt of $21,500 (Wicherski & Kohout, 2005). Thus, the decision to attend graduate school should be carefully considered and discussed with significant others in your life. Then, if you still plan to attend graduate school, be prepared for a lot of work, but also intellectual development as you observe prominent psychologists and are exposed to a world of information and research activity.

SORTING OUT THE LETTERS: MA, PH.D., AND PSY.D.

What degree is right for you? Lots of misinformation circulates about graduate study and the various graduate degrees. In this section, we briefly explore the different types of graduate degrees that a psychology student may pursue.

MASTERS DEGREE

A masters degree typically requires two years of full-time study. There are many different types of masters degrees—the most common are the MA (master of arts) and MS (master of science). Masters degrees in service-oriented fields such as clinical, counseling, and school psychology usually include additional practical experience in an applied setting. Most masters degree programs require a masters thesis based on a research project; however, some programs offer alternatives to the research thesis in the form of qualifying examinations, or a written project. What's the difference between an MA and an MS? The letters MA and MS seldom indicate any great difference in program curricula. Whether a university offers the MA or MS degree depends on the policies of the university, not the characteristics of the program. Many students are unaware that the MA and MS degree are interchangeable and become needlessly concerned that the one set of letters (MA or MS) is better or worse than the other. (This also holds true at the undergraduate level; BA and BS degrees are usually indistinguishable in terms of content.)

Myths abound about the masters degree, as students and advisors often know little about masters degrees in psychology and related fields (Actkinson, 2000). Despite possible biases against, and lack of discussion about, the masters degree in psychology, it is a very popular degree. More students enter masters programs than doctoral programs (Briihl & Wasieleski, 2004). Between 1973 and 1993 the number of masters programs quadrupled (Norcross, Hanych, & Terranova, 1996) and has since continued to increase. About 20,000 students receive masters degrees in psychology each year (National Center for Education Statistics, 2008). Some argue that a form of licensure should be extended to masters-level graduates (Hays-Thomas, 2000). Studies have been inconclusive regarding level of practitioner training and therapeutic outcomes, and economic changes have led to the hiring of more masters-level practitioners (Seligman, 1995; Stein & Lambert, 1995). At least 25 states license masters degree holders to practice psychology, either independently or under continuing supervision (Levant et al., 2001; North American Association of Masters in Psychology, 2004).

What can you do with a masters degree? Depending on the program and curriculum, a masters degree enables graduates to: 1) teach psychology in high school (other certification may be needed) and junior colleges; 2) become more competitive for jobs in government and industry; 3) practice clinical, counseling, or school psychology under supervision; 4) obtain certification or licensure for school psychology (depending on state) and 5) pursue alternative careers in counseling, such as marriage and family therapy, alcohol and substance abuse counseling, or social work. If you're considering a masters in clinical or counseling psychology with the intention of setting up an independent practice, carefully research your options beforehand because requirements for licensure as counselors or marriage and family therapists vary by state (Levant et al., 2001; North American Association of Masters in Psychology, 2004). Be sure to do your homework so that you get the experiences that you need for your chosen field and so that you're not disappointed later.

Masters degree recipients in research-oriented fields such as quantitative psychology, developmental psychology, general psychology, and experimental psychology develop methodological and quantitative skills as well as content knowledge that aids their employment in research positions in university research centers, government, business, and private organizations. Others seek entry into doctoral programs.

Some masters degree programs serve as springboards to doctoral programs. These programs may be slightly more rigorous because they prepare students to continue pursuing their education at the doctoral level. If you plan to obtain a doctoral degree, but some of your credentials may prohibit your acceptance to your desired doctoral programs, two years at a reputable and rigorous (meaning, requires the completion of a research thesis) masters degree program may elevate your credentials to allow you to succeed in your doctoral application. In fact, many students may not be serious about psychology until their junior or senior years of college and may not have the GPA or research experience desired by doctoral programs. One of the authors of this book experienced this dilemma and this route allowed him entry to doctoral study.

DOCTORAL DEGREES

Although a masters degree may allow you to work in some settings, if you're planning on conducting research or teaching at the college level, a doctoral degree is essential. A doctoral degree provides a greater range of flexibility and autonomy, but usually requires five to seven years of graduate work to complete. In clinical or counseling psychology, the requirement for the doctoral degree generally includes a one-year internship or supervised experience.

Two different types of doctoral degrees are offered within psychology: the Ph.D. and the Psy.D. The Ph.D. refers to the doctor of philosophy. The Ph.D. is a research degree that culminates in a dissertation based on original research. The Ph.D. in clinical or counseling psychology is a flexible degree; it trains people for research, teaching, writing, and clinical practice. The Psy.D. refers to the doctor of psychology. It is offered only in clinical and counseling psychology and is considered a professional degree, much like a JD (a lawyer's degree).

How is the Psy.D. different from the Ph.D.? Both are doctoral degrees and both will allow you to practice psychology. They differ in their emphases. The Ph.D., or doctor of philosophy, has a long historical tradition. Most of your college professors hold this degree as it is conferred in nearly all academic fields. The Ph.D. provides training in research and methodology as well as the content of a psychological specialty area. Ph.D. recipients may find employment at universities, medical centers, mental health centers, and in industry and government.

The Psy.D. is a practitioner-oriented degree that emphasizes clinical training or the professional model of training; it is sought by those who want to practice. The Psy.D. degree often is offered at private or professional schools, is generally more expensive than a Ph.D., and is offered in larger programs than traditional scientist-practitioner Ph.D. programs (Norcross, Castle, Sayette, & Mayne, 2004). Most funding for Ph.D. students comes from faculty research grants; there is typically less research conducted in Psy.D. programs, so there are fewer opportunities for research assistantships and other funding to support your graduate education. Professional programs train students to be educated consumers of research rather than generators of research. Because there is less emphasis on research, Psy.D. students tend to earn their degrees a little more quickly than do Ph.D. students (Gaddy, Charlot-Swilley, Nelson, & Reich, 1995; Norcross et al., 2004; Norcross & Castle, 2002).

Practice-oriented students often find the curricula of professional programs to be better aligned with their own interests and career aspirations than those of traditional scientist-practitioner programs. Although some have argued that the Ph.D. is more prestigious than the Psy.D. (Buskist & Sherburne, 1996), you should choose the degree that will prepare you for the career you desire. If you're interested in practicing psychology and do not want to teach in a university setting or conduct research, the Psy.D. may be for you. The only area where graduates from professional schools are at a professional disadvantage is if they apply for positions in research or academic settings. Carefully consider your career objectives to ensure that you obtain the required preparation. For more information about Psy.D. and Ph.D. training opportunities, see Chapter 3.

APPLYING TO GRADUATE SCHOOL

Applying to graduate school is a lengthy and often complicated process. Like most life tasks, it begins with preparation. If you think that graduate school *might* be in your future—even if you're not entirely sure—prepare. Take a conservative approach and obtain the required experiences to ensure that you don't prematurely close doors. The content of your graduate school admissions application takes years to create, so begin early, even while you are still considering whether to apply to graduate school.

What should you do to prepare for graduate school? Consider what graduate admissions committees seek in applicants. Surveys of faculty members who participate in selecting graduate students have found the following to be *very important* criteria in evaluating applicants (Landrum & Clark, 2005; Bonifazi, Crespi, & Rieker, 1997; Keith-Spiegel, Tabachnick, & Spiegel, 1994; Landrum & Clark, 2005):

- The match between the applicant's interests and skills and the program's goals
- Research experience
- Conference presentations and publications
- Whether a member(s) of the selection committee is interested in working with a particular applicant
- The clarity, focus, and content of the applicant's admission essays

The overall fit or match between the student, program, and faculty, as revealed in the admissions essay and in prior research, is paramount. Surveys of faculty have classified the following criteria as *generally important* in selecting applicants (Landrum & Clark, 2005; Bonifazi et al., 1997; Keith-Spiegel et al., 1994):

- Experience as research assistant
- Writing skills
- Knowledge about, and interest in, the program
- Number of statistics, research methodology, and hard science courses taken
- Prestige and status of faculty in undergraduate department, especially of those who are writing letters of recommendation
- Potential for success as judged by interview
- Honors and merit scholarships

Generally speaking, graduate programs look for interest in the program, research experience, and a background in statistics, methodology, and science. Research experience and a broad base of coursework takes years to compile. Begin early. If you ultimately decide that graduate school is not for you, you'll be well-educated and have marketable skills.

THE APPLICATION

The most obvious part of the application is the application form itself. This form asks for your demographic information: your name, address, and so on. Most schools have online application forms and submission procedures. If you prepare your application by hand and "snail-mail" it, remember that neatness counts, so make copies of each application before you begin. You might also scan your applications into the computer so that you can prepare professional-looking forms. If you don't have a scanner at home, plan on spending time in the computer lab at school.

GRE GENERAL TEST

The Graduate Record Exam (GRE) General Test is a standardized test that measures a variety of skills that are thought to predict success in graduate school. The GRE General Test yields three scores: verbal ability, quantitative ability, and analytical writing ability. The verbal section tests your ability to understand and analyze written material through the use of analogies, antonyms, sentence completions, and reading comprehension questions. The quantitative section tests basic math skills and your ability to understand and apply quantitative skills to solve problems. Types of questions include quantitative comparisons, problem solving, and data interpretation. The analytical writing section examines your ability to compose and defend a cohesive argument. The analytical writing section consists of two tasks: "Present Your Perspective on an Issue," in which you address an issue from your perspective, and "Analyze an Argument," in which you critique an argument and discuss how well-reasoned you find it.

Graduate schools consider the verbal and quantitative sections to be particularly important in making decisions about applicants. Therefore, the total GRE score usually refers to the quantitative and verbal scores (with each ranging from 200 to 800) summed to a total of 1,600 possible points. The GRE General Test is administered by computer year-round, but plan to take it in the spring or summer before you apply to grad school. This is particularly important should you not perform as well as you expected or would like, as it allows time for a retake.

GRE PSYCHOLOGY TEST

About one half of doctoral programs require that applicants take the Graduate Record Exam Psychology Test (Matlin & Kalat, 2001). The GRE Psychology Test consists of about 215 questions that tap information from the core psychology courses required in most undergraduate programs. About 40 percent of the test consists of experimental and natural science questions from the areas of learning, language, memory, thinking, perception, ethology, sensation, comparative psychology, and physiological psychology. Social and social science areas of psychology account for an additional 43 percent of the test, including clinical, abnormal, developmental, personality, and social psychology. The remaining 17 percent consists of history, industrial/organizational and applied psychology, measurement, research methodology, and statistics (Matlin & Kalat, 2001). Unlike the General Test, the GRE Psychology Test is administered only three times a year: in April, November, and December.

ADMISSIONS ESSAYS AND PERSONAL STATEMENTS

The personal statement or admissions essay is your chance to communicate directly with the admissions committee. Here you can present yourself as an individual, the person behind the GPA and GRE scores. Your essays will tell the admissions committee about your ability to write, to stick to the task at hand, and to persuade readers. It's the place where you can make yourself stand out because you have the opportunity to talk about your interests, career aspirations, and values. Usually, programs provide a question or a specific topic on which to write. Most questions posed by graduate programs fall into one of several categories, as identified by Keith-Spiegel and Wiederman (2000):

- **Career plans.** What are your long-term career goals? Where do you see yourself 10 years from now?
- **General interest areas.** What academic or professional areas interest you?
- **Research experiences.** Discuss areas in which you might like to do research, research experiences you have had, or both. Describe your research interests.
- **Academic objectives.** Why are you undertaking graduate study? Describe how graduate training is necessary for your goals.
- **Clinical or other field experience.** Describe your clinical experience. How have your field experiences shaped your career goals?
- **Academic background and achievements.** Discuss your academic background.
- **Personal.** Is there anything in your background that you think would be relevant in our evaluation of applicants? Describe your life up to now: family,

friends, home, school, work, and particularly those experiences most relevant to your interests in psychology and you. Write an autobiographical sketch.

- **Personal and professional development.** Describe your values and your approach to life.

Although there are many similarities among essay topics, you should not write a generic essay to send to all programs. Tailor your essay to the specific question and program, because the admissions committee is interested in how well your interests and abilities match the program and faculty. As you write your essay, occasionally stop to make sure that you're answering the question posed by the admissions committee (and not digressing). Many students use the personal essay as an opportunity to explain how they became interested in psychology; remember that your essay will be used by the admissions committee to determine whether you're suitable for graduate study. Do not disclose personal information that might be construed negatively. Certainly, your essay is a personal statement and you should feel comfortable expressing yourself; however, this is not the time to explain that your interest in psychology stems from your dysfunctional family or your own history of pathology.

Seek feedback from others—especially faculty. Faculty are aware of what graduate programs seek and their advice is invaluable. If you seek feedback, be sure to approach faculty early and well before the due date to give them time to read and respond to your essay—and to give you time to revise it. The same philosophy about approaching faculty early in requesting letters of recommendation applies here. Finally, carefully proofread your essays (or have a trusted family member or friend proofread for you as well), as typos are the kiss of death to your application. Your admissions essays are your chance to present your strengths and really shine, so take advantage of the opportunity to discuss your accomplishments, describe valuable experiences, and emphasize the positive.

LETTERS OF RECOMMENDATION

Most graduate programs require applicants to submit three letters of recommendation. The letter of recommendation is a letter, written by a faculty member or supervisor, that discusses the personal qualities, accomplishments, and experiences that make you unique and perfect for the programs to which you've applied. As you might imagine, letters of recommendation are very important parts of your application.

In most cases, your letters of recommendation will be written by faculty in your department. In choosing your recommenders, make sure that the persons you ask to write your letters:

- Know you well and have known you for a long time
- Know your work and describe it positively
- Have a high opinion of you
- Know where you are applying as well as your educational and career goals
- Are able to favorably compare you with your peers
- Are able to write a good letter

Aim for a set of letters covering the range of your skills, including discussion of your academic and scholastic skills, research abilities and experiences, and applied experiences (for example, cooperative education, internships, related work experience). Provide your letter writers with all the necessary information so that they don't have to work at remembering all of the details that they should include. Make an appointment to speak with each of your recommenders and give them plenty of time to write your letter (3 to 4 weeks at a minimum). Provide a file with the following:

- Your transcript
- Resume or vita
- GRE scores
- Courses you've taken with them and grades that you've earned
- Research experiences
- Internship and other applied experiences
- Honor societies to which you belong
- Awards you've won
- Work experience
- Professional goals
- Due date for the application
- Information about the programs to which you're applying
- Copy of the application recommendation forms

When approaching potential recommenders, ask them if they know you well enough to write a meaningful letter. Pay attention to their demeanor. If you sense reluctance, thank them and ask someone else. Remember that it is best to ask early in the semester. As the end of the semester approaches, faculty may hesitate because of time constraints.

The Interview

Once you've submitted your application, the waiting begins. Some graduate programs conduct phone interviews, some conduct on-site interviews, and some don't interview at all. If you're invited for an interview, remember the purpose: the interview gives admission committees an opportunity to meet candidates and see the people behind the GPAs and GRE scores. It's a chance for them to meet you, to see how you react under pressure, and to assess your verbal and nonverbal communication skills. The interview might range from half an hour with one or two faculty to a full day or more filled with meetings with students and faculty, and include small group discussions, larger group interviews, and even social hours or parties.

To prepare for a graduate admissions interview, learn as much about the program as possible. Review the program description, department Web site, and faculty Web sites. Understand the program's emphasis, and be aware of the faculty's research interests. Consider how you will answer common interview questions, such as those in Table 14.1.

In addition to answering questions, you must also ask questions. Admissions committees *expect* you to ask questions, so prepare some thoughtful questions about the program, faculty, and students. Use this opportunity to learn about the program and whether it meets your needs. During your visit, try to get a sense of

TABLE 14.1 | COMMON GRADUATE SCHOOL ADMISSIONS QUESTIONS

- Why are you interested in our program?
- What do you know about our program?
- What are your career goals?
- Why did you choose a career in psychology?
- What are your research interests? Describe your research experience. What are your research strengths and weaknesses?
- What are your academic strengths? What was your favorite course, and why?
- What do you like best about yourself?
- Who would you like to work with? Why?
- Describe the accomplishments of which you're most proud.
- If you were to begin a research project now, what would be the topic?
- Describe your theoretical orientation.
- Discuss your experiences in clinical settings. Evaluate your clinical abilities. What are your strengths and weaknesses?
- Tell us about yourself.
- How would your professors describe you?
- How will you be able to make a contribution to this field? How do you hope to contribute?
- What are your hobbies?
- Describe your greatest academic accomplishment. Personal?
- Tell me about your experience in psychology thus far. What is the most challenging aspect? What is the most rewarding?
- What are your career goals? How will this program help you achieve your goals?
- How do you intend to finance your education?
- What skills do you bring to the program? How will you help your mentor in his or her research?
- Are you motivated? Explain and provide examples.
- What do you plan to specialize in? Why?
- If you're not accepted into graduate school, what are your plans?
- Why did you choose this career?
- What do you know about our program?
- Why did you choose to apply to our program?
- What other schools are you considering?
- In what ways have your previous experience prepared you for graduate study in our program?
- Any questions?
- What do you believe your greatest challenge will be if you are accepted into this program?
- In college, what courses did you enjoy the most? The least? Why?

TABLE 14.2	QUESTIONS TO ASK DURING A GRADUATE SCHOOL ADMISSIONS INTERVIEW

- What characteristics distinguish this program from others?

- Where are recent alumni employed? What do most students do after graduation?

- What types of financial aid are offered? What criteria are used for choosing recipients?

- Are there any scholarships or fellowships available? How do I apply?

- Are there teaching opportunities, such as teaching assistantships and adjunct positions, for current students?

- Do most students publish an article or present a paper before graduation?

- What planned practical experiences are included in the program (for example, internships)? Ask for examples of internship placements.

- What is the relative importance of admissions test scores, undergraduate grades, recommendations, statements on applications, experience, and other requirements?

- Does the department prefer applicants immediately out of undergraduate programs or do they prefer applicants with work experience? If they prefer or require experience, what kind of experience are they looking for?

- How do graduate students obtain research experience? Are they assigned to labs or do they choose labs on their own?

- How are mentors assigned to students?

the department's emotional climate. What do graduate students call professors–'Doctor,' or do they use first names? Are students competitive with one another? Try to get a sense of whether the atmosphere matches your personality. Is it formal or informal? Would you be happy there? Table 14.2 presents some sample questions to help you determine what you'd like to ask.

After the interview, another period of waiting begins. Most programs inform applicants of their acceptance from March through early April. In most cases, your decision on whether to accept an offer is due by April 15. Accepting an offer of admission to graduate school may seem like a happy ending, but it's only the beginning of the next phase of your career.

SUGGESTED READINGS

American Psychological Association (2007). *Getting in: A step-by-step plan for gaining admission to graduate school in psychology.* Washington, DC: Author.

American Psychological Association (2008). *Graduate study in psychology: 2009.* Washington, DC: Author.

Keith-Spiegel, P. & Wiederman, M. W. (2007). *Complete guide to graduate school admissions: Psychology, counseling, and related professions.* Erlbaum.

Kuther, T. L. (2008). *Surviving graduate school in psychology: A pocket mentor.* Washington, DC: American Psychological Association Press.

Mayne, T. J., Norcross, J. G., & Sayette, M. A. (2008). *Insider's guide to graduate programs in clinical and counseling psychology.* Guilford.

Web Resources

Psychology Graduate Applicant's Portal
http://www.psychgrad.org/

Applying to Graduate School in Psychology
http://www.psichi.org/pubs/articles/article_22.asp

Pursuing Psychology Graduate School Information Page
http://www.uni.edu/walsh/linda2.html

A Suggested Plan for Grad School Admission
http://www.uwstout.edu/programs/bap/pgs.html

About Graduate School
http://gradschool.about.com

American Psychological Association of Graduate Students (APAGS)
http://www.apa.org/apags/

Checklist: Is Graduate School for You?
(Adapted from Kuther, 2006)

Answer the following questions honestly:

1. Are you ready to live at or near poverty for the next 2 to 7 years?
2. Does the thought of studying all the time make you ill?
3. Is writing term papers fun?
4. Does public speaking bother (or even scare) you?
5. Do you read psychology books or articles even if they are not assigned?
6. Do you put off studying for tests or writing papers?
7. Do you enjoy reading and studying?
8. Do you hate library research?
9. Will you give up a social event (like a party) to study for a test or to finish a paper?
10. Are you sick of school?
11. Can you concentrate and study for hours at a time?
12. Are your grades mainly B's or lower?
13. Do you read recent issues of psychology journals?
14. Are there other careers aside from psychology that you'd like to explore?
15. Did you earn an A or B in statistics?
16. Does research bore you?
17. Are you willing to work long hours?
18. Are you willing and able to incur significant student loan debt?
19. Do you frequently hand in assignments on time?

Scoring: Assign one point to each odd question to which you answered yes and one point for each even question to which you answered no. Sum the points to obtain a total score. Higher scores indicate a greater potential for graduate study.

REFERENCES

Aamodt, M. G. (1999). *Applied industrial/ organizational psychology*. Pacific Grove, CA: Wadsworth.

Aamodt, M. G. (2007). *Applied industrial/ organizational psychology*. Pacific Grove, CA: Wadsworth.

Ackerman, M. J. (1999). *Essentials of Forensic Psychological Assessment*. New York: John Wiley.

Actkinson, T. R. (2000). Master's and myth: Little-known information about a popular degree. *Eye on Psi Chi, 4*(2), 19–21, 23, 25.

American Association of Marriage and Family Therapy. (2002). *Advancing the professional interests of marriage and family therapists*. Retrieved on July 24, 2008 at http://www.aamft.org/

American Counseling Association. (2008). *American Counseling Association*. Retrieved on July 24, 2008 at http://www.counseling.org/

American Federation of Teachers. (2007). Survey and analysis of teacher salary trends 2005. Retrieved on July 24, 2008 at http://www.aft.org/salary/2005/download/AFT2005SalarySurvey.pdf

American Institute for Graphic Arts. (2008). *Survey of design salaries, 2008*. Retrieved on July 20, 2008 at http://designsalaries.org/calculator.asp

American Psychological Association. (2002). *Undergraduate psychology major: Learning goals and outcomes*. Retrieved on September 19, 2005 at http://www.apa.org/ed/pcue/taskforcereport2.pdf

American Psychological Association. (2007). *Accredited doctoral programs in professional psychology: 2007. American Psychologist, 62*, 930–944.

American Psychological Association. (2008). *2007–2008 APA congressional fellowship program*. Retrieved on July 25, 2008 at http://www.apa.org/ppo/fellows/congressional.html

American Psychological Association. (n.d.). *Introduction to military psychology: An overview*. Retrieved on January 18, 2001 at http://www.apa.org/about/division/div19intro.html

American Psychological Association Center for Workforce Studies. (2008). Doctorates awarded in 2005–2006: Subfield by degree type. Retrieved on July 24, 2008 at http://research.apa.org/doctoraled11.html

American Psychological Association, Division 12: Society of Clinical Psychology. (n.d.) *About clinical psychology?* Retrieved on July 24, 2008 at http://www.apa.org/divisions/div12/aboutcp.html

American Psychological Association Division 16. (2005). *Goals and objectives*. Retrieved on July 28, 2008 at http://www.indiana.edu/~div16/G&O.htm

American Psychological Association Division 22. (n.d.). *What is rehabilitation psychology*. Retrieved on July 29, 2008 at http://www.apa.org/divisions/div22/Rpdef.html

180

American Psychological Association Division 47. (2007). *Becoming a sports psychologist.* Retrieved on July 30, 2008 at http://www.psyc.unt.edu/apadiv47/APA%20Div%2047%20(1)/about/about_becomingsportpsych.html

American Psychological Association Division of Clinical Neuropsychology. (1989). Definition of a clinical neuropsychologist. *The Clinical Neuropsychologist, 3*, 22. Retrieved on July 29, 2008 at http://www.div40.org/def.html

American Psychological Association Research Office. (2003). *PhDs and PsyDs by major degree field: 2001 new doctorates in psychology.* Retrieved on July 28, 2008 at http://research.apa.org/doctoraled03.html

American Psychological Association Research Office. (2008). New doctorates in psychology by subfield: 2001–2002. Retrieved on July 24, 2008 at http://research.apa.org/doc17.html

American Psychology-Law Society. (2004). *Careers in psychology and law: A guide for prospective students.* Retrieved on July 25, 2008 at http://www.ap-ls.org/students/careers%20in%20psychology.pdf

American Psychology-Law Society. (2005). *Careers in psychology and law: Subspecialties in psychology and law: A closer look.* Retrieved on July 25, 2008 at http://www.unl.edu/ap-ls/student/careers_closerlook.html

Amsel, J. (1996). An interesting career in psychology: Acquisitions editor. *Psychological Science Agenda.* Retrieved on January 18, 2002 at http://www.apa.org/science/ic-amsel.html

Anderson, M. B. (Ed.) (2000). *Doing sport psychology.* Champaign, IL: Human Kinetics.

Andrews, C. K. (2005). Trial consulting: Moving psychology into the courtroom. In R. D. Morgan, T. L. Kuther, & C. J. Habben (Eds.), *Life after graduate school in psychology: Insider's advice from new psychologists.* New York: Psychology Press.

Andrews, D. A., & Bonta, J. (1994). *The psychology of criminal conduct.* Cincinnati, OH: Anderson.

Andrews, D. A., Zinger, I., Hoge, R. D., Bonta, J., Gendreau, P., & Cullen, F. T. (1990). Does correctional treatment work? A clinically relevant and psychologically informed meta-analysis. *Criminology, 28*, 369–404.

Anson, R. H., & Bloom, M. E. (1988). Police stress in an occupational context. *Journal of Police Science and Administration, 16*, 229–235.

Appleby, D. (2000). Job skills valued by employers who interview psychology majors. *Eye on Psi Chi, 4*(3), 17.

Attfield, C. (1999). Stock Market: Making the Transition from Acids to Assets. *Next Wave.* Retrieved on June 16, 2002 at http://nextwave.sciencemag.org/cgi/content/full/1999/03/02/2

Augenbraun, E., & Vergoth, K. (1998). Broadcast science journalism: Working in television, cable, radio, or electronic media. In C. Robbins-Roth (Ed.), *Alternative careers in science: Leaving the ivory tower* (pp. 49–62). San Diego, CA: Academic Press.

Ax, R. K & Morgan, R. D. (2002). Internship Training Opportunities in Correctional Psychology: A Comparison of Settings. *Criminal Justice and Behavior, 29*, 332–347.

Balster, R. L. (1995). An interesting career in psychology: A research psychologist in a medical school. *Psychological Science Agenda.* Retrieved on February 1, 2002 at http://www.apa.org/science/ic-balster.html

Bardon, J. I. (1989). The school psychologist as an applied educational psychologist. In R. C. D'Amato, & R. S. Dean (Eds.), *The school psychologist in nontraditional settings: Integrating clients, services, and settings* (pp. 1–32). Hillsdale, NJ: Lawrence Erlbaum.

Bartholomew, D. (2001a). Academia or industry: Finding the fit. *Next Wave.* Retrieved on February 1, 2002 at http://nextwave.sciencemag.org/cgi/content/full/2000/08/10/6

Bartholomew, D. (2001b). Academia or industry: Where would I fit in? *Next Wave.* Retrieved on February 1, 2002 at http://nextwave.sciencemag.org/cgi/content/full/2000/06/15/1

Bartol, C. R. (1996). Police psychology then, now, and beyond. *Criminal Justice and Behavior, 23*, 70–89.

Bartol C. R., & Bartol, A. M. (2004). *Introduction to forensic psychology.* Thousand Oaks, CA: Sage.

Baskin, M. L. (2005). Public Health: Career opportunities for psychologists in public health. In R. D. Morgan, T. L. Kuther, & C. J. Habben (Eds.), *Life after graduate school in psychology: Insider's advice from new psychologists.* New York: Psychology Press.

Beall, A. E., & Allen, T. W. (1997). Why we buy what we buy: Consulting in consumer psychology. In R. Sternberg (Ed.), *Career paths in psychology: Where your degree can take you* (pp. 197–212). Washington, D.C.: American Psychological Association.

Belar, C. D. (1997). Clinical health psychology: A specialty for the 21st century. *Health Psychology, 16*, 411–416.

Belar, C. D., & Deardorff, W. W. (1995). *Clinical health psychology in medical settings: A practitioner's guidebook.* Washington, D.C.: American Psychological Association.

Belar, C. D., Brown, R. A., Hersch, L. E., Hornyak, L. M., Rozensky, R. H., Sheridan, E. P., Brown, R. T., & Reed, G. W. (2001). Self-assessment in clinical health psychology: A model for ethical expansion of practice. *Professional Psychology: Research and Practice, 32,* 135–141.

Bergen, J. (n.d.). *Public relations careers.* Retrieved on July 29, 2008 at http://prfirms.org/index.cfm?fuseaction=page.viewpage&pageid=575

Birmingham, D. & Morgan, R. D. *Helping police manage Type III stress.* In Shelia Holton (Chair), Law Enforcement and Stress: Crossing the Blue Line. Symposium presented at the annual convention of the American Psychological Association, San Francisco, CA, August, 2001.

Boothby, J. L., & Clements, C. B. (2001). A national survey of correctional psychologists. *Criminal Justice and Behavior, 27,* 716–732.

Bonifazi, D. Z., Crespi, S. D., & Rieker, P. (1997). Value of a master's degree for gaining admission to doctoral programs in psychology. *Teaching of Psychology, 24,* 176–182.

Bornstein, M. (2006). Scientific Careers in Psychology in Government Service. In R. J. Sternberg (Ed.), *Career paths in psychology: Where your degree can take you (2nd ed.).* Washington, D.C.: American Psychological Association.

Boulakia, C. (1998). What is management consulting. *Science's Next Wave.* Retrieved on July 5, 2002 at http://nextwave.sciencemag.org/cgi/content/full/1998/03/29/262

Briihl, D. S. & Wasieleski, D. T. (2004). A survey of psychology Master's programs: Admissions criteria and program policies. *Teaching of Psychology, 31,* 252–256.

Brigham, J. C. (1999). What is forensic psychology, anyway? *Law & Human Behavior, 23,* 273–298.

Brodsky, C. M. (1982). Work stress in correctional institutions. *Journal of Prison and Jail Health, 2,* 74–102.

Bruzzese, J. M. (2005). Medical schools and centers: The merger of developmental psychology and pediatric asthma education. In R. D. Morgan, T. L. Kuther, & C. J. Habben (Eds.), *Life after graduate school in psychology: Insider's advice from new psychologists.* New York: Psychology Press.

Bryans, A. B. (1999). An evaluation of the special needs referral. *Early Childhood Research Quarterly, 14,* 483–484.

Bureau of Labor Statistics. (2002). *Occupational outlook handbook.* Retrieved on June 6, 2002 at http://stats.bls.gov/oco/ocoiab.htm

Bureau of Labor Statistics. (2004). *Occupational outlook handbook.* Retrieved on September 27, 2005 at http://stats.bls.gov/oco/ocoiab.htm

Bureau of Labor Statistics. (2008). *Occupational outlook handbook 2008–2009 Edition.* Retrieved on July 24, 2008 at http://www.bls.gov/oco/home.htm

Buskist, W., & Shurburne, T. R. (1996). *Preparing for graduate study in psychology: 101 questions and answers.* Needham Heights, MA: Allyn & Bacon.

Butcher, J. N., & Miller, K. B. (1999). Personality assessment in personal injury litigation. In A. K. Hess, & I. B. Weiner (Eds.), *The handbook of forensic psychology* (2nd ed.), pp. 104–126.

Callan, J. R. (2004). An interesting career in psychology: Engineering psychology in research and development. *Psychological Science Agenda, 18*(10).

Carpenter, J. (2000). *Careers in consumer psychology.* Retrieved on July 29, 2008 at http://www.wcupa.edu/_ACADEMICS/sch_cas.psy/Career_Paths/Consumer/Career05.htm

Carpenter, S. (2001). National Science Foundation boosts cognitive neuroscience. *Monitor on Psychology, 32*(4). Retrieved on January 13, 2002 at http://www.apa.org/monitor/apr01/nsf.html

Carpenter, S. (2002). An interesting career in psychology: Becoming a science writer. Retrieved on July 31, 2008 at http://www.apa.org/science/ic-carpenter.html

Carter, J. E. (2005). Sport psychology: Locker room confessions. In R. D. Morgan, T. L. Kuther, & C. J. Habben (Eds.), *Life after graduate school in psychology: Insider's advice from new psychologists.* New York: Psychology Press.

Chapman, C. N. (2005). Software user research: Psychologist in the software industry. In R. D. Morgan, T. L. Kuther, & C. J. Habben (Eds.), *Life after graduate school in psychology: Insider's advice from new psychologists* (pp. 211–224). New York: Psychology Press.

Cheek, F., & Miller, M. (1983). The experience of stress for correction officers: A double-blind theory of correctional stress. *Journal of Criminal Justice, 11,* 105–120.

Child Life Council (2008). *Summary of the 2008 Child Life Profession Compensation Survey*

Results. Retrieved on July 29, 2008 at http://www.childlife.org/Career%20Center/

Clay, R. A. (2000). Often, the bells and whistles backfire. *Monitor on Psychology.* Retrieved on June 5, 2002 at http://www.apa.org/monitor/apr00/usability.html

Cobb, H. C., Reeve, R. E., Shealy, C. N., Norcross, J. C., Schare, M. L., Rodolfa, E. R., et al., (2004). Overlap among clinical, counseling, and school psychology: Implications for the profession and combined-integrated training. *Journal of Clinical Psychology, 60,* 939–955.

Cohen, J. (2002). I/Os in the know offer insights on Generation X workers. *Monitor on Psychology.* Retrieved on June 5, 2002 at http://www.apa.org/monitor/feb02/genxwork.html

Committee on Education and Training, Division 38. (n.d.). *What a health psychologist does and how to become one.* Retrieved on July 30, 2008 at http://www.health-psych.org/articles/what_is.php

Conaway, A. (2000). *Careers in environmental psychology.* Retrieved on December 20, 2002 at http://www.wcupa.edu/_ACADEMICS/sch_cas.psy/Career_Paths/Environmental/career09.htm

Condelli, W. S., Bradigan, B., & Holanchock, H. (1997). Intermediate care programs to reduce risk and better manage inmates with psychiatric disorders. *Behavioral Sciences and the Law, 15,* 459–467.

Copper, C. (1997). An interesting career in psychology: Social science analyst in the public sector. *Psychological Science Agenda.* Retrieved on January 19, 2002 at http://www.apa.org/science/ic-copper.html

Costello, E. J., Angold, A., Burns, B. J., Stangl, D. K., Tweed, D. L., Erkanli, A., & Worthman, C. M. (1996). The great smoky mountains study of youth: Goals, design, methods, and the prevalence of DSM-III-R disorders. *Archives of General Psychiatry, 53,* 1129–1136.

Czerwinski, M. (2002). An interesting career in psychology: Research psychology at Microsoft. *Psychological Science Agenda.* Retrieved on August 2, 2008 at http://www.apa.org/science/ic-czerwinski.html

D'Amato, R. C., & Dean, R. S. (Eds.). (1989). *The school psychologist in nontraditional settings: Integrating clients, services, and settings.* Hillsdale, NJ: Lawrence Erlbaum.

Danish, S., Petitpas, A. J., & Hale, B. D. (1993). Life development interventions for athletes: Life skills through sports. *The Counseling Psychologist, 21,* 352–385.

Day, M. C. (1996). An interesting career in psychology: Human-computer interface designer. *Psychological Science Agenda.* Retrieved on June 5, 2002 at http://www.apa.org/science/ic-day.html

DeLeon, P. H. (1988). Public policy and public service: Our professional duty. *American Psychologist, 43,* 309–315.

Diddams, M. (1998). An interesting career in psychology: Cognitive and I/O psychologists in the technology industry. *Psychological Science Agenda.* Retrieved on June 5, 2002 at http://www.apa.org/science/ic-diddams.html

Ditton, P. M. (1999). *Mental health and treatment of inmates and probationers* (Bureau of Justice Statistics Special Report, NJC 174463). Washington, D.C.: Department of Justice.

Drogin, E. Y., & Barrett, C. L. (2007). Off the witness stand: The forensic psychologist as consultant. In A. M. Goldstein (Ed.), *Forensic Psychology: Emerging topics and expanding roles.* Hoboken,: John Wiley & Sons NJ.

Dunivin, D. L. & Ingam, M. V. (2006). Military Psychology: A Dynamic and Practical Application of Psychological Expertise. In R. J. Sternberg (Ed.), *Career paths in psychology: Where your degree can take you* (2nd ed.). Washington, D.C.: American Psychological Association.

Edwards, J., & Smith, K. (1988). What skills and knowledge do potential employers value in baccalaureate psychologists? In P. J. Woods (Ed.), *Is psychology for them? A guide to undergraduate advising.* Washington, D.C.: American Psychological Association.

Evans, B. (1998). Why do realtors really leave the profession? *Realty Times.* Retrieved on July 2, 2002 at http://realtytimes.com/rtnews/rtapages/19981012_leaving.htm

Fabris, P. (1998). *Data mining: Advanced navigation.* Retrieved on June 16, 2002 at http://www.cio.com/archive/051598_mining.html

Families and Work Institute. (n.d.) *Work-life research.* Retrieved on July 2, 2002 at http://www.familiesandwork.org/announce/workforce.html

Ferrell, S. W., Morgan, R. D., & Winterowd, C. L. (2000). Job satisfaction of mental health professionals providing group psychotherapy in state correctional facilities. *International Journal of Offender Therapy and Comparative Criminology, 44,* 232–241.

Fisher, C. B. & Osofsky, J. (1997). Training the applied developmental scientist for prevention and practice: Two current examples, *Social Policy Report, 11*(2), 1–18.

Fowler, R. D. (1996). Psychology, public policy, and the Congressional Fellowship program. In R. P. Lorion, I. Iscoe, P. H. DeLeon, & G. R. VandenBos (Eds.), *Psychology and Public Policy: Balancing Public Service and Professional Need* (pp. ix–xiv). Washington, D.C.: American Psychological Association.

Gaddy, C. D., Charlot-Swilley, D., Nelson, P. D., & Reich, J. N. (1995). Selected outcomes of accredited programs. *Professional Psychology: Research and Practice, 26,* 507–513.

Garrett, C. (1985). Effects of residential treatment on adjudicated delinquents: A meta-analysis. *Journal of Research in Crime and Delinquency, 22,* 287–308.

Gehlhaus, D. (2007). What can I do with my liberal arts degree? *Occupational Outlook Quarterly, 51*(4), 2–11.

Gelso, C. & Fretz, B. (2001). *Counseling Psychology* (2nd ed.). Orlando, FL: Harcourt College Publishers.

Gendreau, P., & Andrews, D. (1990). Tertiary prevention: What the meta-analyses of the offender treatment literature tells us about "what works." *Canadian Journal of Criminology, 32,* 173–184.

Gendreau, P., & Ross, R. (1979). Effective correctional treatment: Bibliotherapy for cynics. *Journal of Research in Crime and Delinquency, 25,* 463–489.

Gendreau, P., & Ross, R. (1981). Offender rehabilitation: The appeal of success. *Federal Probation, 45,* 45–48.

Goetnick Ambrose, S. (2006). Science writing: Communicating with the masses. In C. Robbins-Roth (Ed.), *Alternative careers in science: Leaving the ivory tower* (2nd ed.) (pp. 27–38). San Diego, CA: Academic Press.

Golden, C. J., Zillmer, E., & Spiers, M. (1992). *Neuropsychological assessment and intervention.* Springfield, IL: Charles C Thomas.

Goldstein, D., Wilson, R. J., & Gerstein, A. I. (1983). Applied developmental psychology: Problems and prospects for an emerging discipline. *Journal of Applied Developmental Psychology, 4,* 341–348.

Grocer, S., & Kohout, J. (1997). *The 1995 APA survey of 1992 psychology baccalaureate recipients.* Retrieved on August 21, 2000 at http://research.apa.org/95survey/homepage.html

Haluck, R. S. (2005). Design considerations for computer-based surgical simulators. *Minimally Invasive Therapy & Allied Technologies, 14* (4/5), 235–243.

Harris, G. (1983). *Stress in corrections.* Boulder, CO: National Institute of Corrections.

Hart, S. (1996). Producing a great textbook with the help of a developmental editor. *Bioscience, 46.* Retrieved on January 18, 2001 at http://www.aibs.org/biosciencelibrary/vol46/oct.96.hart.html

Hart, S. G. (2002). *A safe and secure system.* Retrieved on June 5, 2002 at http://www.apa.org/ppo/issues/safesecure.paper.html

Hassine, V. (1996). *Life without parole.* Los Angeles: Roxbury Publishing.

Hawk, K. M. (1997). Personal reflections on a career in correctional psychology. *Professional Psychology: Research and Practice, 28,* 335–337.

Hayes, N. (1996). What makes a psychology graduate distinctive? *European Psychologist, 1,* 130–134.

Hays-Thomas, R. L. (2000). The silent conversation: Talking about the master's degree *Professional Psychology: Research and Practice, 31,* 339–345.

Hedge, J. W., & Borman, W. C. (2008). Preparing yourself in graduate school. In J. W. Hedge & W. C. Borman (Eds.), *The I/O consultant: Advice and insights for building a successful career* (pp. 17–21). Washington, D.C.: American Psychological Association.

Herrman, D. (1997). Rewards of public service: Research psychologists in government. In R. J. Sternberg (Ed.), *Career paths in psychology: Where your degree can take you* (pp. 151–164). Washington, D.C.: American Psychological Association.

Hodgins, S. (1995). Assessing mental disorder in the criminal justice system: Feasibility versus clinical accuracy. *International Journal of Law and Psychiatry, 18,* 15–28.

Holland, J. L. (1959). A theory of vocational choice. *Journal of Counseling Psychology, 6,* 35–45.

Huss, M. T. (2001). Psychology and law, now and in the next century: The promise of an emerging area of psychology. In J. S. Halonen, & S. F. Davis (Eds.), *The Many Faces of Psychological Research in the 21st Century* (Chapter 11). Society for the Teaching of Psychology: retrieved at http://teachpsych.lemoyne.edu/teachpsych/faces/text/Ch11.htm

Inwald, R. E. (1982). Research problems in assessing stress factors in correctional institutions. *International Journal of Offender Therapy & Comparative Criminology, 26,* 250–254.

Irwin, J. (1996). The march of Folly. *The Prison Journal, 76,* 489–494.

Job Profiles. (2003). Psychiatric technician. Retrieved on July 29, 2008 at http://www.jobprofiles.org/heapsytech.htm

Kao, L. S., & Thomas, E. J. (2008). Navigating towards improved surgical safety using aviation-based strategies. *Journal of Surgical Research, 145*(2), 327–335.

Kaplan, R. M., Sallis, J. F., Jr., & Patterson, T. L. (1993). *Health and human behavior.* New York: McGraw-Hill.

Kasserman, J. (2005). Management consultation: Improving organizations. In R. D. Morgan, T. L. Kuther, & C. J. Habben (Eds.), *Life after graduate school in psychology: Insider's advice from new psychologists.* New York: Psychology Press.

Keith-Spiegel, P., Tabachnick, B. G., & Spiegel, G. B. (1994). When demand exceeds supply: Second order criteria used by graduate school selection committees. *Teaching of Psychology, 21,* 79–81.

Keith-Spiegel, P., & Wiederman, M. W. (2000). *The complete guide to graduate school admission: Psychology, counseling, and related professions.* Mahwah, NH: Erlbaum.

Kierniesky, N. C. (1992). Specialization of the undergraduate major. *American Psychologist, 47,* 1146–1147.

Kilburg, R. R. (1996). Toward a conceptual understanding and definition of executive coaching. *Consulting Psychology Journal: Practice and Research, 48,* 134–144.

Kirkland, K., & Kirkland, K. L. (2001). Frequency of child custody evaluation complaints and related disciplinary action: A survey of the Association of State and Provincial Psychology Boards. *Professional Psychology: Research and Practice, 32,* 171–174.

Kolb, B. & Whishaw, I. Q. (2003). *Fundamentals of human neuropsychology* (5th ed.). New York: Bedford, Freeman, & Worth Publishers.

Krannich, C. (2002). *Interview for success: A practical guide to increasing job interviews, offers, and salaries.* Impact Publishers.

Kuther, T. L. (1996). Doctoral training in applied developmental psychology: Matching graduate education and accreditation standards to student needs, career opportunity, and licensure requirements. In C. B. Fisher, J. P. Murray & I. E. Sigel (Eds.), *Applied developmental science: Graduate training for diverse disciplines and educational settings,* pp. 53–74. Norwood, NJ: Ablex.

Kuther, T. L. (2002). Ethical conflicts in the teaching assignments of graduate students. *Ethics and Behavior, 12,* 197–204.

Kuther, T. L. (2005). *Your career in psychology: Industrial/organizational psychology.* Belmont: Wadsworth.

Landrum, R. E., & Clark, J. (2005). Graduate Admissions Criteria in Psychology: An update. *Psychological Reports, 97,* 481–484.

Landrum, R. E., Davis, S. F., & Landrum, T. (2000). *The psychology major: Career options and strategies for success.* Upper Saddle River, NJ: Prentice Hall.

Landwehr, H. (2001). An interesting career in psychology: Aviation human factors psychologist. *Psychological Science Agenda.* Retrieved on November 2, 2005 at http://www.apa.org/science/ic-landwehr.html

Lauber, J. K. (1997). An interesting career in psychology: Human factors psychologists in aviation. *Psychological Science Agenda.* Retrieved on June 5, 2002 at http://www.apa.org/science/ic-lauber.html

Lee, T. (2002). Rating the nation's best and worst jobs. *Career Journal.* Retrieved on June 16, 2002 at http://www.careerjournal.com/jobhunting/change/20020507-lee.html

Levant, R. F., Reed, G. M., Ragusea, S. A., DiCowden, M., Murphy, M. J., Sullivan, F., Craig, P. L., & Stout, C. E. (2001). Envisioning and accessing new roles for professional psychology. *Professional Psychology: Research and Practice, 32,* 79–87.

Levine, L. (2002). Biotechnology. *Microsoft® Encarta® Online Encyclopedia.* Retrieved on July 22, 2002 at http://encarta.msn.com/find/Concise.asp?z=17pg=2&ti=761575885

Lezak (2004). *Neuropsychological assessment* (4th ed.). New York: Oxford University Press.

Lipsey, M. (1992). Juvenile delinquency treatment: A meta-analytic inquiry into the variability of effects. In T. Cook, H. Cooper, D. Cordray, H. Hartmann, L. Hedgews, R. Light, T. Louis, & F. Mosteller (Eds.), *Meta-analysis for explanation* (pp. 83–127). New York: Russell Sage.

Lindquist, C. A., & Whitehead, J. T. (1986). Burnout, job stress, and job satisfaction among southern correctional officers: Perceptions and causal factors. *Journal of Offender Counseling, Services, and Rehabilitation, 10,* 5–26.

Liss, M. B. (1992). Psychology and law courses: Content and materials. *Law & Human Behavior, 16,* 463–471.

Lloyd, M. A. (2000). *Master's- and doctoral-level careers in psychology and related areas.* Retrieved on February 1, 2000 at http://www.psychwww.com/careers/masters.htm

Lloyd, M. A., & Kennedy, J. H. (1997). *Skills employers seek.* Retrieved on August 20, 2000 at http://www.psywww.com/careers/skills.htm

Marchant, D. B. (2000). Targeting futures: Goal setting for professional sports. In M. B. Anderson (Ed.), *Doing sport psychology* (pp. 93–103). Champaign, IL: Human Kinetics.

Martinson, R. (1974). What works? Questions and answers about prison reform. *Public Interest, 35,* 22–54.

Matlin, M. W., & Kalat, J. W. (2001). Demystifying the GRE Psychology Test: A brief guide for students. *Eye on Psi Chi, 5*(1), 22–25.

Max, D. T. (2000, December). The cop and the therapist. *The New York Times Magazine,* p. 94.

McCann, R. S. (2001). An interesting career in psychology: NASA research scientist. *Psychological Science Agenda.* Retrieved on August 2, 2008 at http://www.apa.org/schience/ic-mccann.html

McCracken, P. (1998). The path of a scientist's job search. *Science's Next Wave.* Retrieved on June 5, 2002 at http://nextwave.sciencemag.org/cgi/content/full/1998/03/29/265

MSU Career Placement and Services. (2008). *Recruiting trends 2007–2008.* East Lansing, MI: Michigan State University.

Murray, B. (2002). Psychologists help companies traverse the minefields of layoffs. *Monitor on Psychology.* Retrieved on June 6, 2002 at http://www.apa.org/monitor/apr02/layoffs.html

McGovern, T. V., Furumoto, L., Halpern, D. F., Kimble, G. A., & McKeachie, W. J. (1991). Liberal education, study in depth, and the arts and sciences major — psychology. *American Psychologist, 46,* 598–605.

Melton, G. B., Petrila, J., Poythress, N. G., Slobogin, C., & Lyons, P. M. (2007). *Psychological evaluations for the courts: A handbook for mental health professionals and lawyers* (3rd ed.). New York: Guilford Press.

Meyers, A. W., Coleman, J. K., Whelan, J. P., & Mehlenbeck, R. S. (2001). Examining careers in sport psychology: Who is working and who is making money? *Professional Psychology: Research and Practice, 32,* 5–11.

Montell, G. (1999). Another career choice for Ph.D.'s: Management consulting. *Chronicle of Higher Education.* Retrieved on June 5, 2002 at http://chronicle.com/jobs/99/11/99111203c.htm

Morgan, R. D. (2002). Basic mental health services: Services and issues. In T. Fagan & R. K. Ax (Eds.), *Correctional Mental Health Handbook.* Submitted for publication.

Morgan, R. D., & Cohen, L. M. (in press). Clinical and counseling psychology: Can differences be gleaned from printed recruiting materials?

Training and Education in Professional Psychology.

Morgan, R. D., Van Haveren, R. A., & Pearson, C. A. (2002). Correctional officer burnout: Further analyses. *Criminal Justice and Behavior, 29,* 144–160.

Morgan, R. D., Winterowd, C. L., & Ferrell, S. W. (1999). A national survey of group psychotherapy services in correctional facilities. *Professional Psychology: Research and Practice, 30,* 600–606.

Muchinsky, P. M. (2006). Psychology applied to work. Pacific Grove, CA: Wadsworth.

Murphy, C. H. (2007). The average tech manager makes $105,000, our salary survey finds. Have tech jobs bounced back? *Information Week.* Retrieved on August 2, 2008 at http://www.informationweek.com/news/management/compensation/showArticle.jhtml?articleID=199202140

Murray, B. (2000). From brain scan to lesson plan. *Monitor on Psychology, 31*(3). Retrieved on January 13, 2002 at http://www.apa.org/monitor/mar00/brainscan.html

Myers, D. G. (2004). *Psychology* (6th ed.). New York: Worth.

National Association of Colleges and Employers. (2008). *Job Outlook 2008 Survey.* Washington, D.C.: National Association of Colleges and Employers.

National Association of Social Workers (2008). *National Association of Social Workers.* Retrieved on July 24, 2008 at http://www.socialworkers.org/

National Center for Education Statistics. (2008). *Digest of Education 2007.* Washington, D.C.: National Center for Education Statistics.

National Rehabilitation Counseling Association (n.d.). *NCRA.* Retrieved on July 24, 2008 at http://nrca-net.org/

Nielson, J. (2008). Salary trends for usability professionals. Retrieved on July 21, 208 at http://www.useit.com/alertbox/salaries.html

Norcross, J. C., Castle, P. H., Sayette, M. A., & Mayne, T J. (2004). The PsyD: Heterogeneity in Practitioner Training. *Professional Psychology: Research and Practice, 35,* 412–419.

Norcross, J. C., & Castle, P. H. (2002). Appreciating the PsyD: The facts. *Eye on Psi Chi, 7*(1), 22–26.

Norcross, J. C., Hanych, J. M., & Terranova, R. D. (1996). Graduate study in psychology: 1992–1993. *American Psychologist, 51,* 631–643.

Norcross, J. C., Karg, R. S., & Prochaska, J. O. (1997). Clinical psychologists in the 1990's: Part I. *Clinical Psychologist, 50,* 4–9.

Norcross, J. C., Prochaska, J. O., & Gallagher, K. M. (1989a). Clinical psychologists in the 1980s: I. Demographics, affiliations, and satisfactions. *The Clinical Psychologist, 42,* 29–39.

Norcross, J. C., Prochaska, J. O., & Gallagher, K. M. (1989b). Clinical psychologists in the 1980s: II. Theory, research, and practice. *The Clinical Psychologist, 42,* 29–39.

Norcross, J. C., Sayette, M. A., Mayne, T. J., Karg, R. S., & Turkson, M. A. (1998). Selecting a doctoral program in professional psychology: some comparisons among PhD counseling PhD clinical and PsyD clinical psychology program. *Professional Psychology: Research and Practice, 29,* 609–614.

North American Association of Masters in Psychology. (2004). *Licensure Information.* Retrieved on July 16, 2008 at http://www.enamp.org/modules.php?name=Content&pa=showpage&pid=4

Pate, W. E. (2001). *Analyses of data from graduate study in psychology: 1999–2000.* Retrieved on July 5, 2002 at http://research.apa.org/grad00contents.html

Pate, W. E., Frincke, J. L., & Kohout, J. L. (2005). *Salaries in Psychology 2003.* Retrieved on July 29, 2008 at http://research.apa.org/03salary/homepage.html

Patterson, F. (2001). Developments in work psychology: Emerging issues and future trends. *Journal of Occupational and Organizational Psychology, 74,* 381–390.

PayScale (2008). Salary survey report for Job: Early intervention specialist. Retrieved on July 28, 2008 at http://www.payscale.com/research/US/Job=Early_Intervention_Specialist/Salary/by_Degree

Perry, C., Jr., & Marsh, H. W. (2000). Listening to self-talk, hearing self-concept. In M. B. Anderson (ed.), *Doing sport psychology* (pp. 61–76). Champaign, IL: Human Kinetics.

Peters, R. L. (1992). *Getting what you came for: The smart student's guide to earning a master's or a Ph.D.* New York: Noonday Press.

Public Relations Society of America. (n. d.). *About public relations.* Retrieved on June 5, 2002 at http://www.prsa.org/_resources/profession/index.asp

Randall, C. R. (2006). Technical writing: Making sense out of manuals. In C. Robbins Roth (Ed.), *Alternative careers in science: Leaving the ivory tower* (2nd ed.) (pp. 15–26). San Diego, CA: Academic Press.

Resnick, J. H. (1991). Finally, a definition of clinical psychology: A message from the President, Division 12. *Clinical Psychologist, 44,* 3–11.

Roediger, H. (2006). Teaching, research, and more: Psychologists in an academic career. In R. J. Sternberg (Ed.), *Career paths in psychology: Where your degree can take you (2nd ed.).* Washington, D.C.: American Psychological Association.

Roger, R. R., & Stone, G. (n.d.). Counseling vs. Clinical: What is the difference between a clinical psychologist and a counseling psychologist? Retrieved on July 24, 2008 at http://www.div17.org/students_differences.html

Romans, J. S. C., Boswell, D. L., Carlozzi, A. F., & Ferguson, D. B. (1995). Training and supervision practices in clinical, counseling, and school psychology programs. *Professional Psychology: Research and Practice, 26,* 407–412.

Rowh, M. & Suchorski, J. (2000). *Opportunities in Fund-Raising.* McGraw-Hill.

Salary.com (2008). *Salary wizard.* Retrieved on July 28, 2008 at http://www.salary.com

Salzinger, K. (1995). The academic life. *Psychological Science Agenda.* Retrieved on January 18, 2002 at http://www.apa.org/psa/janfeb95/acad.html

Sarafino, E. P. (2002). *Health psychology: Biopsychosocial interactions* (4th ed.). New York: John Wiley & Sons.

Scrader, B. (2002). Industrial/organizational psychology 2010: A research odyssey. In Halonen, J. S., & Davis, S. F. (Eds.). (2001). *The many faces of psychological research in the 21st century.* Retrieved on June 5, 2002 at http://teachpsych.lemoyne.edu/teachpsych/faces/text/Ch03.htm

Sebestyen, G. (2000). Watching the consultants. *Science's Next Wave.* Retrieved on June 5, 2002 at http://nextwave.sciencemag.org/cgi/content/full/2000/07/26/1

Seligman, M. E. P. (1995). The effectiveness of psychotherapy: The Consumer Reports Study. *American Psychologist, 50,* 965–974.

Sheetz, P. I. (1995). *Recruiting Trends: 1995–1996.* East Lansing, MI: Collegiate Employment Research Institute, Michigan State University.

Sherman, C. P. & Poczwardowski, A. (2000). Relax! ... It ain't easy (or is it?). In M. B. Anderson (Ed.), *Doing sport psychology* (pp. 47–60). Champaign, IL: Human Kinetics.

Silva, A. (2003). Who are school psychologists? Retrieved on July 28, 2008 at http://www.nasponline.org/about_sp/whatis.aspx

Simmons, J. (2000). Doing imagery in the field. In M. B. Anderson (ed.), *Doing sport psychology* (pp. 77–92). Champaign, IL: Human Kinetics.

Singleton, D., Tate, A., & Randall, G. (2003). *Salaries in psychology, 2001: Report of the 2001 APA salary survey.* Washington, D.C.: American Psychological Association. Retrieved on September 15, 2005 at http://research.apa.org/01salary/index.html

Smith, L. (2002). Working Extra Hours Pays Off. *Information Week.* Retrieved on June 16, 2002 at http://www.informationweek.com/story/IWK20020426S0002).

Smith, P. M. (1997). An interesting career in psychology: Organizational development consultant. *Psychological Science Agenda.* Retrieved on June 5, 2002 at http://www.apa.org/science/ic-smith.html

Society of Counseling Psychology, Division 17: American Psychological Association. (n.d.). *About counseling psychologists.* Retrieved on July 24, 2008 at http://www.div17.org/students_defining.html

Steadman, H. J., Morris, S. M., & Dennis, D. L. (1995). The diversion of mentally ill persons from community-based services: A profile of programs. *American Journal of Public Health, 85,* 1630–1635.

Stein, D. M., & Lambert, M. J. (1995). On the relationship between therapist experience and psychotherapy outcome. *Journal of Consulting and Clinical Psychology, 63,* 182–196.

Sullivan, M. J. (2005). Psychologists as legislators: Results of the 2004 elections. *Professional Psychology: Research and Practice, 36,* 32–36.

Susman-Stillman, A. R., Brown, J. L., Adam, E. K., Blair, C., Gaines, R., Gordon, R. A., et al. (1996). Building research and policy connections: Training and career options for developmental scientists. *Social Policy Report, 10*(4), 1–19.

Super, J. T. (1999). Forensic psychology and law enforcement. In A. K. Hess, & I. B. Weiner (Eds.), *The handbook of forensic psychology* (2nd ed.) (pp. 409–439).

Taylor, S. E. (1999). *Health Psychology* (4th ed.). Boston: McGraw-Hill.

Tenopyr, M. L. (1997). Improving the workplace: Industrial/organizational psychology as a career. In R. Sternberg (Ed.), *Career paths in psychology: Where your degree can take you* (pp. 185–196). Washington, D.C.: American Psychological Association.

Toch, H. (1992). *Mosaic of despair: Human breakdowns in prison* (Rev. ed.). Washington, D.C.: American Psychological Association.

Torrey, E. F. (1995). Editorial: Jails and prisons – America's new mental hospital. *American Journal of Public Health, 85,* 1611–1613.

Toth, S. L., Manly, J. T., & Nilsen, W. J. (2008). From research to practice: Lessons learned. *Journal of Applied Developmental Psychology, 29*(4), 317–325.

Tyler, R. R. (2000). An interesting career in psychology: Aviation human factors practitioner. *Psychological Science Agenda.* Retrieved on June 5, 2002 at http://www.apa.org/science/ic-tyler.html

Van Raalte, J. L., & Williams, J. M. (1994). *Graduate training & career possibilities in exercise & sport psychology.* Retrieved on July 30, 2008 at http://www.psyc.unt.edu/apadiv47/APA%20Div%2047%20(3)/Sport%20Psych%20a%20Guide/gradtrain.htm

Vesilind, P. A. (2000). *So you want to be a professor? A handbook for graduate students.* Thousand Oaks, CA: Sage.

Watkins, C. E., Lopez, F. G., Campbell, V. L., & Himmell, C. D. (1986). Contemporary counseling psychology: Results of a national survey. *Journal of counseling psychology, 33,* 301–309.

Weinberg, R. A., & Susman-Stillman, A. (1999). Required reading for making a difference in the lives of children and families. *School Psychology Quarterly, 14*(1), 94–99.

Weiner, H. R. (2001). *An interesting career in psychology: Expert witness in employment discrimination cases.* Retrieved on August 2, 2008 at http://www.apa.org/science/ic-weiner.html

Weinstein, M. & Rossini, E. D. (1999). Teaching group treatment in doctoral programs in counseling psychology. *Psychological Reports, 85,* 697–700.

Wetfeet.com. (2005a). *Account management.* Retrieved on July 29, 2008 at http://www.wetfeet.com/Careers-and-Industries/Careers/Account-Management.aspx

Wetfeet.com. (2005b). *Retail: Career overview.* Retrieved on July 29, 2008 at http://www.wetfeet.com/Careers-and-Industries/Industries/Retail.aspx

Wetfeet.com. (2008). *Non-profit and government.* Retrieved on July 29, 2008 at http://www.wetfeet.com/Careers-and-Industries/Industries/Non-Profit-and-Government.aspx

Whitebrook, M. & Phillips, D. (1999). Child care employment: Implications for women's self sufficiency and for child development. *Foundation for Child Development Working Paper Series.* Retrieved on July 2, 2002 at http://www.ffcd.org/wbwp2txt.pdf

Wicherski, M., & Kohout, J. (2005). *2003 Doctorate Employment Survey*. Washington, D.C.: APA Research Office.

Wicherski, M., & Kohout, J. (2007). *2005 Doctorate Employment Survey*. Washington, D.C.: American Psychological Association.

Williams, S. (2005). Executive management: Helping executives manage their organizations through organizational and market research. In R. D. Morgan, T. L. Kuther, & C. J. Habben (Eds.), *Life after graduate school in psychology: Insider's advice from new psychologists*. New York: Psychology Press.

Winerman, L. (2004). Designing psychologists. *Monitor on Psychology, 35*(7), 30–31.

Wiskoff, M. F. (1997). Defense of the nation: Military psychologists. In R. J. Sternberg (Ed.), *Career paths in psychology: Where your degree can take you* (pp. 245–268). Washington, D.C.: American Psychological Association.

Witherspoon, R. & White, R. P. (1996). Executive coaching: A continuum of roles. *Consulting Psychology Journal: Practice and Research, 48*, 124–133.

Woods, D. (2002). *Behind human error: Human factors research to improve patient safety*. Retrieved on June 5, 2002 at http://www.apa.org/ppo/issues/shumfactors2.html

Index